THE NEW MIDDLE AGES

BONNIE WHEELER, *Series Editor*

The New Middle Ages is a series dedicated to transdisciplinary studies of medieval cultures, with particular emphasis on recuperating women's history and on feminist and gender analyses. This peer-reviewed series includes both scholarly monographs and essay collections.

PUBLISHED BY PALGRAVE:

Women in the Medieval Islamic World: Power, Patronage and Piety
　edited by Gavin R. G. Hambly

The Ethics of Nature in the Middle Ages: On Boccaccio's Poetaphysics
　by Gregory B. Stone

Presence and Presentation: Women in the Chinese Literati Tradition
　by Sherry J. Mou

The Lost Love Letters of Heloise and Abelard: Perceptions of Dialogue in Twelfth-Century France
　by Constant J. Mews

Understanding Scholastic Thought with Foucault
　by Philipp W. Rosemann

For Her Good Estate: The Life of Elizabeth de Burgh
　by Frances A. Underhill

Constructions of Widowhood and Virginity in the Middle Ages
　edited by Cindy L. Carlson and Angela Jane Weisl

Motherhood and Mothering in Anglo-Saxon England
　by Mary Dockray-Miller

Listening to Heloise: The Voice of a Twelfth-Century Woman
　edited by Bonnie Wheeler

The Postcolonial Middle Ages
　edited by Jeffrey Jerome Cohen

Chaucer's Pardoner and Gender Theory: Bodies of Discourse
　by Robert S. Sturges

Crossing the Bridge: Comparative Essays on Medieval European and Heian Japanese Women Writers
　edited by Barbara Stevenson and Cynthia Ho

Engaging Words: The Culture of Reading in the Later Middle Ages
　by Laurel Amtower

Robes and Honor: The Medieval World of Investiture
　edited by Stewart Gordon

Representing Rape in Medieval and Early Modern Literature
　edited by Elizabeth Robertson and Christine M. Rose

Same Sex Love and Desire among Women in the Middle Ages
　edited by Francesca Canadé Sautman and Pamela Sheingorn

Sight and Embodiment in the Middle Ages: Ocular Desires
　by Suzannah Biernoff

Listen, Daughter: The Speculum Virginum *and the Formation of Religious Women in the Middle Ages*
　edited by Constant J. Mews

Science, the Singular, and the Question of Theology
　by Richard A. Lee, Jr.

Gender in Debate from the Early Middle Ages to the Renaissance
　edited by Thelma S. Fenster and Clare A. Lees

Malory's Morte Darthur: *Remaking Arthurian Tradition*
by Catherine Batt

The Vernacular Spirit: Essays on Medieval Religious Literature
edited by Renate Blumenfeld-Kosinski, Duncan Robertson, and Nancy Warren

Popular Piety and Art in the Late Middle Ages: Image Worship and Idolatry in England 1350–1500
by Kathleen Kamerick

Absent Narratives, Manuscript Textuality, and Literary Structure in Late Medieval England
by Elizabeth Scala

Creating Community with Food and Drink in Merovingian Gaul
by Bonnie Effros

Representations of Early Byzantine Empresses: Image and Empire
by Anne McClanan

Encountering Medieval Textiles and Dress: Objects, Texts, Images
edited by Désirée G. Koslin and Janet Snyder

Eleanor of Aquitaine: Lord and Lady
edited by Bonnie Wheeler and John Carmi Parsons

Isabel La Católica, Queen of Castile: Critical Essays
edited by David A. Boruchoff

Homoeroticism and Chivalry: Discourses of Male Same-Sex Desire in the Fourteenth Century
by Richard E. Zeikowitz

Portraits of Medieval Women: Family, Marriage, and Politics in England 1225–1350
by Linda E. Mitchell

Eloquent Virgins: From Thecla to Joan of Arc
by Maud Burnett McInerney

The Persistence of Medievalism: Narrative Adventures in Contemporary Culture
by Angela Jane Weisl

Capetian Women
edited by Kathleen D. Nolan

Joan of Arc and Spirituality
edited by Ann W. Astell and Bonnie Wheeler

The Texture of Society: Medieval Women in the Southern Low Countries
edited by Ellen E. Kittell and Mary A. Suydam

Charlemagne's Mustache: And Other Cultural Clusters of a Dark Age
by Paul Edward Dutton

Troubled Vision: Gender, Sexuality, and Sight in Medieval Text and Image
edited by Emma Campbell and Robert Mills

Queering Medieval Genres
by Tison Pugh

Sacred Place in Early Medieval Neoplatonism
by L. Michael Harrington

The Middle Ages at Work
edited by Kellie Robertson and Michael Uebel

Chaucer's Jobs
by David R. Carlson

Medievalism and Orientalism: Three Essays on Literature, Architecture, and Cultural Identity
by John M. Ganim

Queer Love in the Middle Ages
by Anna Klosowska

Performing Women in the Middle Ages: Sex, Gender, and the Iberian Lyric
by Denise K. Filios

Necessary Conjunctions: The Social Self in Medieval England
by David Gary Shaw

Visual Culture and the German Middle Ages
edited by Kathryn Starkey and
Horst Wenzel

*Medieval Paradigms: Essays in
Honor of Jeremy duQuesnay Adams,
Volumes 1 and 2*
edited by Stephanie Hayes-Healy

*False Fables and Exemplary Truth in Later
Middle English Literature*
by Elizabeth Allen

*Ecstatic Transformation: On the Uses of Alterity
in the Middle Ages*
by Michael Uebel

*Sacred and Secular in Medieval and Early
Modern Cultures: New Essays*
edited by Lawrence Besserman

Tolkien's Modern Middle Ages
edited by Jane Chance and Alfred K.
Siewers

*Representing Righteous Heathens in Late
Medieval England*
by Frank Grady

*Byzantine Dress: Representations
of Secular Dress in Eighth-to-Twelfth
Century Painting*
by Jennifer L. Ball

*The Laborer's Two Bodies: Labor and the
'Work' of the Text in Medieval Britain,
1350–1500*
by Kellie Robertson

*The Dogaressa of Venice, 1250–1500: Wife
and Icon*
by Holly S. Hurlburt

*Logic, Theology, and Poetry in Boethius,
Abelard, and Alan of Lille: Words in the
Absence of Things*
by Eileen C. Sweeney

*The Theology of Work: Peter Damian and the
Medieval Religious Renewal Movement*
by Patricia Ranft

*On the Purification of Women: Churching in
Northern France, 1100–1500*
by Paula M. Rieder

*Writers of the Reign of Henry II:
Twelve Essays*
edited by Ruth Kennedy and Simon
Meecham-Jones

*Lonesome Words: The Vocal Poetics
of the Old English Lament and the
African-American Blues Song*
by M.G. McGeachy

*Performing Piety: Musical Culture in Medieval
English Nunneries*
by Anne Bagnell Yardley

*The Flight from Desire: Augustine and Ovid to
Chaucer*
by Robert R. Edwards

*Mindful Spirit in Late Medieval
Literature: Essays in Honor
of Elizabeth D. Kirk*
edited by Bonnie Wheeler

*Medieval Fabrications: Dress, Textiles,
Clothwork, and Other Cultural Imaginings*
edited by E. Jane Burns

*Was the Bayeux Tapestry Made in France?:
The Case for St. Florent of Saumur*
by George Beech

*Women, Power, and Religious Patronage in the
Middle Ages*
by Erin L. Jordan

*Hybridity, Identity, and Monstrosity in
Medieval Britain: On Difficult Middles*
by Jeremy Jerome Cohen

*Medieval Go-betweens and Chaucer's
Pandarus*
by Gretchen Mieszkowski

*The Surgeon in Medieval
English Literature*
by Jeremy J. Citrome

Temporal Circumstances: Form and History in the Canterbury Tales
  by Lee Patterson

Erotic Discourse and Early English Religious Writing
  by Lara Farina

Odd Bodies and Visible Ends in Medieval Literature
  by Sachi Shimomura

On Farting: Language and Laughter in the Middle Ages
  by Valerie Allen

Women and Medieval Epic: Gender, Genre, and the Limits of Epic Masculinity
  edited by Sara S. Poor and Jana K. Schulman

Race, Class, and Gender in "Medieval" Cinema
  edited by Lynn T. Ramey and Tison Pugh

Allegory and Sexual Ethics in the High Middle Ages
  by Noah D. Guynn

England and Iberia in the Middle Ages, 12th–15th Century: Cultural, Literary, and Political Exchanges
  edited by María Bullón-Fernández

The Medieval Chastity Belt: A Myth-Making Process
  by Albrecht Classen

Claustrophilia: The Erotics of Enclosure in Medieval Literature
  by Cary Howie

CLAUSTROPHILIA
THE EROTICS OF ENCLOSURE IN MEDIEVAL LITERATURE

Cary Howie

palgrave
macmillan

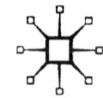

CLAUSTROPHILIA
© Cary Howie, 2007.

All rights reserved. No part of this book may be used or reproduced in any manner whatsoever without written permission except in the case of brief quotations embodied in critical articles or reviews.

First published in 2007 by
PALGRAVE MACMILLAN™
175 Fifth Avenue, New York, N.Y. 10010 and
Houndmills, Basingstoke, Hampshire, England RG21 6XS
Companies and representatives throughout the world.

PALGRAVE MACMILLAN is the global academic imprint of the Palgrave Macmillan division of St. Martin's Press, LLC and of Palgrave Macmillan Ltd. Macmillan® is a registered trademark in the United States, United Kingdom and other countries. Palgrave is a registered trademark in the European Union and other countries.

ISBN-13: 978–1–4039–7197–5
ISBN-10: 1–4039–7197–8

Library of Congress Cataloging-in-Publication Data

Howie, Cary.
   Claustrophilia : the erotics of enclosure in medieval literature / Cary Howie.
      p. cm.—(New Middle Ages)
   Includes bibliographical references and index.
   ISBN 1–4039–7197–8 (alk. paper)
   1. Literature, Medieval—History and criticism. 2. Claustrophilia in literature. 3. Sex in literature. I. Title.

PN682.C545H69 2007
809′.933538—dc22   2006051355

A catalogue record for this book is available from the British Library.

Design by Newgen Imaging Systems (P) Ltd., Chennai, India.

First edition: May 2007

10 9 8 7 6 5 4 3 2 1

Printed in the United States of America.

For at least four of her six years she had been aware of how close at hand everything was, of how whatever she wanted tended to be wherever she was. "Come out," Marcy said. Why should she? What was in the bedroom that was not in the closet?

—Barbara Gowdy, *Mister Sandman*

My answer is as clear as sunrise, but conveniently smaller.

—A. L. Kennedy, "On Having More Sense"

CONTENTS

Acknowledgments		x
Introduction		1
Chapter 1	The Edge of Enclosure	11
Chapter 2	The Verge of the Visible	37
Chapter 3	Spaced Out	69
Chapter 4	Lyric Enclosures	103
Chapter 5	Nothing Between	123
In Closing		139
Notes		153
Works Cited		183
Index		193

ACKNOWLEDGMENTS

Looking back on the *itinerarium* that has led to this little book, I cannot help being reminded of Thomas, the historian whom Flannery O'Connor mocks in a short story titled "The Comforts of Home." He leads a life of safely enclosed, domestic research until his mother abruptly takes in a charity case, a "little slut" who interferes with his careful historiography. "His home was to him home, workshop, church, as personal as the shell of a turtle and as necessary. He could not believe that it could be violated in this way (130)." I have had the good fortune, or perhaps simply the grace, to find myself intruded upon time and again.

My thanks, first of all, to Bonnie Wheeler for her charisma and confidence in this project; to Farideh Koohi-Kamali and Julia Cohen at Palgrave; and to the manuscript's peer reviewer, whose suggestions made this a better book. The foundations of this project were laid during my years as a graduate student at Stanford University, where the Department of Comparative Literature provided me with funding and freedom: two gifts I cannot repay. Sepp Gumbrecht has never ceased, from the sundrenched patios of Palo Alto to the dock of a cottage overlooking Cayuga Lake, to be an inspiring interlocutor, gentle guide, and lover of things sacred and profane. Seth Lerer has been a generous respondent, a connoisseur of comedy, and a model of rhetorical finesse. The death of Brigitte Cazelles in January 2004 made this book's argument all the more urgent. Jeffrey Schnapp introduced me to Pierre et Gilles (who lie under the surface of this book, even as they will shimmer on the surface of the next one). My adventures on that technicolor coast were, and still are, aided and abetted by a host of friends, colleagues, and drinking buddies, especially Dawn Green, Karen Gross, John Hess, Tim Zerlang, Adrienne Janus, Christy Pichichero, and Meg Worley.

Since 2003, I have had the pleasure of taking part in Cornell's Department of Romance Studies, which somehow made room in the French section for someone whose claims to French literature were nothing short of tenuous. I am especially grateful to Richard Klein for his particular brand of intellectual hedonism and Tracy McNulty for her bracing

ACKNOWLEDGMENTS

directness and camaraderie. My small world in Ithaca has been made larger than I would ever have thought possible, and I would like to thank some of the friends who have made it happen: Jason Frank, for his fierce intelligence and love of design; Myrna Garcia, for chocolate; Becky Givan, for tea; Ellis Hanson, for cocktails; Kim Leighton, for so many conversations about love and lack; Kate Morris, for hospitality on both coasts; Diane Rubenstein, for introducing me to Viagra d' Abruzzo; and Lee Strock, for gin and style when I needed both of them badly. Judith Peraino and Masha Raskolnikov are my lovely partners in medieval crime, and they are even lovelier in ways that have nothing to do, thank God, with the Middle Ages.

I am also grateful for the conversations I have had over the years with a community of friends and scholars elsewhere: Bill Burgwinkle, above all, has been an exceptional host, friend, and correspondent throughout the many stages of this book's genesis; I cannot imagine the past six years without him. Let me quickly add my thanks to Bettina Bildhauer, for taking me to the beach; Emma Campbell, for her theoretical audacity and her company in Nice; Holly Crocker, for encouragement when I needed it; Marilynn Desmond, for advice and company across countries and continents; Albrecht Diem, for showing me that historians are not all bad; Noah Guynn, for giving me yet another reason to visit San Francisco; Bob Mills, for daring to write such inspiring stuff and taking a train with me to St. Andrews; Kristina Olson, fellow Virgo; and Marc Schachter. I would never have become a medievalist without Karen Sullivan; my thanks to her as well.

And when it comes to my parents, Cary and Cathy, I am, like my mystics, at a loss for words. Their love keeps me grounded. My brothers and sister-Craig, Scott, Rebecca—confirm that we are destined to be a family of preachers and teachers. Winnie Pounds is the best grandmother in the world. Mark Tendall keeps me dreaming of California.

All these folks surround and disclose my life to me: they make me the claustrophile I am.

★ ★ ★

Grateful acknowledgment is made to the following authors and publishers for permission to reprint previously published work.

Parts of Chapter Two originally appeared in "As the Saint Turns: Hagiography at the Threshold of the Visible," *Exemplaria* 17.2 (Fall 2005): 317–46. Reprinted by permission of Pegasus Press, PO Box 15806, Asheville NC, 28813. Copyright 2005.

Parts of Chapter Three originally appeared in "Vision beyond Measure: The Threshold of Iacopone's Bedroom," *Troubled Vision: Gender, Sexuality, and Sight in Medieval Text and Image* (New York: Palgrave, 2004), pp. 139–53.

"Messiah (Christmas Portions)" [l. 81–92] and "Lilacs in NYC" [l. 52–64, 71–73], from *Sweet Machine* by Mark Doty. Copyright 1998 by Mark Doty. Reprinted by permission of HarperCollins Publishers Inc.

INTRODUCTION

Once inside a book, any book, it's impossible to emerge from it absolutely intact, to be outside it in quite the same way as before. Take the example of Saint Augustine, whose famous response to the injunction to "take and read" in *Confessions* VIII is to open a book of Pauline epistles that he has left with his friend Alypius. Once he opens the book at random and reads Paul's warning against following "nature and nature's appetites," he closes the book again, marking it "with [his] finger or by some other sign." But no sooner has he closed the book than he must open it again, in response to Alypius, who has remained nearby: "He asked to see what I had read. I showed it to him and he read on beyond the text which I had read."[1] Augustine's book, newly marked, is opened to include Alypius, to speak to him just as Augustine has been spoken to. In fact, it is a contiguous sentence that will address itself to Augustine's friend, just as the two men are contiguous to one another within the garden where they have now closed and opened and closed and reopened the Epistles. Their proximity to one another outside the book is, from this moment on, unthinkable outside of their proximity inside the book, the extent to which two adjacent Pauline sentences have not just reproduced but reinforced the fact of these friends' being together.

In the pages that follow, I make a series of gestures that attempt to show just how far inside, just how spatially and textually delimited, we inevitably are. Indeed, I argue that there is, finally, no such thing as solitary confinement. The question of being inside and the question of how it is possible to speak this fragile pronoun, "we," across temporal, spatial, and ontological difference, never cease to overlap and literally to inform one another. Being together *is* being inside. But inside what exactly? And across which bindings and boundaries?

These brief remarks will inevitably constitute a poor excuse for an introduction.[2] Take them, accordingly, as an interrogation of what it might mean to *introducere*: literally, to lead inside. There are at least five principal entrances here: five chapters, each in its way opening onto the next, and each in its way repeating what has preceded it. Chapters 1 and 4 frame and indeed enclose in mostly (but never exclusively) modern terms the engagements with medieval literature in the second and third. The fifth chapter, in turn, embodies an effort to get beyond even the most tenuous distinctions between medieval and modern, immanence and transcendence.³ It will become clear, nonetheless, that it is never really a question of separating out the present from the past; nor of separating the literary from the nonliterary, and specifically from the theological. That, as Gerard Loughlin puts it, "knowledge of the exterior can be gained only inside the enclosure"[4] means, too, that this exterior, like the enclosure through which it's known, must be construed in the strongest possible sense: as transcendent, and not just transcendental; just as the enclosure's boundaries are no mere heuristic, no erasable line, but porous, fleshy, continually renegotiated and intensified.

In this sense I have tried to be inclusive. And in another as well: these readings are grounded in a poetics—but also an ontology—of metonymy; that trope of contiguity, contamination, and guilt by association. Indeed, in the final chapter, metonymy will give way to anaphora, the trope whereby repetition produces relational difference. In the spirit of these figures of speech, then, my readings have relied to a remarkable extent upon the at-hand, the books that have found themselves, through whatever circumstances, in close proximity to me over a course of repeated gestures and journeys. Built in bookstores, bedrooms, and libraries, in the United States and Europe and the places between them, these pages owe their architecture to an understanding of scholarly space whose constitutive incompleteness would rival the libraries of Erich Auerbach's Istanbul. For whatever enclosure seeks to encapsulate or evoke (and these moments will always be simultaneous in their respectively inward and outward reaching), it is never perfect, never self-contained. If this does not strike the reader as obvious—that is, if the reader either desires such perfect enclosure or accepts its inevitability, as an evil foil to good transparency—then the following pages are meant to make this imperfection and incompleteness apparent.

Mieke Bal describes, in terms particularly felicitous for this purpose, the challenge posed by Louise Bourgeois' architectural sculpture *Spider* to "anteriority narratives," especially those of art history:

> For topology destroys linearity by making embedding, not sequence, a principle of narrative time: embedding—an enfolding of one thing within another, a body within a house. Each element of *Spider* comprises both itself and the whole of which it is a part.[5]

Literary history, like art history, depends upon a romance of sequence. What is more, Bal speaks, unsurprisingly but cannily, of the linearity of these historical narratives: the romance of sequence, in other words, is also literally a romance of the line. (These terms quickly fold back into one another: romance, after all, embodies the emergence of a certain kind of linear narrativity in the medieval West, as well as the frustrations and deferrals of this linear logic.) Thus, topology, in Bal's account, offers an alternative to this romance, a logic of emplacement, where the dots—and, crucially, what they contain—are as important as what connects them. Still the logic of "embedding" remains that of synecdoche: part for whole, whole for part, each fully, symmetrically participant in the other. This is where my essay and Bal's part ways: for the link that embedding inscribes between two terms, architectural or bodily or textual, is not so much synecdochic, with all its concomitant symmetries, as *metonymic*, unstable, contingent, about to break out, or break *in*. To "enfold" one thing within another, as Bal suggests, is not necessarily to reduce the enfolded to a bit, a portion, of what enfolds it: a body does not "comprise" its surrounding house any more than, in a ruby ring—to use Bonaventure's metaphor for virginity and humility—the gem "comprises" its surrounding gold.[6] We would say that the gem is *set off* by the gold: enhanced yet distinct, made not to reflect what surrounds it but, by virtue of these surroundings, to glow.

Sarah Spence suggests, via Augustine, what such a metonymic understanding of scholarly storytelling could entail: the "order of love" that organizes Augustinian thought is

> hardly an order at all—at times the text [*Confessions*] seems structured around nothing more systematic than free association. Yet this can also be viewed as a tropic order: issues are ordered by figures of speech, not by discursive logic.[7]

Between topology and tropology, between places and turns of speech, I hope to show the order of embeddedness and enclosure upon which literary histories depend. Although neither Spence nor Augustine would be willing to reduce their tropic, amorous order to one specific figure of speech, metonymy suggests itself as particularly appropriate, inasmuch as, like the memory houses of medieval rhetoricians, it relies so much upon spatial proximity in order to generate meaning. A metonymic, enclosed order may nonetheless seem disorderly, particularly in comparison to the stories that romance philology has been telling itself for the last 200 years. And yet metonymy lurks even within these stories, as canons take shape according to imagined proximities, often geographical, and influence is calculated in terms of books that have or have not fallen into someone's hands, as well as in terms of lines of scholarly descent. The tropic/topic order of these chapters suggests that the genealogies behind the conventions of national, period-based, methodologically-grouped literary study all presuppose a proximity, a touch, between texts worthy of inclusion.

But what radicalizes this suggestion is that its poles—touch and inclusion or enclosure—cannot be stabilized. Metonymy is also metaphor, if by the latter one understands a figure of speech whose dominant trait is *epiphora*, "bringing together two heterogeneous things close to reveal their kinship."[8] Other texts, other heterogeneous things, always impinge—from memory, from the spaces we inhabit—upon the stories we tell ourselves about literature. There is no acceptable hierarchy of contingency. Slavoj Zizek has observed, for example, that "the easiest way to score points automatically" in contemporary academic debate "is to claim that the opponent's position is not properly 'situated' in a historical context."[9] Metonymic reading, embedded and extensive, accepts the inevitability of situatedness but flouts the logic according to which one mode of situating, often historicist, must be privileged above all others, effectively robbing the text of whatever extrahistorical (or, in María Menocal's terms, synchronic) resonance it might possess. Thus, to return to Augustine, what makes the discursive order of this book an imperfect order of love is its resistance, in the name of the alterity of what it describes, to hermeneutic control: like that *eros* which is (in Anne Carson's words) an intensifier of edges,[10] but also (in Plato's words) an eye disease.[11] Claustrophilia (the love of enclosure, enclosed love, embedded touch) is therefore both an object of study and a critical practice that, like it or not, is catching.[12]

To catch, here, means both to spread and to snag. These chapters can be read as a linear argument in which claustrophilia moves from aesthetics, through ethics, to an ontologically resonant critical poetics; yet, as these introductory remarks hopefully make clear, this linearity is at every stage compromised. Each chapter is variously embedded in the others. For this reason, cross-references abound. The argument's formal dimension is thus made not so much to correspond as to rub against and participate in the permeable boundaries that claustrophilia objectively intensifies. To be inside (a chapter, a house, or a chapterhouse) is not to be sealed off: it is to be summoned, paradoxically, into a more concrete, ecstatic relation to what lies not just beyond but within these boundaries. In no respect does the end of the book get past the beginning. The following brief descriptions, weighted as they are on the side of linearity, are meant to indicate the extent to which this enclosed lack of traditional closure (transparent, fulfilling, accompanied by the feeling of having gotten somewhere) nonetheless moves.

Chapter 1, "The Edge of Enclosure," maps out, in sequence, the three primary discursive levels—aesthetic, ethical, ontological—that determine the whole of the book. It begins by characterizing claustrophilia, the love of enclosure, as a specifically aesthetic phenomenon: the work of art is enclosed even as it discloses itself to the viewer; there is something irresistibly resistant about the artwork's relationship to the potentially appropriative gaze. An aesthetic ambivalence—do I or do I not want to be seen?—gives way to an ethical ambivalence: is visibility always virtuous? Will we like what we see? What happens when the enclosive function of the artwork is aligned with sexuality or death? An ethics of interpretation, or even of sensory reception (before and beyond interpretation), requires an intervention into the artwork's constitutive ambivalence. It requires intensifying, not abandoning, the specificity of the sexed body, or the dead letter, as they give themselves equivocally to sight.

This ethics of intensification has distinct ontological consequences: intervention within the compromised appearance of enclosed bodies and texts amounts to participating in these appearances' being-apparent. Interpretation, or aesthetic reception, is thus not entirely discrete from aesthetic production: it reaches across the aporia between seer and seen, to make something more visible, contingently, approximately, and thereby also offers itself to sight. This movement also makes something more hidden, deepening the artwork's depths even as it intensifies the surface. Claustrophilia thus, beyond readerly "response" and deconstructive supplementarity, makes singularity more apparent through participative intensification. It names the strange community in which beings become visible through and close to each other, without ever being reducible to a flat, self-same Being.

Chapter 2, "The Verge of the Visible," dwells in the first and second stages of the claustrophilic sequence outlined in chapter 1. It fleshes out, via the very fleshy lives of medieval hermit saints, the ways in which saintly appearance dovetails with ethical ambivalence, an ambivalence coded sexually. In the Old French lives of Marie the Egyptian and Jehan Bouche d'Or, one witnesses (with an emphasis upon the explicitly spectatorial dynamic established by these texts) bodies exposed and enclosed, stripped and enshrined. Marie's body keeps turning away, evades the gaze even as it offers itself to view; Jehan's body, housed in a hermitage, writes repeatedly in order to avoid the lascivious contexts into which his hands would otherwise be drawn. In each case, sexuality is the site at which a saint's life—and the saint's life as genre—is contested and made most apparent: Marie's constantly averted face is inscribed with her sex; Jehan's hand grasps a surrogate tool. Dwelling with saints, interpretatively or literally, involves a kind of risk, a risk fundamental to aesthesis: remaining within paradox instead of resolving it too quickly; accepting the challenge to touch a *corpus* and be contaminated by it, by the impure (but not purely impure) thoughts it arouses, by the animating impurity of that tact. The ethical ambivalence of saints' lives thus foregrounds the impurity of their very appearance, as written and visible bodies, inviting an intervention that would not shore up one side at the expense of the other but allow both to come as forcefully as possible. The enclosure bodies forth the resistance of contingency to fixity or discretion. It is also a resistance, in Lee Edelman's terms, of metonymy to metaphor.

Metonymy comes to the forefront of the argument in chapter 3, "Spaced Out." In the first place, metonymy provides a way to talk about how, within radical religious enclosure, bodies and discourses impinge upon other bodies, other discourses, and end up mysteriously inside them. It also frames a transition from the aesthetic object, desiring to be seen, to the aesthetic subject, desiring to see. What the eleventh-century monastic reformer Peter Damian and the thirteenth-century Franciscan lyricist Iacopone da Todi share is, first and foremost, a commitment to the spatial complexity of religious life, and its constitutive ethical ambivalence. This ethical ambivalence, spaced out in the hermitage or the wandering friar's monastic prison, is figured most powerfully, as it was for the Old French saints, in sexual terms. For Damian, the resistance of architecture (both literally and figuratively) to transparency animates his condemnation of the sodomites somehow always already inside the permeable ecclesial body; for Iacopone, the mystical cell itself becomes a locus of spatial penetration and, more importantly, inflation, expansion, and abject redoubling.

Aesthetic ambivalence and its ethical consequences, as described in chapters 1 and 2, require this kind of tarrying with the abject, with what refuses to be assimilated into a given ecclesial or discursive structure, in order that participation might not seem to be a mere reduction to immanent unity or selfsameness. Thus Damian's paranoia only serves to reproduce exactly those holes it seeks to cover up, whereas Iacopone's ironic insinuation of his words into the bowels of the church shows how every critique is bound, abjectly and erotically, to its object. A poetics of rimming and limning comes to subtend the participation of tongues in holes, the unworldly in the all too secular, as the discursive means of negotiating the difference within their retraced and retracted sameness (what Iacopone calls their anal "opening"). Metonymies—of tongue and page, body and bed—stretch the space in which vice and virtue come together in a common, if differently shared, moment of arrival: that coming which is also an inauguration of a new space, a third heaven, beyond vice and virtue, heterodoxy and orthodoxy. This new space is one of ongoing transfiguration, as analogically repeated words, gestures, and movements instantiate new materialities, bound to one another and multiplying these boundaries.

Chapter 4, "Lyric Enclosures," takes this multiplication of boundaries, and its underpinning poetics of participative metonymy, as a model for a critical practice that would rub medieval and modern texts together, beyond the dualist distinction between amateurism and scholarly rigor, poetry and prose. Bonagiunta da Lucca's critique of Guido Guinizzelli's use of academic diction in his poetry provides a way to talk about textual proximity, and the extent to which historical moments, genres, and bodies are always dragged from their contingent others while simultaneously giving themselves to be similarly dragged. This traherence, as I call it, never quite gets free of what it ostensibly emerges from, and furnishes the basis for a reading practice that would resist the slavish devotion to the controlled, discrete bloodlines of those patrilinear critical and literary histories that continue to haunt contemporary reading practices. Mark Doty in this way traces the enclosures from and as which bodies and even inanimate objects emerge, belatedly and contingently, to be sensed and desired.

The implications of this are as follows. To touch is to experience a limit and open a connection. Whether this touch is figured visually, hermeneutically, or sexually, it traces the outline of a community of embodied lovers expropriatively given over to bodies, texts, and buildings sensibly intensified by this gift. Neither a mere idealization of aesthetic attention nor a diminishment of eros to interpretation, the metonymic, participative touch (or look, or reading) brings more fully into being the bodies, texts, and buildings it brushes against. The risk of violence remains—when does it ever go away?—but it is important to stress that, if touch is in some way entry, it is thus only inasmuch as appropriation has been thoroughly relinquished. Such an entry, such a touch, requires an ecstatic reorientation of the most basic (and finally damaging) ontological presuppositions: that this body has fundamentally nothing to do with mine; that this body cannot be touched; that this body is impenetrable or forever lost.

More traditionally, it is possible to say that beings not only participate in one another through a shared Being irreducible to any sum of beings, but also draw close to one another as this very Being's proximity, which is to say its increasingly articulate and tangible difference. In nearness, in enclosure, this difference becomes more available to the senses, just as closer inspection of the beloved body reveals this body's greater difference from my own. Nor does the differential intensification of beings as the Being in which they participate occur only through ever more precise scrutiny or meticulous sensation: claustrophilia shows, and hides, the degree to which invisibility and the unknowable take a parallel, if not even greater, ontological risk. Think what it means to reach out, in the dark, toward something or someone you cannot see. I would call this a queer ontology, inasmuch as it expounds a coinherence or traherence of differences, an erotic participation through which they become not identical but singularly shared and mutually, messily incompleted. Resisting both a poetics of attenuation (which would relegate the queer to pure indifference, pure negation, while leaving purity intact) and a mere historicizing of sexualities (whose diachrony disallows the fundamentally erotic approximations of anachronism), such an ontology is committed to the *intensification* of these materialities in their very mystery and withdrawal, these multiple and proliferating enclosed spaces upon which we inevitably, extensively touch. Chapter 4 thus performs, in some small way, the critical intervention demanded by the ambivalence demonstrated in the earlier chapters. If such ambivalence is ultimately inescapable, it can nonetheless be reconfigured, and room can be made for other interventions, other advents.

Chapter 5, "Nothing Between," takes its title from a paradox articulated by the fourteenth-century English anchoress Julian of Norwich in her book of revelations. There is, she repeats, "nothing between" the soul and God. And yet, at the same time, the soul's relationship to God is also one of reciprocal enclosure. I argue here, with Julian and the twelfth-century poet Marie de France, for a rearticulation of not just space but mediation itself. For, if claustrophilia is an erotics of spatial mediation, it is so not in the sense in which (spatial, embodied) means get submitted to (erotic) ends, nor in the sense in which a sequence of discrete moments of spatial appropriation give way to a complex but neat erotic synthesis. If mediation might, in this account, be akin to a sort of being-between, an ontological fact continually reproduced and intensified through embodied erotic practice, it is nonetheless the case that this "between" is both constantly under revision, and irreducible to any given spatial situation. After the inflated cells of Iacopone and Peter Damian, and after the enclosed "infinity" of Mark Doty's bedroom, Marie and Julian provide us with a necessary antidote to thinking that we can finally grasp, cognitively or otherwise, even the relational, dynamic quality of enclosure.

To be more specific: in Marie's *Yonec*, an enclosed lady is visited by a lover who, offering to take communion and thereby prove his devotion, will ultimately lie down beside her, inside her enclosure, and assume her form. In fact, the lover promises to speak at once *to* and *as* his lady, inscribing or, better, vocally articulating a difference at the heart of their shared semblance. It is unclear whether, in this moment, it is a question of one body or two; in fact, I argue, Marie is gesturing here toward something beyond mere fusion, on the one hand, and absolute isolation, on the other; that is to say, beyond the standard antinomies according to which what intervenes between us must separate us entirely or, in the absence of such a separation, not really intervene at all. Julian takes this one step further, making the question less about the discreteness of enclosed human bodies in relation to one another and more about humanity's relationship to divinity, specifically to a divinity made human. When the soul at once surrounds God and is surrounded by him, yet according to a logic of proximity wherein nothing, strictly speaking, intervenes between them, then the erotics of the middle may take on a slightly different cast. God—or, in another version, my lover—does not just enclose me; God is not even merely coextensive with the space I take up; God is, in Julian's words but also in Augustine's, closer to me than I am to myself.

It is possible, in this way, to take in a still more radical sense Catherine Brown's provocative recognition of the "medieval" as "coeval": we are, yes, always between bodies and times, but only because there is, in another way, nothing between us. Our dealings with the world, with difference, are ultimately fumblings, necessary and beautiful, toward an immediacy that is *im-mediate*, in the strongest sense: not beyond mediation but *inside* it. Not, in other words, content with mediation alone: this would be, in the lexicon of visionary literature, to throw out the kernel for the husk; or, in a slightly less lofty register, to underestimate the double sense of getting in someone's pants (where the mediating object can be neither circumvented nor precisely exalted in itself). Rather, claustrophilia's apophatic immediacy, *inside between*, is grounded in the notion, indeed in the experience, that between immediacy and mediation, so to speak, some other kind of relation is not just possible but already at work.

This project, in all the thrownness of its *pro-iectum*, owes its stylistic freedom and generally contemplative tone to the work of countless more traditional studies of medieval enclosure. It does not so much inaugurate as intensify the critical poetics of intervention and relinquishment to which, and within which, it is drawn. I want to mention briefly, in particular, the delicacy of Shari Horner's exposition of looking into the enclosures, both textual and architectural, of Old English hagiography. Her assertion that, for the hagiographer Aelfric in the tenth century, "spiritual truth is found only by looking into—that is, interpreting—literal surfaces,"[13] is crucial for the formulation of the superficial hermeneutic I espouse here, even as I hope not to limit the effects of "looking" to meaning alone. Likewise, Sarah Beckwith's gesture toward "an ethics not of the pure subject . . . but of ambiguity" provided the first provocation to deal with the ambivalence of art as enclosure and enclosure as art.[14] And Richard Rambuss sowed the seed of claustrophilia in his observation that "the history of sacred eroticism is one that is pointed toward a more particularized *emplacement*, not effacement, of its energies and expressions."[15] If this essay breaks with the methodology and tone of Beckwith's and Horner's studies, it does so only to reinforce Rambuss's conclusion—so that a "greater density" might be allowed to intervene.[16]

Anne Carson, typically, says this better than I can. In "Just for the Thrill: An Essay on the Difference between Women and Men," she shows how interiority can also disrupt and disclose:

> The radical for *within* in classical Chinese is an empty box. You can indicate withinness of any kind you like by setting another radical within the box. For example, human love, while it is happening, will seem like something within withinness. . .On the other hand, withinness may spit you out like a glass eye.[17]

To love, one could say, is to think inside the box. Carson provides a radical etymology for being in love, for what this "in" redundantly and necessarily betrays. To be in love is, she says, to be inside, "within withinness." Not just inside, then, but doubly inside. Still, where is the line between enfolded and unfolding? Love's interiority is, after all, limited to "while it is happening," while it unfolds. The box holds up—it holds—only in the tension of three dimensions drawn toward two; it only lasts on the condition that it breaks down. (When love ends, it is a little like recycling.) Here is another way to say this: get too far inside and you may—paratactically—slide right out of love, pop out of its socket. Its surface contains you; its surface excludes you. Spitting and swallowing require each other. But if you are not inside this surface, if you hesitate to go too far, to swallow or be swallowed, then it is not love, and you are neither inside nor outside. God will not even spit you out. Unless, of course, you never stop being enclosed, not for a moment, not even when the box collapses and the socket pops. Claustrophilia bets everything on that glass eye.

Francisco X. Alarcón proposes, in a recent poem called "Eros," an analogous analogy. (Would that be something like "within withinness"?) Key is to door, he says, as tongue is to keyhole. But this keyhole is also, in Spanish, a lock: it is a "cerradura."[18] The way in is always, potentially or actually, blocked. What is more, it consists in the narrowing of an object (door) to its constitutive absence (hole). Only a tongue fits such a narrowly limited, enclosed space, the absence at the heart of you. Only by blocking that already blocked hole—only by, as it were, locking the lock, being enclosed by what is, in itself, the heart of all enclosure—*only thus* can the tongue make it open. According to Adam Phillips, "one of the most striking features of people who suffer from claustrophobia is that, for them, the way out is not through the door."[19] For the claustrophilic reader and the claustrophilic text, the door may not be a way out so much as a place of intensification, in which the riddle of embodiment, penetrability and contact is focused, narrowed, into a deepening and reinforcement of edges. The door may, as for Clare of Assisi, be a way out only inasmuch as it is "sealed up," at once keyhole and lock.[20] In either case, a tongue has intervened to preserve the enclosure and, simultaneously, to open it up. In either case, spat out or swallowed, on the surface or deep within, we make room for joy.

CHAPTER 1

THE EDGE OF ENCLOSURE

Temples

Concealment is tempting. I hide from you; you seek me out. What happens when concealment becomes a matter of space, the kinds of space where I hide, and where, perhaps, I seek to be sought? This is what Stacey D'Erasmo describes in *A Seahorse Year* when Hal, a San Francisco accountant, is confronted with the hidden spectacle of a new lover's back: "Though he has seen Dan's naked back, he's very compelled at the moment by the hidden length of it within the shirt: Dan's back, concealed. It is as if he is standing, blindfolded, before a major work of art."[1] Not only is concealment compelling; it's compelling in an explicitly aesthetic way. Art would seem to name, here, the place where the hidden becomes sensible, where the eyes fail, drop, or are folded out of sight. After all, it is not Dan's back that is blindfolded here—what would it mean to speak of a blindfolded back?—but instead, Hal's eyes. Blindness and folding must be thought together. The limit between Hal and Dan closes like an eye, but it also brings them close. This limit is as simple as a shirt. It is what in the following pages will come to be called enclosure.

The narrative trajectory of this chapter, and of the book as a whole, can be summed up as follows: beginning with the temple, it moves through hermitages and monasteries, prisons and toilets, and ends up in the bedroom. This movement does not so much abandon as preserve each previous place in the itinerary even as it moves on: in this way, the bedroom gets to live up to all the popular clichés according to which it is a church, its bed an altar. As, therefore, simultaneously a movement *into* a kind of spatial density that I am calling enclosure, and a movement *across* the textual landscapes of modern philosophical discourse, medieval devotion, and contemporary gay lyric, this series of essays participates in the claustrophilia it ostensibly describes. And yet, if there is a substantial risk in trying to contain such disparate material in a single argument, it is only through such participative reiteration, a critical enclosure which continually traces its own openings, that coherence is even remotely possible. But what would it mean, then, to cohere? To hold together and thereby to hold forth? The Greek temple, Heidegger informs us, both sets up and sets forth. These are its "earthy" and "worldly" functions: what one might call its vertical and horizontal dimensions, asocial and social. But the dialectic runs deeper: the temple also "holds in protective heed," it is the custodian of what it ostensibly divulges.[2] That is to say, the enclosure persists even amidst what it discloses. This is obvious in one way: who would say that a building's function eliminates its material walls, that the space delineated by and confined within these walls can be abstracted from their material surroundings and the sense, itself so close to the body, of being held? In another way, it is less obvious. For what Heidegger has in mind here, what his text holds even in its offering, is less a claim about material space and more a claim about the intensified mode of enclosure and disclosure particular to the work of art. That every such work should resist the gaze of its public even as it offers itself to this public, that every such work should draw upon a singular relationship with a source, a relationship which is not immediately reducible to the work's historical conditions or immediate environment: this is the core of Heidegger's insight.

I wish to articulate some of the resistance to historicism that comes, in Heidegger, to reside primarily within "earth" as opposed to "world." Such resistance is not, I realize, currently fashionable in an academy where the bottom line for credible scholarship seems to be precisely historicist. Indeed, if Augustine is right in saying that historicism wards off *cupiditas*,[3] then my project remains blatantly lustful in its commitment to the threshold at which "what is" emerges, sensibly, into being. This emergence is an opening in historical time, permitting and defying narrative. This is not to argue for a kind of mysticism of art; all the texts discussed below, medieval and modern, are exempt from claims to oracular truth. On the contrary, what Heidegger is articulating, and what I seek to articulate after him, is a fundamental unsettledness, a complicated and even hostile coincidence of functions, within the work of art: historical and ahistorical, social and asocial, sacred and profane, open and closed. That, perhaps contrary to Heidegger, this unsettledness might not finally be an undecided unraveling; that it takes place against the background of, even amidst, a constitutive coherence, a non-immanent horizon (as the spatial equivalent of what "eternal" is to "time"), is this book's biggest gamble, its unprovable burden of proof.

Yes, I am also unapologetically committed to what lies beyond "documentary evidence" and "critical rigor," beyond "straightforwardness," in Allen Frantzen's usefully contrarian but, I find, impoverished formulation.[4]

THE EDGE OF ENCLOSURE

Frantzen makes the following critique of queer theorists in medieval studies, a critique that says a lot about—or, more strictly, *shows*—the phenomenological presuppositions of a certain kind of historicism:

> The effect of queer theory on the study of medieval literature seems to be that the term has indeed become the point of departure—not for the historical reflections that [Judith] Butler suggests, however, but rather for historical imaginings. They are, in my view, no substitute for rigorous inquiry into the thoughts, words, and actions of medieval people, phenomena that cannot be known through literary texts alone.[5]

The "thoughts, words, and actions of medieval people" are, Frantzen concedes, "phenomena," but these are strange phenomena, for they are not principally appearances; they are, instead, objects of knowledge. Their mode of appearing, strictly speaking, disappears. It is, in fact, Frantzen who performs the most obvious "substitution" here—that of epistemology for phenomenology, and specifically, of a certain empiricism for an account of phenomena according to which those "thoughts, words, and actions" might be experienced precisely *in*—and not before or beyond—their appearing. What is more, the question of the subject or critic's relationship to appearances disappears as well. In the place of the possibility that there may be a complex but real closeness between perceiver and perceived, it appears that a case is being made for a certain critical distance, one that would be coterminous with "rigorous inquiry" and the cult of the evidentiary, which would separate "imaginings" from "reflections." The ambiguity of this vocabulary is telling, for it is not as if "reflection," at least since Narcissus, has ever gotten away from the problem of images, and specifically from the problem of the subject's relationship to and self-constitution through them.

What this amounts to is at once a mere difference of opinion—Frantzen's historicism is, after all, well-articulated—and, quite literally, a way of looking at the world, or, really, the very fact of *looking* at the world, of paying attention to how the world appears. Such attentiveness might, in fact, be more historical than it seems; it may be historical in its very seeming. Hans Ulrich Gumbrecht has argued that the "effort to establish cognitive distance as a condition for 'objective' historical experience can make us blind to our desire for direct experience of the past—which is best served when we do not seek such distance."[6] The earnest and often ascetically driven quest for what can be *known* about the past may, in other words, thwart precisely the desire for *experience* of the past, which animates this very quest. I want, in this way, to assent to Louise Fradenburg and Carla Freccero's felicitous assertion that "the past may not *be* the present, but it is sometimes *in* the present,"[7] but I want to take them still more literally. For no less than everything rests upon the relation between their two italicized words, "be" and "in": between, that is, being and enclosure. Appearances are the edges at which this relation becomes perceptible. To put this as succinctly as possible: if the past *is*, it is only insofar as it is enclosed by the present, and only insofar as this enclosure *appears*.

Enclosures

Somewhere, on account or in spite of Heidegger, we have gotten the notion that enclosure is a bad thing. It would be easy to blame it on Romanticism: the cult of wide open spaces in Leopardi, for example, or the terror of immurement in Poe. But closer inspection, indeed closer thought, reveals that the phenomenon is by no means limited to early modernity: Antigone suffered death by enclosure; Abelard was castrated in his "inner room."[8] Rafael Campo, meditating upon the difficulty of empathy in urban life, hears the wind respond: "*Your heart is human. Never let it close.*"[9] Humanity is open; enclosure is necessarily self-enclosure, closing-out, heartless. What is more, claustrophobia is practically a household word, thanks in part to its tricky relationship with voyeurism, as any viewer of *Big Brother* or *The Real World* can attest. On the big screen, small spaces delight as well: David Fincher's movies—the murder tableaux of *Seven*, *Fight Club*'s sweaty basement, *Panic Room*—have practically constituted a primer in the fascination with, and terror of, enclosed space.

Indeed, not only do fear and fascination go hand in hand when enclosures are at stake; fear is often alloyed with desire. Claustrophobia is, at bottom, in part a denied love of confinement: that is to say, it is always alloyed with claustrophilia.[10] The Middle Ages had a particularly sensitive, and sensory, understanding of this. In the devotional texts discussed below, it will become clear that enclosure was unavoidable for high-medieval religious culture; it was not only secretly desired (through repression) but openly courted, constructed, lived in. Critics have already said similar things with regard to contemporary gay culture: that homophobia structurally reproduces homoeroticism, for example,[11] or that niche marketing—sad symbol of social acceptance—intensifies the very closets it ostensibly opens.[12] And yet what if enclosures are not merely desired but desirable? What if the way out of the closet is, first and foremost, a way in?

These questions carry with and within them certain hermeneutic implications. Geoffrey Galt Harpham has opined that two otherwise strikingly divergent contemporary critics share "an antipathy they define as ethical to the closeted secrets of the text, to those encrypted, unfolding interiorities that are the typical object of the recoding or translation operations . . . by which the literary text is converted into terms and contexts not its own."[13]

A certain fetishism of exteriority, rendering both text and reader *as visible as possible*, goes hand in hand with an aversion to apparently unliterary "terms and contexts" and, more importantly, to the interpretive labor that attempts to translate, bridge, or even juxtapose these terms. My strategy, in the pages that follow, is to foreground not just the resistant and ultimately alluring interiority of bodies, texts, and buildings, but the very question of hermeneutic propriety: it is we interpreters who own and disown; the objects of our "reading" are dispossessed *a priori*, and only able to be inserted into the terms of propriety inasmuch as a given interpreter possesses (i.e., animates) them. What kind of logic could replace, or at least displace, that of the proper and improper? My answer to this question takes the methodological form of a claim that medieval enclosures can and do touch upon those of contemporary philosophy and lyric, in the right reader's hands: a risky claim, inasmuch as it requires a metonymic understanding of poetics, one in which contiguous terms come to participate, not just semantically but also in a sense ontologically, in one another without losing their distinctness. Between mine and not mine, what intervenes is *close to mine*, neither appropriable nor wholly other: within reach, without ever being fully grasped.

Given the high-medieval penchant for "decontextualizing and anthologizing" critical strategies,[14] this approximation of medieval to modern material, with its disregard for historical and discursive purity, is ultimately quite medieval. "Medieval," in this latter sense, indicates not just a historical situation particularly prone to anachronism, but, still more crucially, the inscription of modernity in and as the Middle Ages' own enabling betweenness: its constitutive middle.[15] Therefore, just as fear and desire touch at the point of their shared affective intensity, so too are the Middle Ages and modernity brought close, and made disclosively to touch, within an enclosing critical poetics of metonymy. Enclosure, then, is not a bad thing. As much surface as depth, it is, rather, ambivalent in the most literal sense: enclosure wants it both ways.[16]

It is, after all, fairly evident that those ostensibly impenetrable towers that litter the landscape of Old French narrative are built only to be broken into. Take, for example, Garin's early-thirteenth-century fabliau "The Lady Who Was Fucked and Fucked Over for a Crane" (Celle qui fu foutue et desfoutue por une grue).[17] Love, it seems, has driven a chatelain to lock his beautiful daughter in a tower: "He held her so dear and loved her so much / that he shut her up in a tower. / She had no one with her except her nurse" (Tant l'avoit chiere et tant l'amoit / que en une tor l'enfermoit. / N'avoit o li que sa norrice; 19–21). Yet no sooner has the enclosure appeared than it appears full of holes. One day, inevitably, the nurse leaves the tower in order to fetch, of all things, a plate from the main house for the girl's dinner and, as she does so, leaves the gate open:

> She left the gate of the tower open.
> At that moment a young man passed
> in front of the tower; he was carrying
> a crane that he'd trapped
> and was holding it in his right hand.
> The maiden was at the window
> and spending her time looking outside.
>
> [L'uis de la tor ouvert laissa.
> Atant uns vaslez trespassa
> par devant la tor, qui portoit
> une grue que prise avoit;
> si la tenoit en sa main destre.
> La pucele ert a la fenestre,
> a l'esgarder hors se deporte.] 33–39

The enclosure, here as elsewhere in this study, is doubly permeable; there's no such thing as just one entrance. In other words, where there's a window, there's a gate. The girl at the window engages in a brief conversation with the crane-bearer about the beautiful bird he holds in his hand, and she agrees, finally, to buy it. The price: "un foutre," a fuck (53). The girl, however, doesn't recognize this strange currency and invites her vendor up into the tower to look for the "foutre," which she claims not to have, and which the young man finds, in due course, under her clothes. To make a short story shorter: she gives him a fuck; he gives her a crane. The nurse returns, finds out what has happened, and is duly dismayed, but not dismayed enough to keep from leaving the tower a second time. The girl once again invites the young man back into the tower and demands her "foutre" back. He gives it to her, takes the crane, and leaves.

This dirty little story has a lot going on, perhaps most markedly a kind of resigned cynicism about economic markets and the ability of older feudal structures to resist them. (In the opening lines, Garin claims to have heard the story for the first time "in Vézelay, in front of the money-changers" [a Vercelai, devant les changes; 5].) But no less evident, in this staging of the openness of windows and gates to traversal, is an explicit eroticism of architectural ambivalence. The tower at once resists and solicits penetration. Indeed, there is no phenomenological difference between these two functions, just as there is practically no lexical difference between the traversals of the nurse and the young man: where the latter post-coitally "left the tower and went outside" (s'en issi de la tor fors; 93), the former rues the hour "that she went outside the tower that day" (qu'ele est hui de

THE EDGE OF ENCLOSURE   17

la tor issue; 155). The window and the gate are both the exception to and the rule of enclosure, just as the verb "to go out" enables all sorts of entrances. Moreover, the eroticism of this permeable enclosure is not just any eroticism; it is explicitly an erotics of dispossession: of birds and boys that come and go, and of the bodies and buildings through which they pass.

Ambivalence

An argument such as this one, conducted on the border between literature and philosophy, owes a great debt to Gaston Bachelard, who first sang the praises of interior space nearly fifty years ago in *The Poetics of Space*.[18] Bachelard's text provides both a model and a provocation for what I am attempting to perform here: a model, inasmuch as his concentration on the "psychic positivity of the image" (positivité psychique de l'image) resists, in the name of literary sensibilia, any wholly appropriative critical practice;[19] a provocation, inasmuch as this emphasis deliberately ignores the potentially unsettling effects of such images, resulting in an explicitly "sheltered" account of poetic space.[20] Indeed, Bachelard stresses the fundamental euphemism of his own project:

> The images I want to examine are the quite simple images of *felicitous space*. In this orientation, these investigations would deserve to be called topophilia. They seek to determine the human value of the sorts of space that may be grasped, that may be defended against adverse forces, the space we love.
>
> [Nous voulons examiner, en effet, des images bien simples, les images de *l'espace heureux*. Nos enquêtes mériteraient, dans cette orientation, le nom de *topophilie*. Elles visent à déterminer la valeur humaine des espaces de possession, des espaces défendus contre des forces adverses, des espaces aimés.][21]

There is certainly something attractive, and daring, about such explicit resistance, in 1957, to the cult of angst. And yet Bachelard here is saying more than this: for the "love" that we direct toward specific kinds of space, the mode of our "grasping," cannot possibly be self-evident or univocal. Indeed, he speaks explicitly of "espaces de possession," where it is unclear whether we who find ourselves in these spaces possess or are possessed by them. Similarly, it is a question of "espaces aimés," a plurality of spaces and, perhaps, also a plurality of loves. In this way, topophilia is fundamentally equivocal.

So when Bachelard asserts that "adverse forces," which here represent the threat of abjection, have a space of their own, it is worth remembering this equivocation and asking whether any space is fully, cleanly set apart.

Bachelard argues that "the space of hatred and combat can only be studied in the context of impassioned subject matter and apocalyptic images" (Ces espaces de la haine et du combat ne peuvent être étudiés qu'en se référant à des matières ardentes, aux images d'apocalypse).[22] But what if the enclosed space we love is also an apocalyptic space—which was surely the case for medieval mendicants (at least those who were influenced by Joachim of Flore) and, more recently, for gay bedrooms, clubs, and closets since AIDS? Is it finally all that easy to distinguish "matières ardentes" from the ardent matter, the burning stuff, of amorous affect? If my notion of claustrophilia responds to what Bachelard calls "topophilia," it is not only by fine-tuning the kinds of *topoi* that are at stake; it is, as well, by seeking to articulate a different, more unsettling, kind of love. This kind of love, and the sense organs through which it is produced, fueled, and articulated, would create and respond to "felicitous space" only in the sense of that space which makes one truly *felix*: for medieval Christianity, the space of blessedness, never far from the excessive, uncanny, occasionally bloody space of joy.

There are, nonetheless, also acknowledged moments of ambivalence and dialectical oscillation in Bachelard's text. He assembles countless commonplaces from continental poetry of the eighteenth, nineteenth, and early twentieth centuries in order to communicate a dialectics of inside and outside.[23] To be sure, this communication is itself dialectical, always half withdrawn even as it is offered: "The pure recollection, the image that belongs to us alone, we do not want to communicate; we only give its picturesque details" (Le souvenir pur, image qui n'est qu'à nous, on ne veut pas le communiquer).[24] Bachelard's daydreamer wants to say, with Angela of Foligno, "My secret is mine!" He is also remarkably ambivalent about the ramifications of his reverie. On the one hand, he claims instead to be interested solely in receiving the pure phenomenon: "the phenomenologist. . .brings the image to the very limit of what he is able to imagine" (le phénoménologue. . .porte l'image à la frontière même de ce qu'il peut imaginer) and nothing more.[25] In one of many implicit critiques of Heideggerian bombast, Bachelard declares,

> Such formulas as being-in-the-world and world-being are too majestic for me, and I do not succeed in experiencing them. In fact, I feel more at home in miniature worlds, which, for me, are domesticated worlds.
>
> [Les formules: être-au-monde, l'être du Monde sont trop majestueuses pour moi; je n'arrive pas à les vivre. Je suis plus à mon aise dans les mondes de la miniature. Ce sont pour moi des mondes dominés.][26]

And sometimes, in fact, one has the sense that Bachelard wants merely to suggest a cozy, ultimately psychological (which for him is close to phenomenological) experience of being "sheltered" before being thrown into the world, an experience that more primitive media such as poetry help us recapture. In observations such as these, one can find traces of Bachelard's strict separation of scientific inquiry from solitary reverie.[27] The dreamer's domesticity is an "experience" as opposed to a mode of "being"; it is an "at home"-ness, as opposed to the uncanny, un-home-like "world" of the (scientific) formula.

And yet, on the other hand, it is precisely Bachelard who speaks of unsettledness as an ontological, and not merely phenomenological or psychological, category. "The being of man is an unsettled being which all expression unsettles" (L'être de l'homme est un être défixé. Toute expression le défixe);[28] "man is half-open being" (l'homme est l'être entr'ouvert):[29] in observations such as these, Bachelard seems to attribute the same degree of constitutive complexity and oscillation to the human that Heidegger attributes to the work of art. In both cases, it is a question of the ultimately "half-open" dialectic of disclosure (here, "expression") and enclosure. The importance of this rhetorical, and perhaps not just rhetorical, convergence between the two thinkers is at least twofold: first, the viewer or reader can thus be seen to emerge, to disclose herself and materially resist disclosure, in response to the work of art; second, there might be said to be a specifically aesthetic mode of human being. What is more, the structural symmetry between the emerging reader and the emerging artwork suggests that, in the moment of aesthetic response, what may be at stake is precisely a metonymic relationship, one of contamination by contiguity: the stuff of saints and disease.

Huts and Hagiographies

Bachelard, as it happens, speaks explicitly of saints' lives. In the first chapter of the *Poetics of Space*, among images of the house that could reasonably be described as those of middle-class modernity, he includes an account of Henri Bachelin's daydreams of living in a hut in the woods. These daydreams, provoked by his father's recitation of saints' lives in the family's sitting room, open onto a "centralized solitude" (la solitude centrée), "the opposite of the monastery" (l'antitype du monastère): "Its truth must derive from the intensity of its essence, which is the essence of the verb 'to inhabit' " (Elle doit recevoir sa vérité de l'intensité de son essence, l'essence du verbe habiter).[30] The bourgeois sitting room, when reduced to its "essence"—a reduction figured here as intensification—becomes the saint's solitary hut, as if an aboriginal outline, a primitive enclosure, still organized the stuff of modern family life. So one enclosure participates in another. The suggestion is, then, that no enclosure is self-identical; even, perhaps, that the relationship of metonymic contamination proposed as the emerging reader's response to the emerging artwork, that this same relationship might be seen here, again, in the saint's hut, which is read aloud in the sitting room: comprehended by the place of its reading and infusing this place with its greater spatial intensity. In this way, metonymy (saying "hut" in and for "sitting room") is revealed to be the product not just of contiguity but of enclosure. To touch is, here, also to hold; and—metonymically—to intensify.

Philippe Lacoue-Labarthe, in his reading of Paul Celan's oblique address to Heidegger in "Todtnauberg," speaks of a different kind of hut, although one that is, like Bachelin's/Bachelard's, a condensation or intensification of other enclosed spaces. Here, "der Hütte" is the Black Forest chalet where Heidegger wrote, and where Celan and Heidegger met in 1967.[31]

"Todtnauberg" is really barely a poem; a single nominal phrase, choppy, distended and elliptical, unwilling to take shape, it is not the outline but the remainder—the residue—of an aborted narrative...It is an extenuated poem, or, to, put it better, a *disappointed* one. It is the poem of a disappointment; as such, it is, and it says, the disappointment of poetry.

[A vrai dire *Todtnauberg* est à peine un poème: unique phrase nominale, hachée et distendue, elliptique, ne se formant pas, c'est non pas l'esquisse, mais le reste—le résidu—d'un récit avorté...C'est un poème exténué ou, pour mieux dire, *déçu*. C'est le poème d'une déception: en tant que tel il est—il dit—la déception de la poésie.][32]

The hut marks the place of that disappointment. Lacoue-Labarthe continues:

In the summer of 1967 Celan writes in the guestbook of the *Hütte* in Todtnauberg. He no longer knows who signed before him; signatures—proper names, as it happens—matter little. At issue was a word, just a word. He writes—what? A line, or a verse. He asks only for the word, and the word, of course, is not spoken. Nothing; silence; no one. The in-advent of the word ("the event without answer").

[C'est dans l'été 67, écrit sur le 'livre d'or' de la Hütte, à Todtnauberg. Il ne sait plus qui avait signé avant lui: les signatures, les noms propres, en l'occurence, importent peu. Il s'agissait d'un mot, d'un simple mot. Il écrit—quoi? Une ligne, ou un vers. Il demande juste le mot et le mot, évidemment, n'est pas prononcé. Rien, le silence: personne. Inavènement du mot. ("Evénement sans réponse").][33]

How, then, does Heidegger's hut—the place of the refusal to respond, where poetry is paralyzed, unable to forgive when pardon is not asked for—how does this hut disturb the intensity of inhabitation that figures in Bachelin's daydreams? It confirms, first of all, Bachelard's suggestion that "in the most restricted intimate space... the dialectics of inside and outside draws its strength" (c'est...dans l'espace intime le plus réduit que la dialectique du dedans et du dehors prend toute sa force):³⁴ the simplicity of the hut condenses a cosmic dialectics, the possibility and impossibility of habitation after Auschwitz, after its implosion of the domestic, the enclosed. It is, however, a suspended dialectics, a disarticulation of the question against the non-event of the answer. Yet the hut, for Lacoue-Labarthe's Celan, would then be not merely a "centralized solitude" but the place of social aporia: where words get lost and enclosures collapse into immanence, which is to say, into impenetrable, transparent disclosure. The closed mouth, the closed door would be the sign of the hermit-saint's refusal, of the muteness of abjection.³⁵

Remembering, then, that Bachelin's daydreams were provoked by saints' lives, it is worth noting the brief chapter called "Hagiography" in Lacoue-Labarthe's essay. Lacoue-Labarthe refers here to Gadamer's characterization of the "understanding" at which Celan arrived, following his visit with Heidegger: " 'He understood the audacity of a thought that another ('the man') can hear without capturing its meaning, the risk of a step that moves forward on shifting terrain' " (Il comprit l'audace d'une pensée qu'un autre ["cet homme"] peut entendre sans la saisir, le risque d'une démarche qui s'avance en terrain mouvant).³⁶ Heidegger, saint-like, is misunderstood when the two men are walking together; understood in the aftermath of their encounter. To this hagiography Lacoue-Labarthe opposes the assertion that "Celan had returned from the encounter in a state of despair" (Celan était revenu désespéré de cette rencontre).³⁷ Despair, immortalized by Kierkegaard as the sign of the diabolic, nonetheless prompts Lacoue-Labarthe to repeat: "Yes, the birth of a hagiography" (Oui, naissance d'une hagiographie).³⁸

Is despair then, like the dawn of understanding, the product of that peculiarly intense inhabiting which the hermit-saint performs? Does hagiography mark, does it write, the holy as that which resists the ethical, before whose *ambivalence* despair and understanding are *equivalent*? Despair, for Lacoue-Labarthe an aesthetic (i.e., a formal or non-hermeneutic) category, the resistance to absent meaning, becomes the only language in which Saint Heidegger can be revealed. Bachelard, in fact, asserts that "language bears within itself the dialectics of open and closed. Through meaning it encloses, while through poetic expression it opens up" (le langage porte en soi la dialectique de l'ouvert et du fermé. Par le *sens*, il enferme, par l'expression poétique il s'ouvre).³⁹ Celan "opens up" the hut only to show its resistance to being disclosed: its sensible, but ultimately senseless, refusal of any gaze that would want to penetrate its surface in search of either a formal or a meaning-based answer. In this way (and I hazard this reading in its inevitable misunderstanding) Heidegger's hut is nowhere Celan can be *inside*; there is no possibility of cohabitation.

The Old French life of Jehan Paulus, a hairy hermit, suggests just how ambivalent a saint's hut—or in fact, a saint's den—can be. Jehan, called to solitary contemplation, goes into the woods and takes over "a large den...that a bear had already made" (une grant fosse...que jadis i avoit fait l'ourse; 947–48).[40] The devil, however, envious of the hermit's happiness, unsuccessfully tries to persuade him away from his life of solitary virtue. When rhetoric proves unconvincing, the devil resorts to a surer temptation: he takes the princess of Toulouse from the room where she is "enclosed" (ou la pucele estoit *enclose*; 1097) and deposits her in front of Jehan's cell. She embraces Jehan, who consequently "softens a little" (auques s'amolie; 1136), to the point of "having his way" with her (Que Jehans fist ses volentés; 1140). In the sex panic that follows, Jehan throws the girl in a well and destroys his hermitage. There follows a sort of parody, or at least inversion, of holy itinerancy:[41] Jehan wanders the woods with murderous intent. Even when he repents and confesses his sins to the pope and a random hermit, he is able to receive neither forgiveness nor consolation. Therefore he returns to the woods, where after years of penitential wandering—in a sense, the inversion of his bloodthirsty wanderings, and thus the inversion of an inversion—he is mistaken for an animal by a royal hunting party. Specifically, he is "hairy as a little bear" (Tout pelu si com un oursel; 1622). Caught in this way, Jehan is revealed to be human when the court subjects his body to close scrutiny: after inspecting his head, "They looked at him underneath, and saw thus his human members, legs, body, feet and hands" (Il l'esgarderent par desous, / S'ont veu les membres humains, / Gambes et cors et piés et mains; 1650–52). He is, however, fully integrated into humanity only once he is absolved by a prodigiously eloquent infant, whose testimony is seconded by an angelic voice: "You are entirely delivered and absolved" (Tous ies delivrés et assaus; 1766). This absolution prompts him to reveal his story, but only after a "wise man" (uns sages hom; 1782) tells the king to "command that he be covered" (Commandés que il soit couvers; 1786). The story told, Jehan leads the royal entourage to the woods and miraculously rescues the princess, alive after fifteen years, from the well where she had been thrown.

As even this condensed narrative should make clear, Jehan's life is a lesson in ambivalent categories. He is a man turned bear, whose "body" and "humanity" are both strikingly genital: how else to explain those "membres" that are distinct from, yet analogous to, his other extremities, and the "cors" that lies amidst them, as their hairy inner truth?[42] It is not, however, only a question of private and public parts. Jehan's "humanity" is thus disclosed through precisely those members he shares with all male bears (and many other animals as well). Moreover, he is a good bear gone bad, who is then converted to the good again. His enclosure in the cave is set up in symmetry to the "enclosed" princess, only to be undone, again metonymically, by her disclosure: after all, he "has his way" with her *in front of* the cave, not inside. Disclosure is contagious. It remains his lot for the rest of the poem, as he wanders, first murderously then in penance, through the woods. Yet something must continue to enclose him if he cannot be clearly seen by the royal hunters. Inasmuch as he is mistaken for a bear on account of his thick fur, the text suggests that this persistent enclosure may in fact be the outermost layer of his body, its finest (and most immediately perceptible) material edge. It takes the collective gaze of the court to see the hermit through the hair: a hermit, or human, whose distinction from the animal depends upon his spectacular genitalia, and perhaps the bodily extremities that frame and extend them. That is to say, genital disclosure— the origin of Jehan's tragedy, we must not forget—is what saves him in the end: and this salvation, as revealed by the wise man's command that Jehan be "covered," consists in covering up everything again, in order that Jehan's narrative, and the princess's body it contains, might be disclosed in full.

If for Giorgio Agamben, after Heidegger, "the animal is the Undisclosable that man harbors and brings as such to light" (l'animale è l'Indischiudibile che l'uomo custodisce e porta come tale alla luce), here instead, or perhaps in addition, the animal is that enclosive tissue, that furry envelope, at whose extremities the human comes to view.[43] This is not just to say that saints and animals are the categories against which proper human beings inevitably collide. Nor is it just to suggest that saints and animals both engage in concealed, imperfect forms of the openness to unconcealment, which characterizes an authentically human relation to the world. What Jehan Paulus shows, beyond the risk for human being of an animal (or saintly) non-relation to an "open but inaccessible" world, is that there is, strictly speaking, no proper opening, no disclosure to or for the world without a simultaneous retreat into the body's barely legible enclosure, thick as fur.[44] If "man occurs essentially as an opening to an enclosure" (l'uomo avviene essenzialmente nell'apertura a una chiusura), the opposite is also clearly the case.[45] Not only is the enclosure of Jehan's "membres humains" displayed, opened up for the courtly spectators as confirmation of his humanity and their own; these "membres" are enclosed by their display.

The categorical oscillation in this text is, of course, nothing short of staggering. It is not stopped but merely prodded toward resolution by the speech-acts of the infant and the angel. Their words of absolution, taken together with the layers of enclosure and disclosure within the narrative, suggest the following: first, that sainthood is a state into which one is interpellated, that is, performatively "called," in the sense of the vocative or vocation; second, that sainthood is an interminable tissue of enclosures and disclosures (or enclosive and disclosive moments). Through these moments, what takes place is a reinforcement of the bare spatial point, line, or three-dimensional structure (body, den) through which what is hidden or enclosed *emerges* into visibility, into disclosure. It is my impression that the interpellative gesture is that intervention which saves the saint for the ethical; whereas the ever-intensified point of emergence articulates the saint's aesthetic being, but also its ethical ambivalence. Jehan's hut, after all, does not protect him from temptation or violence: what one could almost call the spatial fetish of sainthood—and my argument applies as much to Heidegger as to Jehan—is, like all fetishes, ethically neutral, aesthetically fascinating, and a symptom of ambivalent desire.[46]

Closure

This account of sainthood, it must be emphasized, runs directly against the admittedly well-intentioned reading given by Edith Wyschogrod, for whom "a saintly life is defined as one in which compassion for the Other, irrespective of the cost to the saint, is the primary trait."[47] She even goes so far as to suggest that the "stylistics of hagiography" in Genet matter less than his "altruism."[48] It is my contention that neither Jean Genet nor Jehan Paulus could care less about altruism; and that it is precisely the interpellative intervention of a reader (angelic or infantile) like Wyschogrod that would save them for ethics. Rather, as Lacoue-Labarthe and Bachelard have shown, enclosures not only protect but forbid; they close in and close out. The appropriate response to these enclosures, Genet himself might add, is not compassion but horror: at the beginning of *Funeral Rites*, his narrator confesses, "I am horrified with myself for containing—having devoured him—the dearest and only lover who ever loved me. I am his tomb" (Aujourd'hui je me fais horreur de contenir, l'ayant dévoré, le plus cher, le seul amant qui m'aimât. Je suis son tombeau).[49] Enclosures are in themselves no more ethical than openness, than transparency; or perhaps they push the ethical to its breaking-point, to the point of betrayal.[50] Intensity is as bound up with abjection as it is with the ideal. What remains to be thought here, among so many things, is whether this ambivalence, figured as intensity or as enclosure, is itself immanent and impenetrable: that is to say, whether ethical effects can be produced by tracing the *emergence* of the enclosure, intervening in its genesis, refusing to make cohabitation subordinate to habitation. To show just to what extent even this critical practice is multiply contaminated, from its elusive origin: such a genealogy would, of course, also be an ontology; it would also be a decision.

The ambivalence of enclosure has received its most thorough ontological articulation in terms of that dialectic—understanding that dialectic here implies no temporal succession or synthetic *Aufhebung*—of holding and putting forth that we have seen, briefly, in Heidegger. After confronting this text once more—a confrontation in both the English and the Italian sense, that is, both an interrogation and a comparison—I hope the return to abjection and pleasure will seem, like sainthood itself, at once an inevitable intensification and the product of intervention. Inasmuch, then, as the Heideggerian functions might also be called enclosure and disclosure, it is tempting to think of a word that might synthesize them into a sort of metaconcept or, preferably, a concept that would not surpass them so much as limn the place where they are stuck together. *Closure*, for example, might articulate (temporarily, and for the sake of reinforcing ambivalence) the barest edge at which the enclosed meets the disclosed; their common, constantly redrawn threshold. But closure, with its already too instinctive connotations of finality and teleology—one need think only of how common it is to speak of "reaching closure" in a particular part of one's affective life—requires an extended reorientation if it is to be useful, and such a reorientation could prove disorienting for the reader. The following paragraphs are an attempt at once to produce such a reorientation and to attenuate its disorienting effects.

Closure—and here is the greatest risk of disorientation—would name, for me, what Heidegger has called the work of art. Contrasting the Greek temple with instrumental equipment, he observes that

> . . .the temple-work, in setting up a world, does not cause the material to disappear, but rather causes it to come forth for the very first time and to come into the open region of the work's world. The rock comes to bear and rest and so first becomes rock; metals come to glimmer and shimmer, colors to glow, tones to sing, the word to say. All this comes forth as the work sets itself back into the massiveness and heaviness of stone, into the firmness and pliancy of wood, and into the hardness and luster of metal, into the brightening and darkening of color, into the clang of tone, and into the naming power of the word. That into which the work sets itself back and which it causes to come forth in this setting back of itself we called the earth.[51]

Hardness and luster, brightening and darkening: what is named here—and what inheres, Heidegger insists, within the very resonance and refusal of the name—is the earth's emergence *and* retreat, its coming *and* going. I give myself to you by pulling away. Earth discloses itself like a fist.

In an episode of the HBO drama *Six Feet Under*, Nate (a funeral director played by Peter Krause) and Lisa (his wife, played by Lily Taylor) are hiking in the southern California mountains. Nate, starved for sex, suddenly presses Lisa against a boulder and swears to her, twice, "I'm going to fuck you on this rock." The rock at once emerges and retreats in Nate's interpellation: as it becomes more emphatically, materially there as the place of imminent penetration, it becomes hermeneutically more impenetrable. What do all those monosyllables mean? Like a word repeated until it is emptied of sense, "I'm going to fuck you on this rock" is at once too clear and virtually inaccessible. And, indeed, like a liturgical utterance—remember Jesus's promise to Peter in Matthew 16:18, that "upon this rock" his kingdom will be built—Nate's words invite material, bodily assent and resist interpretive appropriation. The work of art, likewise, sets forth and up—Heidegger is careful to draw upon both vertical and horizontal movement—just as it sets itself back. At the risk of simplification, one could say that it emerges out of its basic materiality (into meaning, society, intelligibility) only as it simultaneously retreats back into this same materiality; or not the same materiality at all, but a materiality constantly under revision, indissociable from the social, recalibrating its resistance to the world.

One does not need firsthand experience of a Greek temple to grasp what Heidegger is pointing to: every text's advent in the world, every emergence into visibility and comprehension, defies the audience's ear, the viewer's gaze. If the "worldly" dimension of the work of art is necessary for us to receive the work at all, its "earthy" dimension is what keeps us returning to it in frustration, tantalized by what it withholds. Heidegger's most striking intuition here is that this frustrating, tantalizing, earthy aspect of the artwork is precisely its barest materiality; not some "inexpressible" numinous content, but *the sensible fact that it is there*. For Heidegger, color "shows itself only when it remains undisclosed and unexplained."[52] The work of art *shows itself* as the closure, the cloister (we are still in the precinct of the temple), whose materiality participates in and resists its social meaning.

Under the Altar

It might be appropriate to take back—indeed, to withhold—what was just said about not needing firsthand experience, sensory experience, of the Greek temple. Euripides dramatizes, ironically and as irony, a participative and resistant relationship of setting-forth and setting-back in the temple of *Iphigeneia in Tauris*. Installed as a priestess of Artemis by Thoas, king of the Taurians, after her deliverance from Agamemnon's sacrifice, Iphigeneia delivers her opening monologue from within the temple:

> There are rituals here; the goddess Artemis is pleased
> with them: a holy service: only the name is good.

> I must not tell the details, for I fear the god,
> but I sacrifice, by custom known before my time
> in this state, any Greek man who comes upon this shore.
> I dedicate them: the real killing is left to others,
> and done in secret in the temple of this god.[53]

This is a temple where names are apparently at odds with material facts: the "holy service" is holy in name only; Iphigeneia's "dedication" is distinct from the "real killing," which occurs deep inside the temple. Something about the temple resists speech: Iphigeneia must not tell the details of her sacrifice, a synecdoche she corrects by distinguishing between her dedication and the "real killing" enacted by others. Yet, inasmuch as its space is identified primarily as an interior secrecy, the temple is clearly aligned to a greater extent with these others, not only as thing versus word, "real" against unreal (or social), but as Thing versus word, Real against real. The temple's secrecy speaks through Iphigeneia's repeated denials and qualifications; it is the space in which she speaks and the space between her words.

But the materiality into which the temple sets itself forth and back—a materiality whose resonance with the Thing should make clear its nonimmanence, its inability to be reduced to a *materialism*—appears also through the words of Greek men destined for its secrets. Orestes (Iphigeneia's brother) and Pylades (his companion) come across Iphigeneia's temple, whose altar is "brown with bloodstains," "skulls of slaughtered strangers" piled under its edge.[54] In the place of Iphigeneia's secrecy, here we have transparent evidence of bloodshed. In the place of performative language—"I sacrifice," "I dedicate"—here we have empirical observation. Pylades has in fact just declared, "I am looking. My eyes go everywhere": in the place of Iphigeneia's mouth, we have the Greeks' eyes.[55] In the place of Iphigeneia's monologue, we have the Greeks' conversation. In other words, Orestes and Pylades articulate the worldly aspect of the temple that Iphigeneia has left literally unspoken. Yet in doing so— in making meaning of the brown stains as "Hellenic blood," for example— they also underscore the place's simultaneous resistance to sight and hermeneutic appropriation, the uncanny refusal present in the spectacle of blood, which is, in a sense, their own. Their entry into the temple is thus as much an enclosive as a disclosive moment: Pylades's eyes "go everywhere," but they at once glide along the surface and participate in the most unspeakable secrecy. The figure for what I am calling "closure" is precisely the edge of the altar, brown with blood, hanging over a heap of skulls: this edge is the point at which singular speech meets communal vision, the social unfolds and folds into the asocial. Limning this edge, sharp as all edges are, constitutes the close, closing gesture to which all participants in and viewers of the work of art are consigned, an engagement with a temple of which it is possible to say, to see

> ...the surrounding walls, how high they are. Can we go straight up on the temple stair to the door? How can we do this and remain unseen? Can we with crowbars force apart the brazen doors? We know of no crowbars. Furthermore, if we are caught forcing the doors open, contriving entrances, then we shall die.[56]

The work of art—but, we shall see, the saint too, and the lover's body—obliges us to contrive entrances. It is close.

I venture these comments to show, through a text more widely read than the ones to which my argument is largely devoted, something of the ontological complexity of enclosure. *Iphigeneia in Tauris*, of course, closes (in another sense) with a sham ritual, and it is only through Iphigeneia's canny manipulation of the temple's worldly aspect (its symbolic cachet) that its constitutive dialectic of emergence and withdrawal becomes manifest once more. The rites she is about to perform—orchestrating the escape of the Greeks—require "privacy."[57] The barbarian King Thoas, for his part, is a docile spectator: he "want[s] no forbidden sight," and will "hold [his] robe before [his] eyes" when the strangers emerge from the temple.[58] The temple's entrance, obscured by Thoas's robe, is in fact mediated by this robe, as the sign of the temple's emergence into bare, blinding materiality, stone and fabric. As the Greeks cross its threshold, it is emptied of bodies, left to its secrets; it is simultaneously more present, in its bare material inarticulacy, and less meaningful.[59]

> Setting up a world and setting forth the earth, the work is the instigation of the strife in which the unconcealment of beings as a whole, or truth, is won.[60]

It is part of the paradox of the work of art that holding a robe over one's eyes should amount to a participation in unconcealment. That the temple should appear thus, to Thoas's fabric-filtered gaze as to the Greek eyes that "go everywhere," is evidence of its profound ambivalence—in other words, the neutrality, the blankness, of the space it opens and closes. It takes a canny intervention like Iphigeneia's, it takes the decision of desire, to give this space a direction, a purpose; and even such an intervention may ultimately be folded back into the mute recalcitrance of the work. Even as she springs her countrymen from their prison, amidst her liturgical recitations she declares, "Of the rest I do not speak."[61] This is the temple speaking, resting, through her, as the enclosure that persists within escape.

Looking, Being

Adam Phillips has argued that "the escape artist is always involved in some profound acknowledgement of just what it is that they feel confined by."[62] Iphigeneia would thus be an escape artist in both Phillips's sense of escape and Heidegger's sense of art. Her "profound acknowledgement" would consist in letting the temple appear through the Greeks' retreat, even as it retreats from the gaze of the Greeks at the beginning of the play. The temple finally confines and escapes only itself, but it is not without consequences for its audience. Phillips remarks that the early-twentieth-century performer Harry Houdini

> was revealing something horrifying about the nature of fascination; about spectacle as vicarious risk, about the appetites of a modern paying audience. Above all, he shows us, the audience wants to know that it can't see: wants to thrill to its ignorance.[63]

Surely there is a hint of such a thrill in Thoas's eager completion of Iphigeneia's sentences as she urges him *not* to look. This immobilizing, asocial thrill has its place in the language of desire: it is what the fetish provokes and distils.

What I am suggesting here is that Heidegger's work of art has a fetish-component, and that this component poses the largest challenge to any ethical appropriation of the work of art or its analogs, namely saints and beloved bodies. Heidegger observes that "in the earth. . .as essentially self-secluding, the openness of the open region finds that which most intensely resists it."[64] This self-seclusion invites the fetishistic gaze. It can lead either to immobility or to flight. If its most stubborn traces, in Euripides's play, are the skulls under the altar, as the deathly immobility that the artwork in its purity can confer upon the human, and if Thoas's docile gaze cannot get past his robe, transfixed there by what the robe concretizes and suppresses, this only means that disclosure is sometimes, and sometimes fatally, not desirable. But the fact that the Greeks escape precisely on account of the artwork's self-seclusion, its retreat, as it were, into Thoas's robe, testifies to the fact that no enclosure is final, just as no disclosure is hopelessly transparent. The artwork in this way is ethically suspended; this is why it is impossible to say, with Edith Wyschogrod, that saints are transparently ethical. *The artwork demands an intervention*: an intensification of its own constitutive structure—here, its retreat from speech and sight—in order to set something, someone, free.

Not that setting free is necessarily preferable to confinement. Heidegger points out that "beings as a whole are brought into unconcealment and held therein. To hold [*halten*] originally means to take into protective heed [*hüten*]."[65] The churches of the Middle Ages kept scores of bones protectively held under their altars in order that something, preferably divine power, might be thereby unconcealed. Truth as *aletheia* does not necessarily entail the dismantling of every enclosure: unconcealment closes, but it does not close in or close out; it marks a line, a material edge. In the moment when sensation breaks down even as it accommodates the sensible, the unconcealed holds. In *Iphigeneia at Aulis*, Iphigeneia's disappearance is at once the object of an eyewitness account and the visible inscription of the limits of the visible. The messenger avows, "I saw it myself. I was there." He adds:

> Pain welled up in me
> at that, and I dropped my eyes.
> And the miracle happened. Everyone
> distinctly heard the sound of the knife
> striking, but no one could see
> the girl. She had vanished.[66]

The messenger "was there"; in fact, his being-there is coterminous with his sight, a sense that, painfully, abandons itself to the miracle. Dropping his eyes, literally letting go of the material organs of sensation, the messenger also performs the greatest intensification of his scrutiny. Letting go, that is to say, can be an assent to the arrival of the miraculous: sight pushed to its extremes in surrender, eyes responsively popping from their sockets. The miracle marks the material edge of sensation. In this way, it stages the intervention in which our attempts to make something of an artwork inevitably participate. The lady vanishes, but we see it for ourselves; we are there.

— The Miracle and the Fetish —

That the messenger's look, that the look we direct toward artworks and other disclosive enclosures, might produce the miracle it witnesses, without the connotation that this production is somehow subjective (and thus relative)—that, in its directed embodiment, its being-there as being-*toward*, it might enable the advent of not a new perspective but a new spectacle: this is where my argument touches upon, and owes an unspeakable debt to, Kaja Silverman. In her reading of the cave-allegory in Plato's *Republic*, Silverman hints at the miraculous nature of the look:

> We confer this gift of beauty when we allow other people and things to incarnate the impossible nonobject of desire—when we permit them to embody what is itself without body, to make visible what is itself invisible.[67]

Iphigeneia's strange visibility, her saturation of the sensible to the point of vanishing, merely intensifies the kind of vision that Silverman seeks to articulate. The messenger's look is not necessarily the look of love, but it is affectively charged all the same; it is his pain that lets us know he has not merely given up, averted his gaze, but rather has allowed his look to open upon, and thus to receive as a sensible offering, the miracle of Iphigeneia's vanishing salvation.

Indeed, the messenger's painful acquiescence to Iphigeneia's invisibility also resonates with Silverman's more recent critique of the extent to which invisibility, for a certain contemporary "aesthetics of exposure," has come to function in "a purely instrumental relation to the visible."[68] The messenger allows the approach of the invisible, and like Silverman's spectator, sitting before Jeff Wall's light boxes as they go dim and their images fade, permits us to ask: at the limit of sight, what gives itself? Does it (the light box, Iphigeneia's miraculously saved but invisible body) give itself to be seen or known? Does it perhaps give itself as seeing? Or as enclosing and enabling sensation? Nora Gallagher writes, in *Things Seen and Unseen*, "Still, when I recited the Nicene Creed on Sunday morning, the 'unseen' became for me, not a realm of ghosts, but an ignored otherness, a place where you waited and hoped. It was fragile and at the same time luminous. It was as if we were sneaking in under the radar."[69] Iphigeneia's body is at once the inappropriable place where the messenger "waits and hopes" and the structuring absence at the center of his eyes.

Furthermore, relinquishing the appropriative look mitigates against the mere, and ultimately illusory, creation of what Jean-Luc Nancy would call "a little more sense."[70] The Greek temple, like Iphigeneia's vanishing point, marks the place at which presence is offered and withdrawn: in the first case, it is an instance of the earth's material ambivalence, in which Iphigeneia's liturgy intervenes; in the second, it is the miraculous as just such an intervention, revealing the participative link between each organ of sight and the sensible. To light up Iphigeneia's body with painfully extenuated eyes is, however, to take a risk. The body might vanish: and is this necessarily preferable to her corpse, her body reduced to an immanent (which is to say: an empty) shell? It is just this risk that lies behind Silverman's articulation of the look's ability to make what it sees stand in for the "impossible nonobject of desire," that object which I have earlier referred to as the Thing. My argument here can only brush hesitantly and clumsily against psychoanalysis, but it may be worth recalling that the Thing traditionally marks the most intensified site of the Real, that nameless, disordered psychic realm which is fundamentally, even constitutively desirable, but which can never be directly desired. I would suggest that the risk that Silverman's look is running is precisely that of opening up a specific space, within the sensible, for the Real: this means risking the Real's allure, the possibility that the look, once offered, might not want to look away. Slavoj Zizek has seized upon the Lacanian *objet petit a* to designate those objects that the look, given over toward the Real, can neither seize nor relinquish. The *objet petit a* is "the leftover which embodies the fundamental, constitutive lack."[71] In a chapter on "Coke as *objet petit a*" from *The Fragile Absolute*, Zizek specifies the peculiar spatiality of this object: it "exists (or, rather, persists) in a kind of curved space—the nearer you get to it, the more it eludes your grasp (or the more you possess it, the greater the lack)."[72] If the *objet petit a* is a remainder that opens onto an infinitely protracted interstitial space, the Freudian fetish constitutes an attempt to fill in that space, to exhaust ambivalent desire with an ambivalent object. What would happen, then, if we scribbled between Freud's lines, inflating his shiny noses and jockstraps with this risky, billowing space? The fetish, in this newly reinforced sense, would "inherit [an intensified form of] the interest...formerly directed to its [unnameable, unspeakable] predecessor [which it sustains even as it overcomes]."[73] The fetish becomes protracted in its own penultimacy; it is ever more distinctly not quite there yet. In contrast, the messenger "was there"; he saw. Is part of the "pain" with which Euripides's messenger abandons (in both senses) his look precisely this refusal of fetishism in the advent of the miracle?

Therefore, if the edge of closure names the threshold of the visible, the point at which the material both becomes sensible and settles back into its reinforced materiality, disclosed and enclosed, it might seem that the latter of these moments or gestures runs the greatest risk of fetishism. It is difficult to relinquish the saint's relic once you hold it in your hand. And yet paradoxically, in contemporary discourse, there is also a strain of what we might call disclosure-fetishism: there are distinct, if mostly bureaucratic, advantages to "coming out," to "being open" about certain things. In queer discourse, the closet is only a historical curiosity or a contemporary betrayal. I have no intention of making an apology for the closet here, nor for the cult of secrecy more generally; but I do want to suggest that, if the libidinal (indeed, the ontological) risk of productively looking at the site of closure is a certain relentless, almost petrified tenacity, that is, a certain hybrid fetishism, then this risk holds, as it were, no less for disclosure than for enclosure.[74] As the final scene of *Iphigeneia in Tauris* ironically and eloquently makes clear, the god's ostensible appearance can be a vanishing act, just as, in *Iphigeneia at Aulis*, vanishing itself can mark the site of vision. But what is at stake here is more than just a trick of words or light: it is the question of how to hold an object of desire—*for the best*—within a shelter or within a look whose parameters, touching upon the undecidable "strife"

THE EDGE OF ENCLOSURE   33

of the Real made real, cannot be other than ambivalent. My condensation of vocabularies here is, like all condensations, symptomatic, and thus fraught with its own ambivalence. But this should only dramatize critically, in form as well as content, the extent to which (to use the terms of a previous paragraph) the artwork, enclosed and disclosed, demands an intervention. To build upon these earlier terms: there is also a sense in which the artwork stages this intervention. The miracle happens, and we must produce the miraculous. I want to resist for a few more moments the theological implications of this assertion, in order to show that, just as enclosure and disclosure may both be fetishized by the tenacious look, they may both fold into (and open onto) one another and thereby allow the advent of the miracle.

Participation: Here

Responding to Heidegger's "Letter on Humanism," Silverman writes,

> . . .it is only by embracing other people and things that we can free them to be themselves—only by enfolding them within our psychic enclosure that we can create the space where they can emerge from concealment.[75]

Embrace sets free; enfolding makes room. A few pages earlier, in dialogue with Lacan's *Seminar VII*, she argues:

> To each of us, through our particular libidinal history, has been given the potentiality for participating in a unique series of disclosures. This potentiality is not so much a talent as a responsibility.[76]

Enclosure and disclosure thus seem to be moments in an ongoing "history" (which, I would argue, is as much ontological as libidinal) of unconcealment or "emerge[nce]." I prefer the latter term inasmuch as it consolidates both moments better than "unconcealment" can. To be sure, "unconcealment" presents itself as the constitutive negation of the hidden, but "emergence" speaks forth an even greater, and more spatial, paradox: literally *e-mergere*, emergence plunges, immerses, engulfs not into but *out of*: it is enclosure figured as disclosive opening, approximation as distance. In order for other people and things to "emerge" we must in a sense "merge" with them: not in an appropriative fashion, nor in the sense of a *reductio ad unum*—which would be an immersion *into*—but in a sense to which Silverman's choice of words almost uncannily gives a clue. She speaks of "*participating* in a unique series of disclosures," and I would suggest that the merging through which emergence happens, that is, the productive sensation through which the miracle can intervene, resonates with nothing so much as a platonic understanding of participation. In fact, it is only participation that keeps the miraculous from coming as monstrosity.

In the introduction to *Radical Orthodoxy*, John Milbank, Catherine Pickstock and Graham Ward make the following claim:

> By contrast, the theological perspective of participation actually saves the appearances by exceeding them. It recognises that materialism and spiritualism are false alternatives, since if there is only finite matter there is not even that, and that for phenomena really to be there they must be more than there. Hence, by appealing to an eternal source for bodies, their art, language, sexual and political union, one is not ethereally taking leave of their density. On the contrary, one is insisting that behind this density resides an even greater density—beyond all contrasts of density and lightness (as beyond all contrasts of definition and limitlessness). This is to say that all there is *only* is because it is more than it is.[77]

Participation, in this way, radicalizes Silverman's suggestion that participative disclosure can be figured as "psychic enclosure." That is, again in language closer to Silverman's, I incorporate (incompletely) every body lit up by my look, but in allowing for that body's excess of my senses, I incorporate *excorporatively*. This is also true inasmuch as I am myself immersed, complicit, in the sensory emergence of every sensed being. In this way, neither my body nor the bodies around and contiguous to it merely "are." Their sensory proximity and response, and the mutual imbrication that such proximity responsively generates, show (not unambiguously, but show all the same) that *sensed being is shared being*. But not identical, of course; your skin is not reducible to my skin, let alone to my look. What sustains this immersive emergence, this excorporative incorporation, if it is not to amount to a *reductio ad unum*, must exceed both seer and seen—but exceed them as their point of connection. This is what it means to "save the appearances by exceeding them." What remains to be thought, as I have suggested earlier, is the spatial equivalent of "eternal": not a saturated omnipresence but something, I would suggest, more like a fleeting but recuperable deictic "here"—the shared space that exceeds its sharing, sensed only as an intensification that overwhelms the senses. For who, in such a moment, can actually say what it is like to be "here"? Or in that most common of deictic moments, that of saying, "here, take this; here, let me give you a hand," what is sensed is the connection, the outstretched hand, the offered body, summoned not *ex nihilo* but out of material "density," the body's heft distilled into its barest touch.

To be sure, participative accounts of sensation (and here I am speaking above all of Catherine Pickstock's compelling liturgical critique of philosophy) tend to be distrustful of intensification, and to see its relationship to another modern event, "spatialization," as evidence of the impossibility, for secular ontology, of the miraculous, that is, of any non-immanent intervention in the sensory world. "Reacting against the Thomistic framework of *analogia entis*," according to which finite beings participate, paradoxically, in the Being that nonetheless fully transcends them, for Duns Scotus "God is deemed 'to be' in the same univocal manner as creatures, and although God is distinguished by an 'intensity of being,' He nonetheless remains within, or subordinate to the category of Being."[78] This ultimately immanent chain of intensities—in other words, a nondisclosive enclosure—produces an effect that Pickstock describes as an "absolute space"; such a space would be coextensive with a divine sovereignty ever more separate from humanity, and ever more authoritarian.[79] I am suggesting, on the other hand, that the artwork's retreat into its materiality even as it offers itself to the senses, that the mutual distance and approximation through which two bodies immerse themselves *out of* (which is also to say, *emerge into*) each other, sensibly—that these spatial modalities establish a "here" which is not "absolute space" but contingent sharing. But how can the contingent, or contiguous, be shared—how can the negativity that keeps one body from the other, or the artwork's sensibility from itself, be dealt with in ways other than an appropriative overcoming? I would suggest that this is possible only if something intervenes: not to fill in empty space but to point, through the estranging deixis of desire, to the "here" that draws close.

Against and Above

André Vauchez speaks of a "restructuring of the field of the miraculous" (une restructuration du champ du miraculeux) in the twelfth and thirteenth centuries. Theologians emphasized that human prodigies were distinct from divine miracles. Alexander of Hales, the Franciscan who would become Bonaventure's teacher, argued early in the thirteenth century that *immediacy* characterized the miraculous. (A similarly miraculous immediacy will inform the closing chapter of this book.) For Aquinas, the divine action, additionally, occurred not contrary to nature (*contra naturam*) but surpassing it (*supra naturam*).[80] The miracle—and with it, the possibility not just of ethics or community but transcendence as such—would thus seem to partake of the same ambivalence that, we have seen, characterizes the artworks, the bodies, between and into which it intervenes. In order to circumvent this ambivalence (or in order to intervene within the ambivalence, to let something else come in its place), one must think how the *contra naturam* might participate in the *supra naturam*. This participation would not be a relationship, let me stress, of Derridean supplementarity, in which one term would inhere in the other as its antagonistic parasite and retroactive precondition. The participation of the miraculously *against* nature in the miraculously *above* nature would also undo the customary binary according to which monsters are miracles gone wrong, or done wrongly or by the wrong people. Instead, a "greater density" would be found to connect and exceed the "against" and the "above," the sodomite and saint. It is my assertion that the miraculous break with everyday reality as *natura*—that this break only happens when the materiality of *natura* is pushed literally to its point of greatest saturation or density. And what intervenes here is not the immaterial but precisely the material that nature cannot contain. The intensification of enclosure splits the enclosure open, *but splits it open as enclosure*. The body is only fully body when it breaks.

This is not to propose a mysticism of suffering. What I am suggesting, instead, is that death does not ultimately undo. Jean-Luc Nancy affirms, "Touching one another with their mutual weights, bodies do not become undone."[81] For saints and artworks and those particular modes of perceptible being we have come to call "queer," but also in some sense for all of us, whoever we are, death marks the place of an intensification, where the material has not been overcome but, rather, allowed to arrive. That this material arrival, this intervention as advent, might permit the living to live more intensely—to see the beauty in a body's resistance, to strive to emerge not out of but into the beloved, to "save the appearances by exceeding them"—is the both spoken and unspoken desire of the devout. This devotion is, in Richard Rambuss's auspicious title, a "closet devotion"; but more than this, it knows—no, it doesn't know, it *experiences*—that what it loves will not disappear when the door is opened, or when the body withdraws.

CHAPTER 2

THE VERGE OF THE VISIBLE

Hermits in Space

The saints of Old French hagiography are frequently on the verge of the visible. They are, that is to say, poised on the threshold of appearance, at the edges of enclosures whose importance for the senses, and especially for touch and vision, is continually stressed through a kind of holy peek-a-boo. Indeed, Lynne Tillman may just as well have been writing a saint's life when, in *Haunted Houses*, she observes, "She was not given when she gave, she always held back and drew satisfaction from distance."[1] Something is withheld in the offering, and this spatial withholding—distance within proximity—is explicitly satisfying: it gives pleasure. Likewise, the intensification of the material edge across which saints emerge reinforces both the ambivalence of enclosure and its fundamentally paradoxical resistance to immanence. In other words, saints do not just inhabit but mark a place of sensation, of becoming-sensible. The saints' disclosure, however, is first and foremost the disclosure of a threshold. They come to sight (where sight metonymically gives onto the other senses) always in relation to another place, an enclosure whose inside is necessarily invisible: a whorehouse, a hermitage, a robe, some hair. It is, then, a question of disclosure itself as the drawing of this threshold, the way in which saints disclose their own disclosive function. Hagiography never gets beyond this point of emergence.

At the end of chapter 1, I argued that it is crucial, for a sensitive ontology as well as for any queer theory worth the name, that we not reduce what is "here" to what is quantifiable, transparent, or given; that presence persists, even in death (and not despite death), no matter how many times that old warhorse about mourning and melancholia might be trotted out onto the field. Saints, too, must die as well as live. Moreover, it is through their sex that saints most powerfully and mortally emerge. The sexed body, that is, the body as both genitally specific and potentially sexual, makes an essential contribution to the saint's emergence. Leo Steinberg has famously shown how, for Latin Christianity, genital specificity went hand in hand, so to speak, with genital use.[2] In Steinberg's reading of the tradition of genital display in late medieval and early modern depictions of Christ, sexual potentiality is in fact necessary if Christ is to be understood as "prevail[ing] over concupiscence": "Chastity consists not in impotent abstinence, but in potency under check."[3] Whereas the artists who painted Christ's penis may have done so in such a "formally austere" way that there could be no question of "licentiousness" in their treatment—as of course no trace of licentiousness in their subject—the Old French saints' lives tell a different story.[4] Their dramatization of the sexual margins and enclosures of holy life may owe a great deal to Augustinian anthropology, but their form is seldom austere. Sex perpetually threatens to disclose itself together with, or in the place of, sanctity. Hagiography's desire to make visible always edges up against the vision of desire. Saintly emergence, coming out of the (however fantasized or fantastic) enclosure, risks the traversal of this edge, risks its ambivalence.

It goes without saying—but does it, really, ever go without saying?—that what follows is no more capable of immediate vision, or confident of its utter externality to what it sees, or able to dislodge the sexual from its textual body, than the medieval material it examines. What I hope to offer is a theory of sanctity—theory precisely in the etymological sense of *theoria*, a contemplation linked to the senses—which would also be a theory of vision and space, a compromised disclosure of how hagiography brings to light the illuminating process itself: the deepest and most superficial questions that traditional literary-historical modes of inquiry leave unspoken and unspeakable. Let me repeat this rather basic methodological assertion: if hagiography offers an ethically neutral account of the body's emergence into and retreat from vision, where linear sequence is at once distended and abridged, so too will my readings depart from any strict logic of linear concatenation. In fact, in the lives of Marie the Egyptian and Jehan Bouche d'Or described below, it will become clear that it is fundamentally tough to limit the senses: tough to say, for example, that a hand is only touching a pen and not a penis; tough, as well, to say that a monastic body touches according to the protocols of a specific tradition (e.g., Benedictine practice) and not according to some other, stranger and more temporally complicated order of bodily appearance and engagement. Hagiography, confident of the metonymic connections between the sacred and the profane, this world and the next, touches upon and thus infuses critical prose with its own risk, makes even the most foreign modern discourse a participant in its ambivalent, passing visions.

It is in this spirit that I want to point out how Benedict's sixth-century *Rule* distinguishes good monks from bad monks. There are, on the one hand, "cenobites...who do battle under a rule and an abbot" (1.2) and "anchorites or hermits," who are "well equipped to leave the fraternal battle-line for the solitary combat of the desert" (1.3–5). Benedict's apparently straightforward taxonomy, however, quickly turns polemical: the next class of monks is "the abominable one of the sarabaites," who are "like soft lead," living "in twos and threes, or even alone," and whose law "consists in yielding to their desires" (1.6–9). These monks are outdone only by the "wanderers," "always roving and never settling," given over to gluttony (1.10–11).[5]

What are we to make of this sequence? Is Benedict merely showing the ways in which virtuous monastic life (communal or eremitic) can be perverted if left without a *regula*? Or, given his obvious preference for communal life, is this taxonomy to be read as a scale of monastic virtue, with cenobites sliding into ambivalent hermits, and from there into unequivocally abominable sarabaites and, finally, the atopic wanderers? It is not a matter of deciding which is the correct reading of Benedict's text, much less of ascribing these preoccupations to Benedict alone.[6] Rather, what I want to emphasize is that the soft, the abominable, the indeterminately gathered (all descriptions with strong precedents in the biblical rhetoric of sexual transgression) are coupled with the restlessly wandering in a parody of monastic enclosure: the first group eating away at this enclosure from within; the second, roaming around it, refusing to be policed by its rule. The hermit, set loose in space, sometimes living alone, sometimes in "twos and threes," would provide a point of condensation for these anxieties.[7]

Aelred of Rievaulx gives a twelfth-century account of the problem in the first part of his *Rule of Life for a Recluse*. The "monks of old," he writes, tended to choose one of two kinds of solitary life: "some lived alone in the desert," whereas others, acknowledging the temptation of "aimless wandering," chose "to be completely enclosed in a cell with the entrance walled up."[8] Aelred then goes on to say that, in effect, there is no such thing as complete enclosure, no ultimately impermeable wall. Many recluses "think it enough to confine the body behind walls"; meanwhile, "the mind roams at random" and "the tongue too runs about all day."[9] Where Benedict establishes separate categories for hypocrites and wanderers, Aelred inscribes hypocrisy and vagabondage at the very heart of the enclosure. In other words, what was, for Benedict, the excluded, external supplement to monastic virtue actually *inheres*, for Aelred, within the practice and space of that virtue, as its most intimate threat.

Before returning to the hermit's particular condensation of monastic anxieties, it is worth recognizing that this danger supplementing and threatening monastic life—that is, the badly enclosed and the unenclosed monk—has strong resonances with a tradition Benedict and Aelred would have known well: that of the noonday demon. As Giorgio Agamben describes it, the noonday demon—the concentration of sloth, *acedia*, in a particular temporal moment—inspires both bad enclosure and restless vagabondage. Agamben quotes Cassian's *Institutiones* in observing that the slothful demon makes the monk "inert before every activity that unfolds within the walls of his cell," while at the same time "he convinces himself that he will not be at ease until he abandons his cell"; his inertia becomes indecisive movement, as "he begins to look about himself here and there" and "he enters and exits several times from the cell."[10] *Acedia* proves as shifty, over the course of the Middle Ages, as the monks who potentially fall prey to it. Let me merely point to the fact that its erotic implications are certainly strong in the late twelfth and thirteenth centuries. No less a figure than Bonaventure will stress its connection to the "concupiscent instinct,"[11] and the *Ancrene Wisse* famously links idleness to both Sodom and bodily plenitude: "*The iniquity of Sodom: a surfeit of bread and idleness*—that is, the wickedness of Sodom came from idleness and a full belly."[12] Agamben's restlessly inert monk, then, sums up the most apparent aspect, though not the most radical one, of claustrophilia: a particularly intense and necessarily ambivalent erotic relationship with enclosed space, a relationship that hinges upon the metonymic touching between bodies and the spaces that contain and articulate them.

The Body's Turn: Marie l'Egyptienne

In Old French literature, the figures of hermit-saints articulate perhaps most powerfully this intense and intensely ambivalent relationship to enclosure. It is through two Old French lives in particular, those of Jehan Bouche d'Or and Marie l'Egyptienne, that I will attempt to come to terms with the position of hermits in Benedict's taxonomy. This coming to terms will be necessarily elliptical: necessary, finally, because of its mimetic relationship to the spatialized emergence and retreat of the saintly bodies with which I am here concerned. Of course medieval notions of eremitic life change constantly, but I want to argue that the anxieties which constellate around the figure of the hermit remain fundamentally the same. Moreover, inasmuch as the medieval lives of hermit-saints situate themselves almost exclusively in patristic times (i.e., not long before Benedict), the real question becomes one of the ways in which certain modes of monastic life lend themselves to historical and sexual fantasy.

In matters of sexual fantasy, few saints can rival Marie l'Egyptienne. The Old French versions of her life have been separated by Peter Dembowski into two dominant and contrasting threads: one closer to Sophronios's patristic *vita*, with Zosimas, the monk who discovers Marie, at centerstage; and one in which Marie "plays the principal role," which typically means lots of lingering over the saint's squalid past.[13] It is this latter tradition, with its "hyperbolic" and "perverse" account of the sins from which Marie is saved, that interests me here.[14] Over the course of 1,532 octosyllabic lines, Marie's twelfth-century hagiographer tells the story of an Egyptian whore who travels to the Holy Land, is converted before an image of the Virgin, and flees to the desert, where she is discovered by a monk to whom she tells her story. The nature of Marie's sin is described with a strikingly precise theological vocabulary: "Molt fu esprise de luxure" (l. 63): she was, that is, greatly seized by *luxuria*, that fundamentally undefinable and all-encompassing category of sexual sins.[15] Indeed, it may even be possible to see a hint of Romans 1.24 ff. (the famous passage in which God "gives up" the Romans to their unnatural desires) in the description of Marie's catholic tastes: "She gave herself up to all men" (A tous homes s'abandonoit; 70).

These might, admittedly, be small details in a narrative whose delight in the body of a fallen woman couldn't be much more obvious. Simon Gaunt, with characteristic understatement, speaks of "an eroticism which is often far from restrained."[16] After all, there is a full courtly catalogue of Marie's beauty at ll. 157–92, which begins with her ears and proceeds downward until, after breasts, arms, hands, and fingers, it arrives at her "cors," literally her "body," as if it were just another part like all the others. What, then, does "cors" signify, for this hagiographer and his audience? If "body" fundamentally means *lower* body, what happens to the entire sign-system of a text that is at bottom nothing more than a sustained meditation upon the saint's corporeality? A disembodied saint is not a saint at all. But what about a perversely embodied saint?

I'm not being entirely fair to Marie here. It is true that her body undergoes a profound transformation—indeed, almost an undoing—when she escapes into the desert. Where she had been "white as a flower" (blance comme flour; 113), she becomes, in her newly holy nakedness, totally "blackened" (noirchie; 625, 662). The description of her penitential body even warrants two more lines than her voluptuous courtly form had received. Yet, as much as I want to believe that this text has given up staging Marie's "cors," it turns out that, in the poem's second half, devoted to Marie's encounters with the desert monk Zosimas, the "cors" is alive and well, just under a different name. In fact, the ability of a name to mean something other than what it seems to mean has, by this point, already been highlighted by the poem. In her prayer to the Virgin in Jerusalem, Marie confesses, "We have one name, that is, Marie; / Our life is quite different" (Un non avons, ce est Marie, / Molt est diverse nostre vie; 465–66). Marie speaks grammatically of only one "life," symmetrical to the one name, yet strangely "diverse." One name can thus signify the internal diversity of a life, or a *Life*, while preserving the faintest connection between them. By looking at where Marie's "cors" (or its equivalent: nothing is univocal here) reappears in the edifying second part of the text, it is my aim to suggest that there is an alternative life written within this hagiographic text—a hagiography that is not (quite) one.

Specifically, Marie's body returns as shadow and figure. Zosimas leaves his monastery near the river Jordan for Lent, and goes out into the desert to find "hermits" (hermites; 83). His search is very brief, in narrative terms at least, for after twelve lines he sees Marie's shadow. The text, however, is more coy than this: it is at first a shadow "which was either a man's or a woman's / But it was [in fact] the Egyptian woman's" (Qui estoit ou d'ome ou de feme, / Mais ele estoit de l'Egyptienne; 825–26). Faced with Zosimas's ignorance, the audience nonetheless never loses certainty that "it [or she] was of the Egyptian woman": the rendering-stable of gender ambiguity is shown to be *staged* within the text for an audience who already knows what's coming. Zosimas prays to God to protect him from "male temptation," which one is almost tempted to read as *male* temptation, whereupon "He saw Marie's form; / Marie's form he saw / Openly, without covering" (Le figure vit de Marie; / De Marie vit le figure / Apertement sans couverture; 838–40). For all its obvious voyeurism, the passage shows remarkable rhetorical finesse. The chiasmus—or anadiplosis[17]— in the first two lines gives way to a different sort of redundancy in the third, but the effect is nonetheless to reinscribe the relation between the "figure," barely more determinate than an "ombre," and its owner, with Zosimas's vision serving as the hinge between them. The vision is meant to be doubly unambiguous: not only do we witness it, as it were, backward and forward; its object is displayed both "openly" and "without concealment" (to be sure, the "couverture" is also Marie's absent clothing).

It is something akin to this staging of visibility's becoming-unambiguous that Simon Gaunt describes in his account of how the male audience of this *vie* "watches a holy strip show in which the stripper is first allowed to do her act, and is then punished for her lack of shame, allowing the male audience to enjoy the show, then to feel righteous."[18] Gaunt's description, however, only addresses half of the text's erotic charge: I would argue that the strip show, in Marie's life, does not stop at her conversion. As this encounter with Zosimas more than amply suggests, the text's scandal is that of an *eroticized penitent body*. Zosimas has seen (doubly) Marie's "figure," but the text continues to dramatize the visual aspect of the encounter: Marie has only her long tresses to cover her, but it's a windy day, and "When the wind raised them / Underneath appeared her frost-bidden flesh" (Quant ce li soslevoit le vent, / Dessous paroit le char bruslee; 846–47). This intermittent apparition of Marie's sun-burned, frost-bitten flesh occurs even while

Marie keeps her face, and her "faiture," turned away from the monk. She laments to God: " 'I don't dare turn my face to him / Nor do I dare to turn my features / For I am a naked creature' " (Jou ne li os torner mon vis, / Ne lis os torner me faiture, / Car jo sui nue creature; 868–70). Yet when the narrative sums up Marie's unwillingness to turn her exposed body to Zosimas, it merely notes that she "didn't dare turn her face toward the man" (n'osa son vis torner vers l'ome; 872). Could Marie's "vis" play, in reverse, the same kind of synedochic role that her "cors" played earlier in the text? The poem's solution to the predicament of the exposed saint suggests so: Zosimas throws her a piece of his clothing, and Marie "covered a great part of her body" (de son cors covri grant partie; 886). There can be little doubt that the hagiographer has in mind a "partie" as much qualitatively as quantitatively distinguished. It is, in effect, the textual equivalent of the reproduction through fragmentation that occurs with the cult of relics: once Marie's "cors" appears reduced to its genital "partie" and her face comes to stand in for her "faiture," it's difficult to see anything other than Marie's genitalia on display throughout the poem.[19]

Of course, men have been leering at saints for ages; this should come as no surprise. Even Karl Uitti has this to say about the thirteenth-century version of *Alexis* in which the saint's wedding night is more of an occasion of temptation than in the earlier versions:

> We are not unmoved ourselves, and in our temptation we come to understand the purport of Alexis' renunciation: it is made real. In this way also, then, the clerkly redactor places his *clergie*—here his mastery of *descriptio*—at the service of the saintly paradigm.[20]

Uitti's "we" shows the extent to which there is no strict separation between a saint and her audience, the extent to which it is, finally, always a question of how "we" go about constituting our commonality, our community, in the first place; and how this community might be fundamentally constituted through vision and desire, through the fact of being moved by and toward what we see.[21] More specifically, it is clear that everyone subsumed in this "we" must find saintly *imitatio* more compelling than *admiratio*—must, in other words, feel *close* to the saint. In such a proximity, even the homosocial community potentially created around the wife's scapegoated body would be undone by what Uitti calls "temptation," but what I would prefer to call the fraught status of being "with" a saint, of coming to terms with the extent to which "we" can cohere around or be commensurable, in any sense, with sanctity.

Yet, still more crucially, in his essay Uitti addresses Marie before turning to Alexis: Zosimas is, in his reading, "the clerkly witness to Marie's sanctity."[22] If *clergie* is, then, the sign of transhistorical homosocial community—or perhaps of community *tout court*—in Uitti's reading of the thirteenth-century *Alexis*, here it is too, yet with the following difference: whereas Alexis, as saint, provides the identificatory pole that holds the other scholarly and homosocial identifications in place, here it is the saint's *own* nudity that provides the spectacular basis for clerical community. This may be evidence merely of the difference between male and female saints' lives; or it may show "us" how, by refusing an exclusive, homosocial identification with Zosimas's gaze in the name of a common *clergie*, by refusing to scapegoat Marie's excessive genitality, it is possible to readdress without foreclosing the old *imitatio/admiratio* question. More specifically, it is possible to ask whether this vexed question isn't really first of all a question of visibility and enclosure. [23]

The visibility of Marie's body touches upon a more thorough narrative discovery: when Zosimas begs Marie, "Disclose your life entirely to me" (Descouvre me tote te vie; 1009), the saint responds:

"I will not by any means hide it from you.
When you saw me naked,
Even then my life wasn't hidden from you.
I will now tell you the whole story
Such that nothing will I hide from you."

["Je ne le te celerai mie,
Quant tu nue m'as esgardee,
Ja me vie ne t'iert celee.
Trestoute le te conterai
Si que ja rien n'en celerai."] 1014–18

Marie promises to hide nothing. That her *life* should have remained unconcealed when Zosimas saw her naked *body* indicates just how closely Marie's materiality is connected to her narrativity. (It is worth remembering that it is precisely in her embodied "life" that Marie diverges, earlier in the story, from the Virgin who shares her name.) There is also the sense here that nothing will be hidden because nothing *has been* hidden. In contrast to a narrative logic that would see in Marie's repentance an utter break with her past, here it is precisely this past, with its excess of exposure in both saintly and sinful ways, which makes the present and future exposure possible. Certeau sums up this peculiar narrativity, in which temporal distinctions are necessary but ultimately subordinate to an already-determined self-showing, when he asserts *both* that "hagiography postulates that everything is given at the outset" (l'hagiographie postule que tout est donné à l'origine) *and* that "there is no becoming other than manifestation" (il n'y a devenir que de la manifestation).[24] Marie's future manifestation is, yes, part of a process, but it is a process reinforced by its past, a past whose flagrant sexuality is its most salient feature.

Brigitte Cazelles and Phyllis Johnson describe Marie's cultivation of pleasure before her repentance as a "reverse asceticism,"[25] but it is not so much the reversal as the continuity or participation of her past in the ascetic present that shines forth as her body comes again and again to sight. And the effects of this continuity are not limited to Marie alone. Even Zosimas, returning to the river for another glimpse of the saint, is doing nothing fundamentally different from "the young men" (li jovencel) who "in front of her door, at the entrance / Fought often for her" (devant son huis a l'entree / En faisoient mainte melee; 131–32). Indeed, it is precisely these tricks' desire for exclusivity that reappears in Marie's avowal that she is a sight for Zosimas and him alone: "Since God showed me to you / By you I want to be hidden" (Se Dex m'a a toi demoustree, / Par toi volrai estre celee; 1045–46). The naked saint, before her death, only does a solo show.

The implications of this erotic solitary vision are amplified by the spatial dynamics of saintly visibility in general throughout the text. The young admirers crowded outside Marie's doorway transpose this solitary vision to a public sphere, and the transition implied by the threshold as the figure of access to Marie's not-yet-converted body recurs in the text's repeated return to images of entrances and exits. Yet before my critical method begins to look like just another case of "demonstrating" bodies to a privileged community of viewers, let me emphasize that Marie does have one reliable technique for keeping Zosimas's searching gaze at bay: she *turns*. Not only does she not dare, on first meeting Zosimas, to turn her "vis" toward him (872); when Zosimas asks for her blessing, she turns her "vis" to the east in order to ask God for His blessing on both of them (945); and after promising to meet Zosimas in a year's time, she turns and reenters the desert: "Now the lady has turned from him, / She has entered into the great desert" (Or s'en est la dame tornee, / El grant desert s'en est entree; 1083–84).

If anything, it is this turning that distinguishes the mode of visibility of Marie's body before repentance from its mode afterward. To be sure, this is part of an eastward movement, which in vernacular lives serves to concretize the soul's conversion, a movement that Cazelles and Johnson have aptly called "orientation."[26] Taking a cue from the way in which "orientation" purposefully does not decide the edifying content of what it describes, I would suggest that one think of Marie's turning not as a merely *converted* undoing of *perversion* but, more fundamentally, as evidence, in the most strongly visual sense, of her *version*, of her slippery position both as saint and as object of vision.[27]

By calling attention to the way in which Marie's turning coincides with her reentry into the "desert" (i.e., the solitude of the desert) after her encounter with Zosimas, it is no longer possible to postpone a discussion of entrances in the text more generally. Indeed, the importance of Marie's life for an argument about claustrophilia might seem to depend directly upon such a discussion. Marie's conversion, of course, is provoked by her inability to enter the "temple" in Jerusalem: "They entered into the temple / The whole company entered inside / But Marie could not enter at all" (Dedens le temple en sont entré, / Dedens entra le compaignie, / Mais ainc n'i pot entrer Marie; 372–74). The double "dedens" only serves to reinforce Marie's inability to accede to that sacred inside. In fact, it seems as though knights with swords are keeping her from crossing the threshold, knights whose presence echoes that of the Alexandrian tricks who "Gave each other great blows / with halberds and swords" (Des gisarmes et des espees / S'entredonoient grans colees; 135–36). One kind of privileged interiority thus excludes the other: the brothel and the church are, not surprisingly, symmetrically incompatible. Marie, seeing that "the entry was impossible / withdrew into a corner" (nient ert de l'entree, / En une angle s'es reculee; 387–88), and it is from this oblique position, huddled in a corner, that she begins first to lament her state, then to pray to an image of the Virgin. It is important to note that Marie's angularity serves as a kind of provisional interiority: one could almost say that she withdraws to the boundary, attempts, in her "angle," to create as interior a space as possible outside the "temple." This withdrawal, and the "angle" that best figures it, nonetheless reaches its zero-point in the sight of the Virgin's image, "figured on the wall" (En le maisiere figuree; 415). Only by seeing this image and praying to it will Marie be subsequently permitted to enter the "temple" both "without doubt" (sans dotance) and "without hindrance" (sans destorbier; 543–44).

So what does the text suggest about vision and the threshold by predicating Marie's entry into the "temple" upon her angular prayer to the Virgin "figuree" in the temple's external wall? First of all, vision both results from a particular location (Marie's sudden devotion is indissociable from her semi-enclosed yet oblique position vis-à-vis the Virgin's image) and has specific local consequences. The image is in some ways more of a door for Marie than the actual entrance to the "temple"; certainly it is initially open to her in a way that the temple door is not. Is oblique vision, then, the remedy to Marie's proud attempt to enter the temple in a more straightforward way? And do her subsequent turnings, in the desert, from Zosimas and from her readers, testify to the necessarily oblique character of all saving visions—that is to say, is Marie's own "figure" at best only obliquely visible? Marie will return to the Virgin's "image" once she has entered the temple and received communion, and it is from this image that she will receive instructions to go to the monastery of Saint Jehan.

The image thus frames Marie's entrance and exit, on the one hand, and serves as a hinge between an enclosed sacred space and a quintessentially (if far from simply) open one, the desert, on the other. Frame and hinge, object of vision and agent of conversion, the Virgin's image (an image of a Marie) spatializes vision as it allows Marie to visualize a new, salvific relationship to space.

Marie's vexed visual relationship to the threshold of the "temple" (which, when she emerges from it, is redubbed a "moustier") finds its foil in the expulsion of the monks from the monastery of Saint Jehan for their Lenten penitence. At line 701, the focus of the narrative switches abruptly to the desert monk Zosimas, or more specifically from "Marie" to "an abbey" (une abeie), the rhyme nicely underscoring the architectural significance of Marie's body. The hagiographer chooses to stress monastic virtue with language oddly similar to that used to describe Marie's dalliance with her fellow pilgrims en route to Jerusalem: "Neither by day nor by night / Were they [the monks] ever found in bed" (Ne il de jors ne il de nuit / Ja ne fussent trové en lit; 715–16). (Compare this with Marie's preconversion itinerary: "She never spent an entire night / In one bed only" [Ele n'iert mie tote le nuit / Nient seulement en un lit; 317–18].) The monks are never in their beds; Marie is never in one bed for long. It is as if enclosure, in the monastery or in the pilgrims' ship, establishes boundaries within which there is significant fluidity vis-à-vis spatial conventions; and that this fluidity can be ordered virtuously or viciously. (This is another way in which the description of Marie's "reverse asceticism" is apt.) The monastic enclosure, however, is opened up every Lent, when the monks kiss and are sent out of the monastery into the desert: "The abbot commanded them to kiss each other / Then opened to them the monastery door / And sent them into the forest" (Commandoit les entrebaisier / Puis lor ouvroit l'uis del mostier, / En le forest les envoioit; 741–43). This ceremonial and salutary expulsion both contrasts with Marie's initial inability to accede to sacred interiority and echoes the way in which the image/threshold opens itself for Marie and sends her into the wilderness. Marie thus shares with the monks a particularly fraught relationship with spatial thresholds.

In a similar vein, Certeau describes a fourth-century Greek account of the discovery by a hermit of an idiot woman who works in a monastic kitchen: "All the facts related in the story are either exits or entrances" (Toutes les actions racontées par le récit sont des sorties ou des entrées), Certeau observes.[28] These entrances and exits have, moreover, a specific direction. The hermit advances; the idiot woman retreats. In a sense, it is this dynamic that is at work in Marie's life as well: she is that oblique, shifting saint sought out by the monk's more penetrating gaze. Yet whereas Certeau's idiot woman is the abject around which monastic life takes shape, and is exposed as such by the hermit's penetration of the monastery's least public spaces, Marie only stays inside the temple in Jerusalem long enough to receive communion, and she never again sets foot in any enclosure. If her reaction to her initial inability to cross the temple's threshold is a kind of withdrawal to an oblique, marginal position that I have called "angular," after she leaves the temple she withdraws *not* to the abject heart of sacred community but beyond the pale of monastic distinction and ritual. Marie's lingering genitality would then also be a mark of the extent to which she cannot be assimilated into the spatial hierarchies upon which monastic order depends.

To be more specific, whereas the monks are able to inscribe this relationship within a liturgical calendar and a communal practice (note the reciprocity of their kissing, "entrebaisier"), Marie is destined to obliqueness, turning, and solitude. The rendezvous that Zosimas and Marie fix for the following year might then be seen as an attempt to give Marie a place within monastic rhythms, and the fact that Zosimas and Marie "both looked at each other for a long time" (molt s'entregardent ambedui; 1188) on the occasion of their reunion may suggest just such a monastic spirit of communal recognition. But Marie continues to escape the secure monastic dialectic of open thresholds and certain return: when they are first scheduled to meet again, Zosimas fears that she has stood him up; and when she does appear, it is with such a frenzy of turning that clearly something is about to happen: "she turned toward the holy man" (vers le saint home s'est tornee; 1252); "With this word she turned away" (A icest mot s'en est tornee; 1273). She will, in fact, die before Zosimas sees her again.

That Marie's corpse should be the final statement of her obliquely seen and seeing sanctity is suggested not only by the fact that "she held her face toward the east" (sen vis avoit vers orient; 1375) but by her body's precarious nudity even after death. Her body, itself now a threshold for the believing gaze, refuses to relinquish the genital surplus, crystallized in its turned "vis," which made it an unruly spectacle in life—unruly, too, in its inability to be recuperated into the monastic rule. But how specifically does Marie's corpse take up space, and what relationship does this have, if any, to its visibility? That is, does Marie's corpse continue in any way to turn after death?

> Thus was she stretched out on the ground
> And since she was entirely naked
> She crossed her hands across her chest
> And enveloped herself in her tresses
> And closed her eyes fittingly,
> Her nose and mouth likewise.
> And she goes off to everlasting paradise

Where no devil would dare go.
Into the angelic company
Went the soul of Marie.
Her body remained all naked:
Except for a little cloth, all torn,
Which covered a part of it,
She was poorly shrouded.

[Dont s'est a le tere estendue
Si conme ele estoit tote nue,
Ses mains croisa seur se poitrine
Et s'envolepa en se crine
Et clost ses iex avenanment,
Sen nés et se bouce ensement.
En paradis s'en va durable,
Onc n'i osa venir deable.
En l'angeliel compaignie
S'en ala l'ame de Marie.
Li cors de li remeste tot nu,
Fors d'un drapel tot desrompu
Ki en covroit une partie,
Povrement fu ensevelie.] 1295–308

The striking characteristics of Marie's body at her death are its extension and its enclosure. She lays herself down on the ground and envelops herself in her hair, closing her eyes, nose, and mouth. Her body, so prone to its own internal metonymies, here is literally prone to the most basic external one: as an extension of the earth from which it was made and to which it will return. But Marie's body also reveals itself here as the enclosure that has trumped the sacred interiority of churches and monasteries: sealing off her sense organs, pulling her hair around her, Marie withdraws this time into *herself*. This most unfathomable, solitary, and ultimately invisible space prompts the text to attempt to resocialize and revisualize Marie: on the one hand, it introduces an "angeliel compaignie" to relieve her solitude; on the other, it returns to her body's nudity, which despite being complete, "tot nu," is broken up by a broken "drapel." Zosimas, of course, had given Marie a "drapel" on the occasion of their first meeting, and it would seem that its coquettish framing of the "partie," which earlier in the text served as a sign of genital spectacle, attempts to reintroduce this monastic visual logic in the wake of Marie's death.

Yet in the end, Marie's corpse is *not* convincingly reassimilated into any order of the visible, precisely because it is at once feminine and masculine in its nudity, "tote nue" (1296) and "tot nu" (1305); it is self-enveloped (1298) and partially covered (1307). Her body's visibility is fundamentally undecidable even within the ostensibly clerical structure of the hagiographic text. Brigitte Cazelles assigns to Marie the uncanny status of a "mirage," inasmuch as she is "separated from the world" (séparée du monde) according to a "principle of distancing at once aesthetic and ethical" (principe de distanciation à la fois esthétique et éthique).[29] I would merely add two things to Cazelles's observation. First, this distancing is not immediately distinguishable from a self-enclosure: perhaps then it is at once a drawing-near and a withdrawal. Therefore, just as Marie offers not so much a conversion or a perversion as a *version*, perhaps here too she offers less a spectacular withdrawal or drawing-near than a *drawing*. Second, this drawing, this indifferent *graphein* at the heart of hagiography, is not only aesthetic and ethical but, before and perhaps beyond these, erotic. It is not just that Marie arouses the desire of her viewer; she arouses the desire to *see*, a desire for visual plenitude, which will only ever be frustrated and enticed by her constant turnings, between enclosure and exposure, between part and whole.

Hand to Mouth: The Hermit Writing

Regardless of whether or not "we" finally know what we're seeing, Marie at least constitutes one of the more recognizable saints in the Old French canon. The same cannot be said of Jehan Bouche d'Or, whose verse life nonetheless provides some especially astonishing uses of sex, space, and visuality. Jehan's *vie*, in 870 octosyllabic verses, has been attributed by Cazelles, the text's only recent interpreter, to the north of France around the beginning of the thirteenth century.[30] As she makes clear, the content of the *vie* is such as to frustrate any source-critical approach: "*Jehan Bouche d'Or* is thus connected to an undercurrent of legend, without flowing from any precise source" (JBd'O se rattache donc à un substrat légendaire, mais sans découler d'une source précise).[31] It is thus an especially useful text to place alongside the life of Marie, especially in the face of Duncan Robertson's claim, regarding the latter, that "the comparison of an Old French poem with its immediate Latin predecessor(s) remains always an indispensable step in the critical appraisal."[32] The "concern for the concrete" (souci du concret) that Cazelles locates in Jehan's life draws the reader's attention toward the elements that, beyond the technicalities of transmission, would have proven most compelling for its medieval audience: elements that Cazelles rightly calls "folkloric," but that I would prefer here to describe, in the vein of the preceding analysis of *Marie*, as *graphic*, that is to say, concerned with the concrete texture of hagiographic production and the sensory qualities of saintliness. At the risk of overstating the obvious, let me once more insist that the oft-pursued question of *where saints come from* has meant the general neglect of *how saints come*: Jehan's body, like Marie's, is the site of metonymies,

THE VERGE OF THE VISIBLE   51

which serve first and foremost to stage its becoming visible. The convergence of image, architecture, and bodily exposure in Marie's life get taken, in Jehan's, to another level, as the text redoubles the metonymies of sanctity in the altogether profane form of a pregnant princess.

After a short prologue extolling the virtues of "divinite" over against courtly romance (4), the narrator, Renaut, goes on to explain that our hero, Jehan, is a "chaplain of holy life" (capelain de sainte vie; 25) in the service of a royal family.[33] The princess becomes pregnant (93–94) and, at the devil's prompting, blames Jehan (159–60), who is dragged off to a savage and deserted island (256 ff.). However, before going into exile, he warns the princess that she will not be delivered of her child "until you see me again" (adont que me revoies; 254–56). Exile—and, we will see, enclosure—amounts to invisibility within the logic of the poem; the saint will be able to save his accuser only once he is made visible again. In the meantime, the text goes to great lengths to guarantee that, if the saint falls outside the royal field of vision, he will nonetheless fail to fall outside that of his hagiographic admirers.

All the same, this is a narrative full of enclosures: visibility is thus the effect of overcoming a limit, a spatial obstacle; it is something one has to work for. If, for Ellen Swanberg, the emphasis on prayer in version T of Marie's life "affirms the transportive power of intermediaries, and language is the fundamental intermediary," Jehan's life concretizes mediation not just verbally but also in terms of a dialectic of enclosure and visible disclosure.[34] Jehan's exile is, from the beginning, literally enclosed: the island where the king's men abandon the saint is "A rocky place...enclosed by the sea / The surroundings were all full of woods" (Uns rochiers...de mer enclos / De bos estoit tos plains li clos; 207–08). Though it scarcely makes sense to say so, Jehan's island is enclosed inside and out: surrounded by sea, packed full of trees. He will inhabit a nesting doll of containment.

When he is left on the shore, Jehan prays to God in what amounts to a resumé of salvation history, referring to hell as "that wretched enclosure" (la vil closure; 290). On the edge of another "vil closure," Jehan prays in such a way as to suggest that this enclosure can be redeemed:

His prayer was said in Latin:
I have written it in the vernacular
So that laypeople may learn it,
Lock it up in their hearts and understand it.

[L'orison fu en latin dite:
Por ce l'ai en romans escrite
Que li lai le puissent aprendre,
Fermer en lor cuer et entendre.] 323–26

Not only does the text foreground its vernacular mediation of the Latin prayer, a phenomenon remarkable enough for its inversion of the dominant associations of vernacularity with oral culture and Latinity with writing; it suggests that the lay audience should effectively enclose (literally close, "fermer") the prayer in its heart, as if in an internal, willing imitation of Jehan's own external, forced enclosure. It is surely significant that this moment of communication between lay devotion and the saint's physical trial takes place on the shore, at the limit of the sacred (if still scary) space of exile and the profane world that has sent Jehan there. The mediating model of saintly prayer thus becomes accessible to its audience just as Jehan's enclosed exile will ultimately make his saintly efficacy accessible, and sensible, to the princess.

However, before addressing the moment of disclosure that the poem ultimately builds up to, it's worth emphasizing the detail with which the text constructs Jehan's enclosure. Left on the island, Jehan builds a hermitage:

> He brings some branches and leaves
> And makes an enclosure, an entrance and a door.
> When the friend of God had done this,
> He crossed himself, and placed himself inside:
> He would like to write some good work there.
>
> [Des rains et de la foille aporte,
> Closure i fait, entree et porte.
> Quant ce ot fait li Deu amis,
> Si se segna, dedens s'est mis:
> La voldra alcun bien escrivre.] 351–55

This *closure* is, indeed, a monastic cloister. Furthermore, it marks a moment of transition in Jehan's career. If he is at first a chaplain and priest ("capelains" at 160 and "fals prestres" at 243), and by the end of the story has been appointed bishop of the city, this in-between time of exile is his time of monastic, or really eremitic, retreat. Cazelles points out that eremitism, in Jehan's life as in the structurally similar *Jehan Paulus*, is at best a temporary, intermediary stage resolved, finally, into profane society: "in the two *Jehans*, eremitism is nothing but an initiation and a stage on the way to sanctification. This passage from private to public corresponds to the final recuperation of the saint by society" (dans les deux *Jehan*, l'érémitisme n'est qu'une initiation et une étape dans la sanctification. Ce passage du privé au public correspond à la récupération finale du saint par la société).[35] The "closure" that Jehan builds, then, can be seen as a concretization of this intermediary character, a solitary structure that the saint must pass through on the way to reintegration and mass devotion. (He will, in the end, be rescued so that the princess can have her baby. Women will pray to him for help in childbirth.) The eremitic phase consequently adds another layer of enclosure, a narrative and temporal one, to the material enclosures into which Jehan retreats on account of his exile.

The text is scrupulous in its account of the hermitage: there is no "closure" without an "entree," no "entree" without a "porte." The hermitage is not hermetically sealed; rather, its entrance is foregrounded, in its dual character as opening and obstacle, door and frame. The ambivalence of the threshold is thus constitutive of the enclosure, into which Jehan promptly enters, crossing himself beforehand and, afterward, setting himself to write. The symmetry between crossing, or literally "signing," oneself and "aucun bien escripre," with the enclosure's doorway intervening between them, lends to the cumulative effect of mediated visibility an added emphasis on mediated linguistic practice. The desire to write, in fact, echoes an earlier line of the text, when Jehan has gathered his writing materials in preparation for exile: "For he'd like to write some good work" (Car alcun bien voldra escrire; 226). Jehan's enclosure is the site of writing, and it is the *sight* of writing that will confirm Jehan's virtue.

Signing oneself thus amounts to staging, with and in the body, the visibility of mediating signification. This is, after all, a text in which the characters are signing themselves every time you look: the king (at 166 and "more than a hundred times" [plus de cent fois] at 637); the queen (at 587); and Jehan himself, repeatedly: upon hearing the princess's accusation ("He crosses himself / and knows not what to say" [Il se seigne, ne set que dire; 199]); on the island, after his prayer (322); in the course of dealing with the devil (437); upon returning from exile (741); and when delivering the princess from her seven-year labor (812). In each case, signing oneself is a way of mediating, either productively or receptively, what cannot be directly signified: productively (one might say performatively), as when Jehan delivers the princess of her child; receptively, as when Jehan "ne set que dire" and can accept the new knowledge of his exile only through corporeal contortion.

This insistence upon a kind of body language is intensified by the poem's attention to liturgy. When he enters the space and time of monastic life, Jehan also intones the offices proper to this life. Having said compline and kept a vigil for the dead,

> He said matins at dawn;
> When the morning was bright,
> He rendered to God in a most holy manner
> prime, terce, and the midday service;
> In his heart he vowed and promised

That, as long as he had breath, he would sing mass;
He recited the epistle and gospel.
Afterwards, he chose one of his writing-books
And got his scriptorium ready:
He would like to begin a holy story,
In the name of the powerful celestial king.
He would by no means be idle:
He who is softened by idleness
Is made to think many a foolish thing.

[Matines dist a l'ajornee;
Quant clere fu la matinee,
A Deu moult saintement rendi
Et prime et tierce et miedi;
En son cuer fait veu et promese,
S'armes eust, il cantast mese;
Epistle et evangile dist.
Apres un des quaiers eslist,
Si apresta son escritoire,
Comenchier veut un saint estoire
El non del poissant roi celestre.
Il ne voldra mie useus estre:
Qui en huiseuse s'amolie,
Penser li fait mainte folie.] 375–88

Jehan, who "spent the whole night praying" (fu tote nuit a orison; 372) and says matins at daybreak, accedes to a sacred temporality in which the difference between night and day is subordinated to a succession of prayers and liturgical offices. His recitations explicitly take place "from hour to hour" (a ore dusc'a ore; 369), in a sequence that one might be tempted to call cyclical, if it didn't give way to an account of writing and the dangers of idleness. Cazelles, in fact, when discussing Jehan's "immobile body," describes him as "beyond the reach of cyclical time, of time put into action" (hors de portée du temps cyclique, du temps mis en actes).[36] The cyclical, in Cazelles's account, would seem to carry with it echoes of a kind of pagan fatalism, determined by cycles of destruction and regeneration. Jehan's break with this order could not be clearer: the princess's interminable pregnancy testifies to his defiance of reproductive logic. Yet if, at least in this eremitic in-between time, Jehan falls outside of a secular cyclical temporality, his recitations "a ore dusc'a ore" also break with linear temporality. There is no progress here. However, taking into account the way in which the narrative moves from liturgy to writing to the threat of idleness, perhaps one could suggest that the particular temporality of Jehan's eremitic enclosure is one of _differential repetition_, a practice at the threshold of mere reiteration and revolutionary innovation. Liturgical gesture blends into writing (one is tempted to say that it participates, in the strongest sense, in writing) and writing, in turn, blends into the accretion of virtue. One practice is continually, differently inflected, and its teleology is minimal, just enough to keep the repetitions from the kind of determinism that Cazelles describes.

Yet, Jehan's body is not exactly "immobile" here, not least because of the way in which liturgical gesture is made to permeate written practice. There is, however, stronger evidence for the potential mobility of Jehan's body. The idleness that threatens Jehan with "mainte folie" would have explicitly somatic effects. As he writes a saint's life or holy life (392: "sainte vie"), the devil appears, turning over his inkpot and exclaiming, "Now your hands will be idle!" (Or seront huiseuses tes mains!; 422). The devil knows that this liturgically inflected writing can be addictive:

He knows well that if the life is written,
In which now he takes such delight,
That he will read it many times;
And after this one he'll write another.

[Bien sot, se la vie est escrite,
Ou il ore tant se delite,
Que soventes fois le lira;
Apres cestui altre escrira.] 397–400

Jehan's differential repetition of recitation and writing is here spelled out as the way in which, out of sheer delight, writing one life and reading it can easily give way to writing (and reading) another. However, Jehan's hands, if left idle, *are capable of sinful repetitions*, and it does not take much searching to discover what the text has in mind.[37] Jehan's desolate cry, "Alas! Now I've lost everything / Since my ink lies all over the ground" (He! las, ore ai jo tot perdu, / Puis que mes enques gist par terre; 408–09), makes him into a kind of anti-Onan, dismayed at the graphic sterility inflicted upon him. The text then confronts us with the image of the compulsively masturbating saint, engaged in a parody of repeated writing. The startling suggestion is that there might be precisely a *temporal* affinity between the one set of gestures and the other, and a consonance with the effective, largely self-referential body language of signing oneself. As in Marie's life, one can't help asking what takes priority: the "vis" or the "faiture," the sign of the cross or the masturbating hand.

Earlier, I spoke of Marie's *version* and her *drawing* in an effort to describe the bare point of material contact between the genital and the sacred. Keeping in mind the way in which Jehan's *vie* stages the threshold (of exile, of enclosure), it may be similarly possible to argue for the bare materiality, the *graphic* quality, of hagiographic space. God resolves Jehan's inklessness by changing his spit to gold, in a scene that foregrounds visibility as an effect of crossing a bodily threshold: he has been chewing his pen in consternation, and when he takes it out of his mouth, he notices that it has changed color:

> From his mouth he withdrew
> The pen that was moistened:
> All infused with gold color
> He saw his tool filled.
> The priest drew his hand before his eyes,
> And looked at it for a long while.
>
> [De sa bouce a retraite fors
> La penne ki ert atempree:
> De color d'or bien destempree
> A veu tot le tuel plain.
> Devant ses ex a trait sa main,
> Longement l'esgarda li prestre.] 462–27

The miracle that saves Jehan from idleness, as it makes a spectacle of his hand and mouth, reinforces the connections between writing and recitation, respectively embodied languages of hands and mouths. And the connector, as it were, is Jehan's pen, his "tuel." Note how careful the text is to foreground the movement of the pen *outside* of Jehan's mouth, in front of his eyes; and then to show how contemplating the "tuel" leads to contemplating the "main" that holds it. The body is *implicated* in the mediating act of the instrument it holds. What is more, the body *sees* its implication: Jehan looks at his hand/tool "longement," for a long time. Continued linguistic production, here staged in its barest technicality and materiality, depends upon the passage, mediated by the prosthetic pen, from the inside of the body to its scrutinized outside; but this outside is not one of complete detachment. The page of hagiographic production is, I believe, as contiguous to the writing hand as that hand is to its "tuel," and as this tool is to the mouth that gives it the ink, bodily writing matter, with which it can compose. This is thick stuff: the body is a writing machine, but the written text is also an extension of the body, with all the possibilities for metonymy that we have seen actualized in Marie's *vie*.[38] Cazelles notes that "what is foregrounded here is writing as technique" (c'est ici l'écriture comme technique qui est mise en avant),[39] but the technical is here also corporeal, and explicitly a visualized movement across the boundaries between mouth, pen, hand, and page.

Jehan's life is not by any means the only high medieval text concerned with the ambivalently and spectacularly erotic cooperation of tongues and tools in the act of linguistic production as holy life. Seth Lerer's provocative reading of the twelfth-century *De vita sua* of Guibert of Nogent takes as its point of departure a story Guibert tells about a masturbating pilgrim who, driven to despair by the devil, cuts his penis off and then slits his throat. Brought back to life, he bears the scars of his ordeal on both his throat and his groin:

> The pilgrim's missing penis leaves its sign not only where it was anatomically (in the groin) but where it should be figuratively (in the voice). As a sign on the throat, it spreads the miracle abroad; it speaks, effectively, of the forgiveness of God and may be said to function as a kind of tongue for the revived pilgrim. It is, as well, a figure for the written sign itself, and for the enterprise of writing.[40]

The genital "sign on the throat" is, to be sure, the sign of an absence, a pastness: and yet the resurrected body overcomes these aporias and discloses itself as spectacularly and salvifically sexed precisely insofar as its sex is missing, or at least displaced. But it is not a question of mere displacement here, nor of a random inscription of the genital at the site of the voice; instead, if Guibert's pilgrim speaks with his (absent) dick, it is because there is a metonymic connection *among* bodily extremities and *between* these extremities and the objects, *verbum* or *vellum*, they touch and form.

It is, strangely enough, to theology that one must turn for the most explicit elaboration of the grounds for such sexualized metonymy. Touch—most concretely embodied by the hands and tongue, those most extreme and most articulate parts of the human body—is, for Aquinas, the only one of the five senses possessed more intensely by humans than by animals.[41] That the lowest of senses would also be the most human, and that its organs would be proper, not accidental, instruments of the embodied soul, makes the touching hand (and tongue) especially fitting vehicles for the Incarnation.[42] This is why the Eucharist is primarily a matter of touch (and taste, "a more intimate mode of touch").[43] If the *convenientia* or fittingness of the Incarnation is, therefore, analogically related to and participatively present in each instance of touch, and indeed each instance of sensation,[44] but most immediately apprehensible in the work of the hands and tongue, what is to keep the devout imagination from extending the analogy to another corporeal instrument which would, as well, seem to be a kind of "proper accident," less articulate than tongue or hand, perhaps, but just as vulnerable and just as intensely (if negatively) bound to the intellect? This is not to argue, along quasi-Manichaean lines, for the sacrality of sperm or sex. Instead, what Jehan's life and Guibert's story suggest, in light of touch as incarnational *convenientia* or fittingness, is that metonymy *is a close fit*. Though the pilgrim's penis is never reducible to the throat that bears its trace, and though Jehan's fingers press his stylus in a way nonetheless distinct from more masturbatory manipulations, they are nonetheless brought close by a theology (and not just an everyday erotics) in which the most intimate transactions between soul and world—specifically bodily, sensory transactions—partake to some degree in the divine.

The Threshold of the Visceral

But there are other bodily enclosures, and thresholds, in the text. When the narrative takes up the princess's end of the story again, it jovially remarks that "She was hidden away in a room / Shut in like a recluse" (En une chambre estoit repuse / Enserree conme recluse; 543–44). The princess, bedridden at this point for three years, is doubly locked up, "enserree" (a term that will be used to describe her, four years later, when Jehan is finally brought back to the city; 808). That is, she is confined to her room inasmuch as she cannot move; but her body is itself a confining space, with its ever-growing "fruit" (810) locked up inside. As long as Jehan remains within his island enclosure, the undelivered child will remain inside the princess, and the princess herself will remain inside her chamber. The threshold of the hermitage becomes thus an echo of the entry to the princess's bedroom and, more importantly and obscenely, of the genital door whose opening precipitated the entire situation, and that is for the time being firmly stuck.

The question then becomes whether we're meant to see the hermitage when we see the princess's body, or whether in fact we're supposed to see the princess's body writ large in Jehan's enclosure. This question, of course, redoubles that of Jehan's repeated manual-oral activities. The text's love of parodic equivalences makes it nearly impossible to decide. It is, then, a matter of that bare materiality, touching equally upon virtue and vice, which I have called graphic, a drawing, a version. Having acknowledged the text's fundamental indifference to the resolution of these equivalences and their underlying materiality, it is nonetheless possible to argue that there is, ultimately, an irreducible genitality to both religious and courtly life. This kind of reading would resonate with the symmetries between monastic and courtly culture that Georges Duby outlines in *A History of Private Life*: if the novice monk's emergence into full monastic life entails a three-day retreat into the folds of his cowl, "emulating Christ's withdrawal into the tomb," the courtly bed is "the family womb," itself a locus of withdrawal and transformative regeneration.[45] Duby elsewhere speaks of courtly lovers as living "within an invisible enclosure, where they constructed, in the midst of a crowd of familiars, a more private cell."[46] In fact, the body is the term that monastic and courtly enclosures have in common, a body that is in both contexts "a fortress, a hermitage," at whose gates one must keep watch.[47] And it is not only that the body is a hermitage; the religious enclosure is also a body, "the mouth of the people, from which emanated the chants and prayers of all mankind."[48]

These observations are admittedly vague, but their claims are explicitly corroborated by Jehan's *vie*. They also show how the movement between sacred and profane spaces and metaphors can be staged in either direction. Fundamental to Cazelles's argument about the folkloric elements of Jehan's life is an emphasis on the desacralizing function of Jehan's recuperation into profane society, an emphasis to which I am obviously sympathetic: in many ways, by bringing together devotional literature and texts more explicitly committed to the *saeculum*, I am merely extending its implications. Yet it seems important, as well, to point out the ambivalence with which my notion of the graphic attempts to cope, and that Certeau illustrates with customary vividness in his discussion of Bosch in the *Mystic Fable*. He says that the bodies of Bosch's triptych "form flowery downstrokes and dropped initials, a chain of forms and strokes, in short, a *beautiful but illegible handwriting*" (forment des jambages et des lettrines, un enchaînement de formes et de traits, en somme une *belle écriture mais illisible*).[49] Just as the represented body, for Certeau, in a sense *shimmers* with the graphic stuff of which it is made, and just as "animate merges with inanimate, outside with inside, mind with body," in Jody Enders's account of the architecture of mnemonically inflected embodiment,[50] so too do body, language, and architecture each display the other, in Jehan's vie, as their underpinning and determinately complex structure. Of course, the very logic of predication says too much here, for what is at stake is a kind of co-inherence, more or less like one of those postcards you can buy in the Vatican that, turned one way, show the Virgin, and turned another way, show Jesus, but seen straight on, show a horrifying (or humorous) hybrid of the two, at once obscene and centerstage.

Intensifying this co-inherence (the Vatican comparison would work better if Aiden Shaw—or a similarly illustrious porn star—replaced Jesus) is the crucial technique of Jehan's hagiographer and Jehan *as* hagiographer. For the theological resonances of the passages between bodies, archiectures, and manual/oral languages in the text make for even wilder, and more pleasurable, reading. We can't forget that hagiography is something that gives pleasure: the reading and writing of lives is something in which Jehan "takes such delight" (tant se delite; 398). Jehan's seminal writing, miraculously self-regenerative, also has strong Christological overtones, especially if one accepts Certeau's description of Christ's body as something whose " 'being there' is the paradox of 'having been' here previously, of remaining inaccessibly elsewhere and of 'coming back' later" (son 'être-là' est le paradoxe d' 'avoir été' ici autrefois, de 'demeurer' inaccessible ailleurs et de 'revenir' plus tard), a body "structured by dissemination, like a text" (structuré par la dissemination, comme une écriture).[51] Jehan's body, reproduced metonymically in microcosm (as pen, ink, word) and macrocosm (as hermitage and island), is never merely in one place at one time, while remaining always a unifying structural principle beneath these extensive dispersals. This is a logic of the ultimate, an eschato-logic. Its bare extension is, paradoxically and constitutively, also an enfolding: the other half of the theological story that Jehan's life tells can be found in his prayer for the princess to deliver her baby, and more specifically in its invocation of Jonah and the whale.

Jehan prays:

> O beautiful Lord God, just as you kept
> Jonah safe in the belly of the fish,
> And me against the beasts
> Who seemed so savage:
> As truly as you did me this honor,
> Which must be narrated very well,
> Now I pray that this afflicted woman
> Whom you've kept locked up until now
> Might be delivered by your might:
> Render me the fruit in such a way
> That it might come to term. . .
>
> [Biaus sire Dex, puis que Jonas
> El ventre del poisson gardas,
> Et moi as garde vers les bestes
> Qui tant par estoient rubestes,
> Si voir con ceste honor m'as faite,
> Qui moult bien doit estre retraite,
> Or te proi de ceste esgaree
> Que jusques ore as enserree:
> Delivre le par ta poissance;
> Rent moi le fruit de tel samblance
> Con il aferist al termine.] 801–11

The most basic theological resonance of any invocation of Jonah would be, of course, his typological significance as a figure of the entombed and resurrected Christ. (It is Christ himself, in Matthew 12:40, who establishes the figural connection.) Given the gravity of this typology, it is all the more striking that the text should call the princess a whale whose Jonah awaits delivery: her distended womb is thus a fishy tomb, her suspended reproductivity the sign of a death to be miraculously overcome. What is more, the text explicitly sets up Jehan's hermitage, the place into which he takes refuge from his savage (but miraculously domesticated) surroundings, as the tomb-like equivalent to the princess's typologically enhanced body. To risk a reading that might be too close for comfort, it is also possible to see in the "jusques ore," the "up to now," of the princess's pregnancy a temporality in distinct contrast to, but nonetheless echoing, the "dusc'a ore" of Jehan's scribal-liturgical repetitions. Her bedridden body would then be the incarnation of idleness, and specifically of idleness as a vice both temporal and spatial.[52]

This packed passage, in what amounts to an astonishing sleight of hand, manages also to link these metaphysical concerns to more purely, but never simply, physical ones. For, if the princess's vagina is a fish's mouth, it is also analogous to the point at which God's miracles in the hermitage are discovered: a point defined by Jehan as *visible* ("en tel *samblance*") and *written* (or actually, more ambiguously and piquantly, *graphic*: "Qui moult bien doit estre retraite").[53] By invoking God's "poissance" to free this "poisson," Jehan connects writing and vision and genitality, and brings this multiply determined corporeality to bear upon the temporal-spatial suspension that his prayer seeks to undo. Theological resonance thus produces a body whose genital, graphic, ocular mouth is that of Christ's tomb, the place of his absence and the womb of the world. The ramifications of this are startling, inasmuch as the perverse body is here shown to be a remarkably heteronormative site: the resurrection of this bachelor Messiah, with his injunction to leave behind family and friends and follow him, would amount to a gross act of cosmic breeding.

The inscription of the princess's body and Jehan's enclosure within the story of Jonah is, in fact, even more apt than it first appears. The context for Christ's establishment of a figural link between his entombment and Jonah's being swallowed has explicitly to do with signification, in ways that are revealing for the enclosed and disclosing body languages of Jehan's *vie*:

> Then some of the scribes and Pharisees answered him, saying: Master we would see a sign from thee. Who answering said to them: An evil and adulterous generation seeketh a sign: and a sign shall not be given it, but the sign of Jonas the prophet. For as Jonas was in the whale's belly three days and three nights: so shall the Son of man be in the heart of the earth three days and three nights.
>
> [Tunc responderunt ei quidam de scribis et Pharisaeis dicentes magister volumus a te signum videre; qui respondens ait illis generatio mala et adultera signum quaerit et signum non dabitur ei nisi signum Ionae prophetae; sicut enim fuit Ionas in ventre ceti tribus diebus et tribus noctibus sic erit Filius hominis in corde terrae tribus diebus et tribus noctibus.][54]
> Matthew 12:38–40

It is not difficult to see how the medieval ear would pick up the affinities between Matthew's gospel and Jehan's ordeal. In the place of a "generatio mala et adultera," we have an unwed, pregnant princess, whose specifically *generative* capacity is foregrounded even as it is not yet brought to term.

More importantly, the text establishes a contrast between the demanded visual sign and the "signum Ionae" that the scribes and Pharisees will instead receive: instead of immediate sensory satisfaction, Christ promises delay, enclosure, and the mediation of his story by another. Jehan's *vie*, so invested in bodily signification and the mediations of the flesh, thus demonstrates that the saintly sign is one that does not refuse mediation. The princess's bloated body shows that the refusal of mediation results not, as one might presume, in immediacy, but in a kind of reinforced or redoubled mediation: mediation occurs in spite of oneself. The body encloses and is enclosed, in language and in architecture, and this enclosure is also an extension, its depths thereby perpetually brought to the surface as it spreads out.[55] Sin amounts to a refusal of the threshold across which what passes (meaning or revelation or children) must pass, a refusal of the material intermediary that alone makes the passage possible. The sign of Jonah here amounts to the fact that what I've called the graphic, the mere material version, is itself holy, inasmuch as it allows for, and opens onto, a fundamentally mediated disclosure.

Let me be clear about the mode of this mediation: this is no *Aufhebung*, no resolution of opposites; rather, it is the barest material reaching across a spatial or bodily or linguistic threshold, an emergence that is itself an inscription and thus, in the terms of chapter 1, an emergence *into*. If, as Emma Campbell has argued with respect to the life of Alexis, sanctity may require a revision of gift economies, so that "inviting" divine reward no longer amounts to "expecting" it, so too does the emergent, literally nascent threshold of sanctity here extend an open invitation.[56] When the princess gives birth to her child, who after seven years in his mother's belly emerges as a fully grown seven-year-old, she is putting in act, one might even say *ecstatically*, the sketchy boundary between the miraculous and the (reproductively) profane. What is taking place here is nothing less than an intensification of place itself; what is becoming visible is nothing less than just this visibility, impure, sudden, and inevitably compromised.

This is not to say that hagiography does not occasionally resist these compromises. In the thirteenth-century life of Saint Marina, one finds an attempt to conflate the architectural threshold with unambiguous genital exposure. A certain brother Marin, thrown out of his monastery for alleged "lechery" (lescherie), spends the rest of his life "in front of the gate" (devant la porte) of this same monastery. Upon his death, it is revealed that Marin was actually Marina all along: the monks surround the body at the doorway, take off *his* clothes to reveal the woman inside. The text announces this coyly, with merely a final "e": "Then they all perceived that / what she had been hiding among them so well" (Lors ont jlz tous aperceu / Que bien c'estoit entr'eulx celee; 1039–40).[57] Everyone looks at Marina; everyone sees both how well she was hidden and what she was hiding. The immediate perception of genital specificity (and the saintly "hiding" thereby disclosed) must occur in a communal setting reminiscent of Uitti's "we," controlling what might otherwise offer itself in greater complexity, and ambivalence, to a solitary, roving gaze.

But in fact, even as the monks look collectively, and directly, at Marina's no longer mediated "e," the text's own indirection proves that immediate vision is impossible. For Marina's genital truth is perceptible only in writing; her "e" is inaudible. The visible materiality of the hagiographic text thus occupies the place of Marina's venerable vagina; the transformation, via recitation, of text into audible performance would then amount to a kind of cunnilingus. Such observations may appear slight, to say the least, but they show to what extent the sensibilia of hagiographic language are linked to an always ambivalent genital exposure. When the monks discover Marina's "e," they ask her corpse, "How did you hide yourself?" (Comment vous est vous celee?; 1057). Not *why* did you hide, but *how*; we want a technique, we want to see how it happened, we want to see more. The certainty of what they are seeing is set off balance by this ever-curious "comment," its quest for a saintly technique that would also be one of unambiguous exposure.[58]

I have shown how the technicality of writing that Cazelles foregrounds in Jehan's vie is also a bodily practice; here, likewise, the technique of holiness, which these monks desire to make the object of collective knowledge, is accessible only through the written sign of genital specificity. And not just any written sign, but an all but superfluous "e" whose temporality the text makes explicit: the monks protest, "We didn't think that she *was* a woman" (Ne cuidions pas qu'elle *fut* femme; 1047). Marina's sex, in all senses of the word, is a thing of the past, dead, yet resurrected through her *vie*. The saint's "life" is thus analogous to the sign of Jonah, the site through which an enclosed body is thrown into a new, transformed materiality, which bears, and bares, the trace of the orifice it has traversed. Despite the monks' desire for immediacy, it is, as in Marie's life, a fundamentally *turned*, dynamically resistant body that generates their vision and their desire. Hagiography thus writes the saint's body as an object of erotic knowledge and display, an object that normally remains hidden "entr'eulx," among "them" but also among "us" in Uitti's sense, a genital secret whose frustrating (because dead) disclosure we call miraculous.

The Threshold of the Visible

The hagiographic threshold is a place both risky and risqué. It marks, within and as the saint's life, the barest crossing over from enclosure to exposure, the site of becoming visible. Visibility thus appears as the point at which the sacred and the erotic touch, fold upon and extend each other. Saints and whores, sacred revelation and genital display participate in a foregrounding of the mediately sensible, a staging of naked sensation as aporetic passage. Marina's technique, together with its dead genital sign, echoes Jehan's writing in exile; these lives, in addition to Marie's dervish-like turning, could be said to constitute an account of experience in the barest sense, by which I mean a compromised inasmuch as mediated, that is, *enclosed*, traversal of the senses, especially vision. Such a traversal constitutes vision even as it moves toward it: in this way, to ape Jean-Luc Nancy, it spaces vision out.[59]

Ironically (given its ludic character) hagiography, in fact, may go further than the altogether somber account of experience that Philippe Lacoue-Labarthe gives in *Poetry as Experience*, the essay on Paul Celan first discussed in chapter 1. Reading a series of translations of Celan's poem on Hölderlin, "Tübingen, January," Lacoue-Labarthe observes:

> I propose to call what it translates "experience," provided that we both understand the word in its strict sense—the Latin ex-periri, a crossing through danger—and especially that we avoid associating it with what is "lived," the stuff of anecdotes. Erfahrung, then, rather than Erlebnis. I say "experience" because what the poem "springs forth" from here—the memory of bedazzlement, which is also the pure dizziness of memory—is precisely that which did not take place, did not happen or occur during the singular event that the poem relates to without relating: the visit, after so many others since the joiner Zimmer's time, to the tower on the Neckar where Hölderlin lived without living for the last thirty-six years of his life—half of his life. A visit in memory of that experience, which is also in the non-form of pure non-event.
>
> [Ce dont il est la traduction, je propose de l'appeler l'*expérience*, sous la condition d'entendre strictement le mot—l'*ex-periri* latin, la traversée d'un danger—et de se garder, surtout, de référer la chose à quelque 'vécu,' ou à de l'anecdote. *Erfahrung*, donc, et non pas *Erlebnis*. Je dis *expérience* parce que ce dont 'jaillit' le poème, ici—la mémoire d'un éblouissement, c'est-à-dire aussi bien le pur vertige de la mémoire—, est justement ce qui n'a pas eu lieu, n'est pas arrivé ou advenu lors de l'événement singulier auquel le poème se rapporte, mais qu'il ne rapporte pas: cette visite, après tant d'autres depuis celles du menuisier Zimmer, à la tour au bord du Neckar où Hölderlin vécut, sans les vivre, les trente-six dernières années de la vie, la moitié de sa vie: visite en mémoire de cela, qui est aussi dans la forme nulle du non-événement pur.][60]

Lacoue-Labarthe argues for a "strict" understanding of experience, one in which danger and its traversal are opposed to everyday life, the "vécu." But what if we were to take the negativity of this experience seriously, more seriously, even, than Lacoue-Labarthe's insistence upon this strict "condition"? If the poem springs from "that which did not take place," there might also be a sense in which this negative emplacement cuts through the lofty rhetoric of a Hölderlin—or a Celan—to haunt even the more ordinary places of writing. That is to say, if saints' lives show us, first and foremost, the manifestation of a place and a body, of a body's taking place literally out of nothing, then this traversal of the negative—of the no-man's land figured as desert or womb—produces not a pure positivity but a compromised appearance that is precisely "the stuff of anecdotes." Saints are less pure than Lacoue-Labarthe's "non-event."

To speak of a saint's "life" is, on its own, a complex task. Jehan wishes to begin a "sainte vie" (392), but the text allows for substantial uncertainty as to whether this is first and foremost Jehan's own life or the hagiographic enterprise in which he hopes to be engaged. Similarly, the "vie" that Marie exposes to Zosimas cannot be altogether separated from her "vis," which, in turn and in turning, evokes her genital "faiture." It seems, therefore, only fair to seek even greater complexity by suggesting that these saints' lives may be brought crucially to bear on exactly that distinction which Lacoue-Labarthe wishes to make, between the risky *Erfahrung* and its thresholds, on the one hand, and *Erlebnis* on the other. That is to say, hagiography restores the risk of compromised narrativity, of the never-quite-linear emergence from enclosed speech/body/space into visibility, to the "non-event," which Lacoue-Labarthe establishes as dangerously, because dizzily, constitutive of poetic language. From the saint's life to the saint's lived experience, one crosses "that which did not take place," semen unspilled, vaginas barely turned away or dead before they could ensnare, as the foundation of sacred narrative.

Hagiographic language thus exposes how, in each saint's passage to visibility, the threshold is more fundamental than either its apparently preceding enclosure or its apparently successive exposure. The saint's body, written, sexed, liminal in the most literal sense, would mark, in itself and through the architecture that gives it a place and thereby amplifies it metonymically, a point of passage as close as possible to an *a priori*. Saints' lives risk exposing the ambivalence at the threshold of the articulable, where the genital and the holy are merely two inflections of a more fundamental "non-event," a coming-to-sensation that is also a coming-to-presence. What is more, hagiographic "experience," as this risked passage, turns Lacoue-Labarthe's ultimately tragic reading (Hölderlin's madness and Heidegger's Nazism as the impossible, unspeakable sources of speech) into a comic one: it discloses, *enclosively*, the generative character of the threshold, exposing itself as a perverse linguistic opening of a difficult to determine womb. It is for this reason that, in contrast to Lacoue-Labarthe's "non-form" (one could as easily say "non-place," "non-body," "unspoken"), I wish to emphasize the way in which saints' lives *come*, in every possible spatial and sexual sense. Hagiography is almost tantric, but perversely, *generatively* so: saints give birth, coming, without ever having come.

No one speaks of this kind of advent more eloquently than Lacoue-Labarthe's friend and frequent collaborator, Jean-Luc Nancy. In his introduction to *The Birth to Presence*, he notes (but obviously with nothing like bland designation):

> Joy, *jouissance, to come*, have the sense of birth: the sense of the inexhaustible imminence of sense. When it has not passed over into ornamentation or into the repetition of philosophy, "poetry" has never sought to create anything else. The coming and going of imminence.[61]

It is in the spirit of Lacoue-Labarthe and Nancy—if against their privileging of modern, serious, self-consciously literary literature—that I want to suggest that hagiography is prototypically poetic in just this sense: as experiential crossing, as generation through coming—in fact, through coming and going, just as Marie turns away, just as Marina's body is always already a dead body. Sense, and here especially vision, is always coming, has never yet completely *taken place*; coming dovetails nicely here with what I've already called the in-between. That is, if hagiographic vision often directs itself between the legs of its object, it is nonetheless a vision that *only comes from between the eyes*. This coming, this vision, gives pleasure: Jehan takes delight in the lives he writes, offering himself as a source of delight, opening one life onto another in a kind of co-coming, a stuttering emergence. The reader of hagiography is thus touched by the hagiographer's pen, and more importantly, by the contact of hagiographer and saint: Marina's "e" *is* the hagiographic text, dead and generative, the sign of Jonah.

If Certeau is right, and there is always theology within hagiography,[62] it is only if God is a name for these metonymies, these overlapping concatenations. For Lacoue-Labarthe, "Intimacy, in its very differance, retreats from all subjects. It is nothing but the gaping of the subject. And the gaping is language. Language in the *interior intimo meo* that onto-theology confused with God" (L'intimité, dans sa différance même, est en retrait de tout sujet. Elle n'est rien que la béance du sujet. Et c'est le langage, cette béance. C'est lui l'*interior intimo meo* que l'onto-théologie confondait avec Dieu).[63] The enclosures of hagiography, at least those addressed here, are not merely linguistic; hermitage, body, text, they disclose the way in which "gaping" is not just absence but *access*, not just caving in but *unfurling*, and above all mark the indifference between them, at the heart of the visible. Saints bloom: this kind of assertion in one way draws upon all the worst feminine stereotypes within the philosophical literature of and on (especially female) saints; however, it also concretizes the material coming-to-be that saints inaugurate, expose, and limn. God, perhaps, is then a way of saying the liminal within what is most interior and what is most exposed: linguistic only if this "saying" is understood in its metonymic relation to bodies and spaces. Hagiography, of course, gives way to kitsch: God is the blooming of the saints; God is what makes the flowers bloom.

Thom Gunn, yet another strange name to evoke in an essay on saints, distils the hagiographic threshold into erotic spacing. (Distilling, spacing; contracting, expanding: it is once again a question of marking, and crossing, a threshold. Of *expanding* this threshold.) In a poem called "Touch," he offers an antidote to Lacoue-Labarthe's preoccupation with language, and thus a warning against a purely linguistic interpretation of what I've called the graphic. Gunn's speaker sinks into "an old / big place," a bed or a bedroom, but this place "seeps / from our touch / in continuous creation." Gunn's place seeps from touch, produced by and escaping touch, and isn't a defined place so much as a space or spacing, a tactile spacing, the spacing-out of touch. Touch generates a space in which bodies will then extend into a "dark / enclosing cocoon," which will also be a "dark / wide realm."[64] There is no difference here between a cocoon and a realm, between enclosure and expansion: this indifference is precisely that of our saints. It is worth noting that, in an early poem entitled "Here Come the Saints," Gunn writes of the saints' "abrupt and violent / Motions" as they go "into the terrible dark wood."[65] Our walking, in "Touch," in the "dark wide realm" is not entirely discrete from these more menacing peregrinations, but the space that opens up within an embrace, that sudden narrow wideness, ultimately and, I would argue, comfortingly makes room for the violent and the plaintive, the exhausted and the amorous. The logic of "Touch"—and its lesson—is that a bed is bigger than a forest, or at least more enclosively expansive.[66]

Likewise, the "everlasting life" or "permanable vie" to which virtually all hagiographies sooner or later allude[67] consists of a kind of transitive, expansive enclosure. In acceding to what is "permanable," what is literally through-dwelling (*per-manere*), the saint literally crosses through the enclosure in order to arrive at, constitute, and space out *vie* in all its senses: life, face, sex, text. Life everlasting is thus only accessible, for now, as a confined traversal, compressed turning: a space and a line. Hagiography, on the verge, touches it; touches it on the verge. In the process, hagiography traces the threshold of the visible: coming, experienced, a compromised miracle.[68]

Hagiography thus traces the outline of claustrophilia, its barest bones. For to draw this compromise is also to draw it out. To insist on showing the muddled miracle is, within limits, to give it space. More than this: to make these saints appear, to assist their appearing (where assistance would have the double resonance of help and witnessing), is to desire the phenomenal limits of their appearance. It is, in other words, to desire the boundaries and borders between or through which they come. Jehan, Marie, and Marina dwell in the interstices of permanence; the verge of the visible, where they appear, is just the phenomenon of this dwelling, the sense of that space between one *virga* and another, between pens and pricks and points of emergence. There is only a rough outline to go by, only a shadow, a vowel, some spit. But these slim signs emerge because they are enclosed, because they are, more precisely, on the edge of enclosure.

CHAPTER 3

SPACED OUT

The Coming Community

We have seen, ambivalently, how the disclosure of sainthood depends upon a set of architectural, bodily, and discursive enclosures. Dependence, in fact, understates what is more precisely a co-inherence of disclosive and enclosive functions, at once withholding and giving the saint to sight. What is more, saintly disclosure and enclosure have been shown to be mutually and equivocally bound up with the risk of sex (understood as both the mere—though obviously never mere—genital "there" and what one does with it). This chapter seeks to intensify, through a reading of radical Italian devotional literature, the erotic cachet that enclosed spaces, and the bodies and texts that touch upon them, contain and disclose for medieval culture.

This argument is, then, in a sense historically specific: the thirteenth century witnessed, chiefly but not exclusively in the proliferation of paramonastic orders such as the Beguines and initially disclosed (i.e., unenclosed) orders such as the friars, an extraordinary engagement with religious space and its discursive and bodily ramifications. But this argument is also, in a sense that the last chapter began to elaborate, a specifically rhetorical interrogation of the very enclosedness of historicity. Metonymy, in fact, will come to name those proximities through which, in a way not unlike the princess's deliverance of her seven-year-old child by Jehan's prayers, enclosure is saved from impenetrability. This is why the holy body, in the texts by Peter Damian and Iacopone da Todi discussed below, must be sullied with sex, and critical prose with its various others—literature, obscenity, every discourse too rigid or too soft. If chapter 2 sought to make concrete the claims about the ethical (here, specifically sexual) underpinnings of aesthetic ambivalence elaborated in chapter 1, in this chapter I am concerned to intensify the ethical until it opens upon an erotic ontology, an account of being as desire and participative relation. It is hoped that the rhetorical mode of this intensification, especially its stress upon metonymy, will enchain any potentially hypostatic moment (in which enclosure becomes an apparently transparent and essential metaphor) into a syntax, a relationship of contiguity. Ever quick to contaminate, metonymy will, additionally, be the bridge from the Middle Ages to modernity, from one sexed body to another (and to the spiritual), and from a binary logic of opposition, according to which metonymy itself is situated against metaphor, to a tertiary logic of participation.

In other words, enclosure refuses to be reduced to stasis. Even within the confines of the hermitage, saints seem constantly to be moving: for Jehan Bouche d'Or as for the monks described by Agamben, the question is always whether the body will move itself virtuously or viciously; it is never a question of not moving at all. In this way, the enduring trope of the *odeur de sainteté*, the pleasant scent of the saintly corpse, could constitute a further elaboration of this enclosed (entombed) resistance to stillness and immanence. That enclosure *moves*, both in the sense of eliciting certain bodily responses and in the sense of itself embodying a kind of response, is the central argument of what follows, and it requires, first of all, a concrete account of how spatial boundaries, for medieval religious, engendered experiences of bodily intensity. Experience here, as earlier, marks a less pure, more compromised form of the movement across danger elaborated by Lacoue-Labarthe: if enclosure moves, this movement is a risky business.[1]

It is by now a commonplace of Italian scholarship that Iacopone da Todi, by no means a household name outside of Italy, is very much a man of his times.[2] Born into a bourgeois family in the booming mercantile economy of thirteenth-century Umbria, he forsakes worldly fortune (and learning: he is said to have perhaps studied Law at the University of Bologna) and pursues a penitential life as, first, a wandering preacher and, later, a Franciscan with sympathies for the radical, Spiritual wing of the order.[3] In the conflict between the cardinals Iacopo and Pietro Colonna and Pope Benedict VIII, he takes the part of the cardinals, for which he is jailed in 1298. He composes a large part of his *laude*, devotional poems generally in heptasyllabic dance meter, from his monastic prison. Following his death in 1306, it becomes difficult to discern the authentic from the inauthentic among those poems attributed to him. Yet, even within the corpus that modern scholarship has deemed more or less certainly of his hand, Paolo Canettieri observes that "it is not in fact possible to make Iacopone's literary production fit into a unifying frame, either thematically or metrically" (non è infatti possibile far rientrare la produzione di Iacopone in un quadro unitario, relativamente ai temi come alle forme metriche utilizzate).[4] Iacopone thus gives a unifying name to a heterogeneous group of texts, in a paradox of authorship and authority that would no doubt have suited his taste for contradiction. Such heterogeneity may, however, also be fairly typical of Italian devotional poetry in general, where singing itself could constitute, in Jennifer Fisk Rondeau's words, "an alternative space," discontinuous with other facets of the life of singers (and thus with their other songs as well).[5] Iacopone remains, for Lino Leonardi and Francesco Santi, "second only to Dante in the *duecento*, for both the dimensions of his body of work and its manuscript diffusion" (secondo solo a Dante, nel Duecento, sia per l'ampiezza dell'opera, sia per la diffusione manocritta).[6]

If I am concerned primarily with asking how enclosed space is sensed, embodied, and rhetorically produced in Iacopone's lyrics, there is another tradition, generally (so far) neglected by the secondary literature, which can give concrete weight to the erotic enclosures of Iacopone's poems. Iacopone is, after all, the preeminent Italian poet not just of ascetic mortification but of masculine desire for a male God. This latter position cannot be easily extricated from, on the one hand, the sophisticated accounts of erotic union in the writings of contemporary women, and, on the other hand, the Cistercian commitment to the rhetoric of the Song of Songs. The homoerotic implications of the latter, as John Boswell and others have already observed, are perpetually on view in the writings of Aelred of Rievaulx. In fact, Boswell cites a passage from Aelred's *Mirror of Charity*, which indicates that homoeroticism is intensified by enclosure: "It is in fact a great consolation in this life to have someone...whom you draw by fetters of love into that *inner room* of your soul, so that though the body is absent, the spirit is there, and you can confer all alone, the more secretly, the more delightfully."[7] Therefore, it is not impossible to argue that Iacopone belongs, via this literature of erotic enclosure, to an eremitic (which is to say, a hyperenclosed, hyperdisclosed) tradition that includes the French lives discussed earlier, and was particularly strong in high-medieval Italy.

Benedict VIII's predecessor was, after all, the "angelic" Pope Celestine V, immortalized by Dante at *Inferno* 3.60 for the "great refusal" (gran rifiuto) by which he left the papacy mere months after his election. In the pseudonymous "autobiography" of Celestine, also the founder of an order of "poor hermits" who had much in common with the strict, Spiritual wing of the Franciscans to which Iacopone ultimately belonged, eremitic space proves decisive for the experience (both sensory experience and experience as risk) of eremitic sexuality. The hermit's life, in this text, is explicitly *not* one of absolute solitude. Recounting Celestine's life as the young Peter of the Morrone, the *vita* explains:

> The youth desired ever more to serve God and especially to serve him in the hermitage. He did not know that a hermit could live with a companion, and indeed he thought that a hermit had to remain always alone, and he had a great fear of the night on account of phantasms.[8]

These phantasms, it turns out, are less bogeymen than the classic temptresses of ascetic literature. They sleep naked on either side of him, and the material result is something that prompts him to take off his tunic in the morning. In fact, Peter's life is obsessed with seminal flow, not just in the case of the dirty tunic, but also in terms of its implications for ritual purity and, most indicatively, how it makes sin perceptible. Among the guests that the experienced hermit entertains are two men, both of them case studies in the kinds of intense coming-to-sensation that can occur among hermits in the confined space of the cell:

> One of them suffered a grave illness, which was this: while he slept he would suddenly get up and scream and run outside from place to place and hide in any hiding place he was able to find and nobody was able to restrain him. But from that day on, he felt nothing of the sort. Another, on the other hand, suffered from a spiritual weakness, such that each night he would have at least two nocturnal emissions. And from that day he was so freed from that vice that he never felt anything again.[9]

> [unus illorum patiebatur magnam infirmitatem, que talis erat: dum dormiret, subito excitabatur et vociferabat, et fugiebat fugiens de loco ad locum, et ascondebat se in quocumque pertuso poterat, et nemo poterat eum tenere: set ab illo die nunquam talia sensit. Alius vero patiebatur spiritualem infimitatem, ita quod omni nocte ad minus duabus vicibus in pollutionem cadebat: qui ab illo die ita a vitio liberatus fuit quod nunquam ex eo aliquid sensit][10]

These men, with their two companions, stay with Celestine for three days, as witnesses to a miraculous ringing of bells in the middle of the wilderness. The "infirmitates" that the miracle resolves—both of them questions of "feeling," sensation—are strikingly symmetrical.[11] In both cases, the body moves in mysterious ways. Whereas the first man explodes into audibility and then seeks to hide himself, the second explodes into visibility—and probably tactility and smell. This latter might, on analogy with Celestine's own trials, seek to hide the tunic that (like Thoas's robe in Euripides) at once hides and reveals, serves as evidence and screen. The second guest's wet dreams are thus in more than one sense a coming-to-sensation, but given that at least five men are sharing the cramped space of Celestine's cave, it is impossible to think of them as solitary acts.

The communal ramifications of "polluti0nes" are not generally the concern of clerical literature on the subject. As Dyan Elliott has shown, the thirteenth-century concentration of sacred power in the priestly mediation of the Eucharist put a premium on the purity of these mediating bodies.[12] Celestine's life even provides as prominent a theologian as Jean Gerson, two centuries later, with grounds for exculpating the wet-dreaming cleric: in an echo of contemporary Franciscan discourse,[13] Celestine dreams that he is ascending a hill with a donkey who shits uncontrollably along the path; nonetheless, he is reassured that the donkey's offense is entirely forgivable.[14] I would argue, however, that in the context of the eremitic life, mediation is less crucial a category than it is for Gerson, unless it is precisely the mediation of ascetic witness that each hermit performs for the other. Therefore the transactions between eremitic bodies would appear to be threatened by the explosive, disrupting logic of "pollutiones," inasmuch as they are instances of both seminal excess and oneiric instability.

To put it otherwise: how is a wet dream like a scream? It is an instance of sensory intensity *as experienced suddenly from outside*. Accordingly, just as the screams of the first visitor give evidence of his "grave illness," it is clear that Celestine's second visitor is not the only one in the cell to "feel" his body's excessive movement. It is also clear that this shared sensation owes much to the spatial confines of the hermitage: sperm, virtuously or viciously emitted, can only fly so far. Enclosure abets the communal experience of the individual body's excess.

Holes in the Wall: Peter Damian

If we restrict ourselves to specifically Italian piety, and especially its radical/eremitic varieties, we can find in the work of Peter Damian an even more outstanding case for the intertwining of sex, space, and sensation. Writing two centuries before Iacopone and the pseudo-Celestine, Damian is a monastic reformer whose provocatory temperament bears an uncanny resemblance to Iacopone's. His life of Saint Romuald, the founder of the Camaldolese reform of Benedictine monasticism, is specifically concerned with the dangers of monastic enclosure. The Camaldolese, not unlike the near-contemporary Carthusians, accommodate both eremitic (solitary) and cenobitic (communal) modes of monastic life. Accordingly, it might at first seem strange to put urban, evangelical Franciscanism alongside such an order. Yet not only does Iacopone's reforming rhetoric resonate with Damian's, but no less an authority than Jean Leclercq has made explicit the extent to which Damian's relation to Romuald resonates with the early Franciscan relation to Francis.[15] Indeed, if Cécile Caby is right in suggesting that thirteenth- and fourteenth-century "inurbamento," the gradual gravitation of monastic orders toward the ever more important Italian cities, meant that eremitism would eventually become "lived and conceived first and foremost as 'a state of the spirit rather than a form of life,' "[16] Iacopone's fundamentally asocial account of penance and illumination might be seen as a concrete attempt to effect something like an urban return to an eremitic "form of life." Morever, Caby suggests that the mendicants, and in Italy particularly the Franciscans, are to a large extent responsible for this reinvigoration of urban religious life: "If eleventh- and twelfth-century eremitism flees the town in search of the desert, the eremitism of the late Middle Ages, in the wake of the decisive experience of St. Francis of Assisi, is always marked by an urbicentrism."[17] And yet, even prior to these radical spatial transitions, Italian eremitism, thanks largely to Damian, felt strongly the ways in which monastic space affects, and can be manipulated by, monastic bodies. That these manipulations are often sexual should—in the wake of Jehan Bouche d'Or and Marie—come as no surprise.

Romuald, in Damian's *vita*, is as cantankerous as Damian himself: he wanders the Italian hills building hermitages, visiting monasteries, and routinely beating the shit out of wayward monks. One of these monks decides to get even, or, I would argue, to approximate with a speech act the beatings that Romuald has administered:[18]

> Romuald had a certain disciple by the name of Romanus, a man of noble birth but utterly ignoble in his way of life. The holy man used not only to chide him for his fleshly uncleanness but would often discipline him by giving him a severe beating. This wicked man dared to bring a trumped-up charge against Romuald for a like offence claiming that he had shamelessly blasphemed against the temple of the Holy Spirit and that the holy man had sinned with him in the same kind of vicious companionship.[19]

> [Habebat namque quemdam discipulum, Romanum nomine, qui nobilis quidem fuerat genere, sed omnino degener actione. Hunc itaque vir sanctus cum pro suae carnis immunditia non modo verbis argueret, sed saepe etiam verberibus gravissimis coerceret, ausus est diabolicus vir titulum illi ejusdem reatus opponere, et impudenter contra sancti Spiritus templum sacrilego ore latrare, dicens videlicet sanctum virum una secum ex eadem contagione peccasse.][20]

Leyser's translation, though clear, softens the implications of Damian's rhetoric. Romanus literally "barks" (latrare) against the temple of the Holy Spirit; he accuses Romuald of partaking of the same "contagion" (ex eadem contagione) of which he is himself guilty. There is, consequently, little ambiguity about the nature of Romanus's "fleshly uncleanness" (carnis immunditia): he is a sodomite. The equation of heretics with dogs, and sodomites with heretics, is a commonplace of clerical invective: think, for example, of the manuscript variants in the Old French *Le chevalier au barisel*, in which an evil lord prompts the local hermit to announce, "You are worse than a heretic" (Tu es pire que erites) or, in other versions, "You are worse than a sodomite" (Tu es pires que sodomites).[21] Moreover, Mark D. Jordan has argued that it is precisely Damian who coins the term "sodomia," on analogy with "blasphemia," after centuries of "thinning and condensing" variously understood vices into a difficult to define, yet crucial, theological category.[22]

In fact, Damian's infamous Letter 13, the *Liber Gomorrhianus* (1049) draws extensively upon understandings of sodomy as contagion, blurring the boundaries between disease, rhetoric, and architecture as he attempts to root out the sodomites among his flock. Sodomy, comprising everything from masturbation to anal sex, is repeatedly figured in the *Liber* as disease: "a cancer of Sodomitic uncleanness is slithering through the clerical orders" (Sodomiticae igitur immunditiae cancer ita per clericalem ordinem serpit) whose members are frequently "contaminated with this pus-seeping contagion" (hac purulenta contagione foedati).[23] As if the snake metaphor hadn't already made clear that this is a sexually transmitted disease, Damian goes on to rewrite the sinfully penetrated body as the corrupt body of the church: taking a cue from the narrative of Sodom and Gomorrah, in which the Sodomites are blinded by light at the door of Lot's house, Damian asks:

> He who, unworthy of the order, strains to break in on the Office of the sacred altar, what else does he seek, if not, having relinquished the threshold of the door, to enter through opening a hole in an impenetrable wall? And since their feet are not permitted to enter freely, these same men, while they promise themselves to penetrate the sanctuary successfully, are forced instead, frustrated by their own presumption, to remain in the external vestibule. And they can hit their heads against the rock of Holy Scripture as much as they want, but it will be in no way permitted them to find an entrance allowed by divine authority; and while they attempt to enter where it is not permitted, they do nothing other than grope in vain the wall they cannot see.

> [Qui enim indignus ordine ad sacri altaris officium conatur irrumpere, quid aliud quam relicto ianuae limine per immeabilem parietis obicem nititur introire? Et quia liber pedibus non patet ingressus, hii tales, dum sibi spondent, ad sacrarium posse pertingere, sua presumptione frustrati coguntur potius in exteriori vestibulo remanere. Et fronter quidem possunt in sacre scripturae saxa percutere, sed per divinae acuctoritatis aditum nequaquam permittuntur intrare atque dum ingredi, quo non sinuntur, attemptant, nichil aliud faciunt, quam obtectum parietem inaniter palpant.][24]

The sodomites, here reduced to a venomously vague "these guys" (hii tales), aspire to be masters of perverse penetration. They have abandoned the doorway in order to make their own hole in the wall. What is fascinating about this contention is not only its staging of anxieties not that different from those of contemporary culture's heteronormative custody of the so-called back door, but the fact that Damian must insist upon the sodomites' inability to achieve their aim. They are both inside and out.

Kept in the "outer vestibule" (exteriori vestibulo) and limited to stupid surface contact, "groping in vain" (inaniter palpant), they are nonetheless, by virtue of their serpentine transmissions of disease, obviously successful in surreptitiously breaking down barriers. Indeed, the sodomites' bodies are reduced here to their extremities, those organs most capable of boundary-breaking: heads, feet, hands. The remaining extremity, the most extreme perhaps, is notable for its absence. But Damian's rhetorical practice is thereby revealed as one of a palpably present absence ("inaniter palpant"), the clerical dick as the missing term that holds the puzzle, specifically the continuous impenetrable surface of the church, together.[25]

To speak of continuity is thus to speak of metonymy. It is worth recalling that, for the pseudo-Ciceronian *Rhetorica ad Herennium*, metonymy ("denominatio") is "the figure that draws from an object closely akin or associated an expression suggesting the object meant, but not called by its own name" (Denominatio est quae ab rebus propinquis et finitimis trahit orationem qua possit intellegi res quae non suo vocabulo sit appellata).[26] The metonymic "oratio" (which could not have failed also to invoke prayer for as savvy a rhetorician as Damian) thus remains not just near ("propinquis") but in fact borders, touches upon ("finitimis") the things of which it speaks. A substitutive relation ("non suo vocabulo") draws forth ("trahit") semantic continuity from contiguity. I am belaboring the obvious here in order to show just how far Damian's guiding *metaphor*—the church as male body that only appears to have been penetrated, remaining somehow miraculously intact—overlaps with an overall poetics of *metonymy*, in which the gap between "exterior vestibule" and "interior altar" is closed by nothing other than the absently present clerical penis.[27] Damian's desire for the slick, smooth surface of the ecclesial wall attempts, that is, to plug up its holes. It is a gesture, I have to say, not unlike that of contemporary pornography, with its flawlessly depilated centerfolds and video stars: in the service of total visibility (not to mention the cultivation of youth as beauty) a stunningly smooth surface is presented to the viewer, a surface whose two-dimensional holes beg to be (already) filled by the absently present spectator's dick.[28] Damian says, similarly, "Fill in the blank," and yet he simultaneously asserts that this blank, already somehow filled, locks us outside the body/building of the church.[29] The male ecclesial body thus reveals itself as always already fucked, always already filled, in order to make itself immune to further penetration. To put it in terms all too resonant with mystical discourse, this body is *too full*, overflowing with surface, excessive; the kind of body whose surfaces invite the groping they only subsequently claim to resist.

That metonymy should fundamentally undermine Damian's assertion of the impenetrable church is further underscored by the way in which his ever-allusive prose echoes, in the passage cited above, the first intonations of the Latin rite. The opening liturgical declaration, "introibo ad altare Dei"

(Psalm 42:4), itself a metonymy not only for the church as a whole but for that transcendence upon which the divine altar materially, eucharistically opens, becomes in Damian's hands a fragmented, inverted structure. He substitutes for the approach to, and inside, the altar a *forced* entry ("conatur irrumpere") and postpones "introire" until a situation in which, in fact, "irrumpere" would initially seem more appropriate: the moment of attempted penetration of the impenetrable ecclesial/bodily wall. It is, on the surface, a clever attempt at once to stage the desired disorder of the sodomites and to protect the altar, through a displaced "introire," from the wayward entry Damian condemns. The formal *inversions* are meant to effect a *conversion*, from the penetrating and penetrated sodomitic body to the impenetrable body of the church. Yet what Damian effectively does here, not unlike the author of the life of Marie l'Egyptienne, is to reinscribe the threshold at which inversion and conversion touch: a threshold figured here explicitly as the "ianuae limine," which, contrary to Damian's assertion, is never "relicto," never left behind. To keep this reading even more carefully on the surface—as it were, *hypersuperficial*—let us say that Damian foregrounds the gap between entry and breaking-and-entering even as he makes them rhetorically equivalent, by framing them both as frustrated attempts ("conatur...nititur") to sexualize liturgical movement and language. That such movement and language would be continuous with the physical church is evident in Damian's emphasis upon the altar, a tangible as well as symbolic space, as that term which crystallizes the ambivalence of these frustrated entries. But is it not precisely Damian who here sexualizes liturgy? In an economy of metonymy, is the rhetorician immune to discursive penetration? Has someone already plugged Damian's hole? Damian has bound himself doubly: he can either talk like a sodomite or, through his failed attempt to do so, act like one. It is in this sense that liturgical rhetoric binds one metonymic term (body) to the other (building) and effects the transition from the impossibly fuckable to the actually fucked. To push the logic of these inversions and rhetorical/metonymic contaminations to their (absently present) extreme, it is as perhaps the apotheosis of fabliau-like blasphemy that Damian asserts, "I will come into the altar of God."[30]

If the altar of God is also an asshole—indeed, if Damian has converted it into such through his inversions—it is by no means the only orifice that gets entered, liturgically or otherwise, in the course of this text. In paragraph 23, Damian addresses the sodomite directly: "But now, O Sodomite, whoever you are, I must come to you face to face" (Sed iam te ore ad os quisquis es, sodomita, convenio).[31] I translate "ore ad os" as "face to face" out of deference to tradition, but it is perhaps unwise to overlook the most literal meaning: Damian comes to the sodomite *mouth to mouth*. In a letter so concerned with orifices and modes of entry, it is best not to underestimate this oral metonymy. Remembering the parodic conflation, in the life of Jehan

Bouche d'Or, of the modes of temporal suspension characteristic of the pregnant princess's genital door and the orally lubricated repetitions of the saintly scribe, it is possible to ask how Damian's mouth-to-mouth confrontation with the sodomite can be differentiated from a kiss. To take up the language of the previous chapter again, what is the barest point at which vice is undone by, or transformed into, virtue? As Carolyn Dinshaw has shown, a kiss is rarely just a kiss: it is not always, as in *Gawain*, a potential fuck, but it *is*, I would argue, the very image of an enclosed opening: the trace, the outline, of what resists and intensifies sensation.[32]

Damian thus hopes with his rhetoric to convert the rhetorically deceptive and deceived citizen of Sodom. Yet by mirroring, and thus inverting, the sodomite's position, putting his mouth to the sodomite's while nonetheless insisting on a full-frontal encounter, is Damian nonetheless trying to "pass"? At the same time, if its teleology is the only thing that redeems this mouth-to-mouth encounter, and the sodomite is an indefinite "whoever" whose city overlaps with the boundaries of the hermitage,[33] can Damian be sure of the end of his saving kiss; can he be sure who is kissing whom? I am tempted to suggest that, just as eros is for Plato an "eye disease,"[34] so too is sodomy for Damian a mouth disease—indeed, if we consider the rhetoric of the passage cited above, a foot and mouth disease.[35] Yet to perceive this disease, in Damian's text, is already to be infected by it, to perceive that one has already been kissed, stepped across: taken from the front as from behind.

We will need to return to the space this kiss figures. The kiss is, after all, one of the strongest symbols in monastic theology: in the wake of the Song of Songs, it figures the soul's union with God. Yet before engaging with the Song tradition in light of Iacopone's poems, it is necessary to return to Damian's life of Romuald for two last observations. First, Romanus is not just implicitly a sodomite; he is explicitly a "sarabite": after the sodomy scandal, "he soon got, through simony, the episcopal see of Nucero. He occupied it for two years; in the first year as he richly deserved everything got burned" (Ille autem Sarabaita reprobus, qui sancto viro crimen intenderat, episcopatum postmodum Nucerinum per Simoniacam haeresim acquisivit, et per biennium illum occupans, in primo anno incensam aedem...vidit).[36] At the beginning of my discussion of French hagiography, I mentioned that Benedict's Rule sets out four types of monks. Sarabites are the third type, mentioned just after hermits. In a way that resonates with the indefinite character of Damian's sodomite, "quisquis es," Benedict's sarabite is difficult to define and fundamentally disordered:

> The third kind of monk is the abominable one of Sarabaites, who have not been tested by a rule, as gold is tested in a furnace, nor been taught by experience, but are like soft lead. They keep faith with this world by their

actions, but manifestly lie to God by their tonsure. These people live in twos and threes, or even alone; they have no shepherd, they shut themselves up in their own sheepfolds, not those of the Lord; and their law consists in yielding to their desires: what they like or choose they call holy, and they reckon illicit whatever displeases them.[37]

[Tertium vero monachorum teterrimum genus est sarabaitarum, qui nulla regula approbati, experientia magistri, sicut aurum fornacis; sed in plumbi natura molliti, adhuc operibus servantes saeculo fidem, mentiri Deo per tonsuram noscuntur. Qui bini, aut terni, aut certe singuli, sine pastore, non dominicis, sed suis inclusi ovilibus, pro lege eis est desideriorum voluptas: cum quidquid putaverint vel elegerint, hoc dicunt sanctum; et quod noluerint, hoc putant non licere.][38]

Like the sodomite, the sarabite is a slave to "voluptas" and "mollities": pleasure for its own sake and, still more tellingly, that "softness" which has been associated with sexuality ever since the Pauline lists of vices. At 1 Corinthians 6:9, for example, we find among those who will not inherit the kingdom of heaven "neither fornicators, nor idol-worshippers, nor adulterers, nor the soft, nor those who lie with men" (neque fornicarii neque idolis servientes neque adulteri neque molles neque masculorum concubitores). A quick glance at the modern renderings of the Greek *malakoi*, which the Vulgate translates as *molles*, shows the range of significations that readers have come to find in this elusive "softness": they are "male prostitutes" (NRSV), "sexual perverts" (grouped together with the "concubitores" in the Revised English), "boy prostitutes" (New American), and, best of all, the "self-indulgent" (New Jerusalem).[39] As Mark Jordan sums up the debate,

Modern exegetes have quarreled over whether this refers to "passive" male homosexuals, male homosexuals generally, the effeminate (what that might mean), or (male?) masturbators. The quarrels are endless because the passage gives no evidence for concluding them.[40]

Seen through this philological lens, the sarabite appears still more undefinably vicious, more similar to the "quisquis es" of Damian's sodomite. Romanus's career as a simonist gives us further pause: not only for its sibilance (sarabite, simonist, sodomite) but for its illicit introduction of money into affairs of the church, a prohibited entry which echoes that of usury, a vice classically bound up with sodomy in Dante and elsewhere. Simony, the selling of ecclesial offices and favors, is itself, for the French Dominican William of Peraldus (*Summa de vitiis*, pre-1250), explicitly a kind of "spiritual sodomy." Romanus's "uncleanness" would seem, then, to be a matter not just of infected bodies but of the infected body of the church.

Returning to Romuald, it is possible to see in his life the very conditions of visibility upon which hagiography relies, as well as the ambivalence that inheres within them. Long after Romanus has disappeared from the scene, Romuald is tormented by a devil; he prays for help, and the devil flees his hermitage, sending a plank flying from the wall:

> In his little house, Romuald thus showed openly how great a flame of cruelty burned against its inhabitant, and how in a certain way what he had secretly endured in the spirit remained written on the wall.[41]
>
> [In habitaculo igitur patenter ostendit quanta adversus habitatorem flamma crudelitatis exarsit, et quodammodo scriptum reliquit in pariete quod occultum gerebat in mente.][42]

Romuald's diminutive dwelling is here figured explicitly as a site of transition, indeed of emergence, from the hidden to the visible, from the "occultum" to what is shown openly, "patenter." What is more, the modality of this disclosure appears to be specifically *textual*: in the careful parallelism of the second phrase, "scriptum reliquit in pariete" lines up perfectly with "occultum gerebat in mente," the written as proof of the secret, the wall as evidence of the spirit. Damian thus appears to stage the written wall through which alone sanctity can be seen, and to foreground the compromised way in which this textual disclosure takes place: the hermitage's wall is opened up, only to be reinforced as itself spectacular. Romuald's body emerges into visibility through this new threshold of the building, which encloses and metonymically extends it, as the small "habitaculo" to Romuald's "habitator." Yet is there not as well some echo here of the sodomitic drive to open doors in walls where there are none? If Romuald's spiritual trial is written on the wall as precisely this wall's hole, its constitutive absence, does it not also reinscribe the saint not just in but *as* an ambiguous architectural frame? Such a frame, necessary for the transition from occult to cult, nevertheless would constitute a *surface hole*, something against which the worshipper, or disciple, or sodomite could only grope in vain.

Thus, to return to Damian's corporeal church in light of Romuald's open enclosure, it is possible to ask how the male body and the hermitage must make themselves transparent to the devout look, and to what extent this look can keep from approximating (or, in language more similar to Damian's, straining to approximate) penetration. Is the only access we have to the spectacle of sanctity, as worshippers and interpreters, one of breaking a hole through an impenetrable wall? Damian's logic, I would argue, puts his audience in this double-bind because it simultaneously affirms the transcendence of body by building and vice-versa—what one could also call, more platonically, participation—and reduces body and building to an immanent identity. The body of the church is ultimately unable to escape the sodomitic bodies that have always already penetrated it, just as the saintly body is unable to escape those architectural perforations that contaminate it with the signs of sodomy. In such an economy, there is no room—literally no space—for real transcendence. Sodomy looks like sanctity; sanctity looks like sodomy. Now, the *Rhetorica ad Herennium* specifically lists enclosure as one of the primary modes of metonymic substitution: metonymies occur in cases of "content...designated by means of container" and "container...designated by means of content" [Ab eo quod continet id quod continetur...ab eo quod continetur id quod continet].[43] Accordingly, the hermeneutic maneuver by which one understands a metonymy appears to entail either an opening-up of enclosure or a closing-up of the disclosed. Yet if this disclosive/enclosive act occurs at once, and with regard to the same two terms, then what remains is, at best, a static identity. Church and male body are equally transparent and opaque to one another, and in just the same way. The devout look is excluded by this transparency only if one understands by exclusion the refusal to see anything new. The three-dimensional structures of body and building are collapsed, here, into an exhausted, specular plane.

Close to the Knives: Iacopone da Todi

To get beyond this specular identity, to release metonymy from its centrifugal pull, what is called for is, most simply, a poetics of participation. Dalibor Vesely, in his essay "The Architectonics of Embodiment," describes a "primary" tradition subsequently displaced by the early modern fetish for purely technical proportion. According to this (largely platonic) tradition, "the reality of the world is not structured around identifiable independent entities such as isolated human bodies or isolated architectural elements and their corresponding meanings. Rather, it is structured through degrees of embodiment..."[44] In Vesely's understanding, the relationship between bodies and buildings is one of neither discrete isolation, nor collapsed identity, nor immanent and strictly insignificant proportion. Rather, buildings and bodies participate in embodiment and mediate embodiment, in their respective degrees, to one another. Proportion thus appears to be more like that *convenientia* which, according to Aquinas, aesthetically organizes the basic relationship of creation to Creator.[45] I would extend the implications of this rhetorically. For metaphor, as proper comparison, always occludes catachresis, or improper comparison, and simultaneously establishes the catachretic utterance as its contaminant/supplement.[46] The church is a body: this appears to be a metaphor. The altar is an asshole: this appears to be a catachresis. Metonymy, however, *exposes* the contiguous second term with which it exists in a relation of mediating participation. Just as embodiment structures the mediating relationship between bodies and buildings, so too could holiness be said similarly to shine through the sodomite's body, the saint's body, and the church as the *extension* of both of these. It is merely a question of how brightly: it is a question of degree.[47]

Iacopone da Todi, stern moralist that he is, nonetheless betrays, in his lexicon of "esmesuranza" (literally, what is without measure), the extent to which vice and virtue are connected along just such a scale of degrees. "Esmesuranza" is famously the term with which Iacopone characterizes mystical ecstasy. A typical utterance lies at the heart of laud 92, "Sopr'onne lengua amore," when Iacopone asks, "Measureless Love, why are you driving me crazy?" (Amor esmesurato, perché me fai empascire?; 92.145).[48] Yet, even as the crucial phrasing of the divine "beyond" remains the "ultra esmesurato" (39.90), Iacopone can argue that a brief moment of earthly delight may have as its reward measureless punishment, or measurelessness *as* punishment ("penar 'n esmesuranza"; 19.48). Indeed, laud 44, "O anema mia, creata gintile," uses "esmesuranza" more synthetically, to describe both the heart's callous self-surrender to the senses (44.32–35) and the transcendence that it forfeits in doing so (44.57–58). The "esmesurato" can thus be mapped, I would argue, onto the semantic field of the outrageous, comprising both offense and excess.

It is worth recalling that Dante uses the term only once, to indicate not divine transcendence but excessive pride. At the entrance to the pit that will lead the pilgrim and Virgil to hell's final frozen circle, Dante asks, "If it is possible, / I'd like my eyes to have experience / of the enormous one, Brïareus" (S'esser puote, io vorrei / che de lo smisurato Brïareo / esperïenza avesser li occhi miei). Virgil informs the pilgrim that he will have to content himself with another giant, Antaeus: " 'The one you wish to see lies far beyond / and is bound up and just as huge as this one, / and even more ferocious is his gaze' " (Quel che tu vuo' veder / più là è molto / ed è legato e fatto come questo, / salvo che più feroce par nel volto).[49] Dante thus presents Brïareus's "smisuranza" as a (denied) object of vision, located "più là," in a beyond that mirrors, and reverses, the divine "ultra esmesurato" of which Iacopone speaks. Similarly, Iacopone's confession that, for love of God, "I go down this path as though I were lost" (Como smarrito sì vo per la via; 89.127), turns on its head the (still-to-come) Dantesque inflection of *smarrimento*. The measureless thus marks the place at which virtue and vice are difficult to tell apart, where conversion and perversion, as in the life of Marie l'Egyptienne, meet at the barest point of turning.[50] Here, however, it is less a question of the in-between space of an almost imperceptible turn than of spatial extremity: the seat of the *Deus absconditus* in the very belly of hell.[51] Francesco Santi observes that, for

Iacopone, "the Crucified is placed so to speak at the extreme boundary of the cosmos: on this side, nothingness; on that side, the all" (il crocefisso è posto per così dire al confine estremo del cosmo: al di qua è il niente; al di là è il tutto).[52] Even the most abject forms of nothingness—here figured as the "lost" sinner or the "measureless" hell-bound giant—participate in this "tutto," which should not be understood metaphysically but, instead, as the very name of participative recuperation.

Measure is a crucial category of sensation for no less a thinker than Bonaventure, to whose treatise on *The Soul's Journey to God* Iacopone's angelology, but also much of his neoplatonic repertoire in general, is heavily indebted (e.g., lauds 77, 84). According to the first chapter of the *Itinerarium*, the sensory perception of the world takes account of things in themselves, "see[ing] in them their weight, number and measure" (videt in eis pondus, numerum et mensuram). Measure is defined as that "by which things are determined" (quam limitantur) and is associated, through the ensuing parallelisms, with "order" (ordinem) and "activity" (operationem). But Bonaventurean measure is, above all else, one means of rising from creation to Creator: "From all these considerations the observer can rise, as from a vestige, to the knowledge of the immense power, wisdom, and goodness of the Creator" (Ex quibus consurgere potese sicut ex vestigio ad intelligendum potentiam, sapientiam, et bonitatem Creatoris immensam).[53] It is clear that Iacopone shares Bonaventure's association of measure with order: in a famous moment of mystical back-talk, Iacopone responds to God's demand to "set this love in order" (ordena questo amore; 89.147) by asserting, "When you gave yourself to me so immoderately, you took all moderation from me" (Quanno sì esmesurato me tte davi, tollivin' da me tutta mesuranza; 89.189–90). Yet if measure, precisely in its limiting quality ("quam limitantur"), allows the observer to rise up to God, why does Iacopone need to emphasize the measureless? That is to say, isn't Bonaventure's notion of measure already, and sensorially, ecstatic?

This is, in fact, the lesser-known antecedent to Iacopone's poetics of the measureless. For, as Elena Landoni has most recently observed, Iacopone is responding here to the rhetoric of Occitan lyric as well: in his famous exposition of the virtuous "mean" or "middle way" (laud 43, "O mezzo virtüoso, retenut'a bataglia"), Iacopone "clarifies unequivocally that to reach that 'mean' one must laboriously pass through a stage of being caught up, without reservation or remainder, in the two opposite extremes of love and hatred...and so on: a radical reversal of reasonable, aristocratic *mezura*."[54] Landoni makes fleeting reference to the late troubadour Guilhem de Montanhagol when describing the reluctance of even late Occitan verse to relinquish a courtly commitment to *mezura*; her suggestion is especially useful for the topographies, indeed the *claustrographies*, with which I am concerned. For, if Montanhagol's sincere lover "is not immoderate" (non es desmezuratz), and this moderation is situated *between* two terms, "too much and too little" (entre .l trop e .l pauc mezura jatz), Iacopone's "virtuous mean" (mezzo virtuoso) is still more dynamically spatialized.[55] In laud 43, the mean is a "travaglia," an ordeal, and Iacopone's sequence of opposites results less in synthesis than in a sense of fundamentally unstable, dynamic aporia. Whereas Montanhagol's restful *mezura* lies down, "jatz," as if suspended in a hammock, Iacopone's "mezzo" consists of a series of unhappy cohabitations: "love and hatred staying in one heart" (amare et enodiare enn un coraio stante; 43.5), "pleasure and displeasure convened in one heart" (placere e displacere en un cor convegnire; 43.9), "hope and despair staying in one house" (sperare e desperare stare enn una masone; 43.13), "security and fear abiding in one court" (escecurtà e temore demorar 'nn una corte; 43.17). What is more, these spatially compressed conflicts are redoubled by the senses: Iacopone warns, "Hearing about this and enduring it are two different things" (Altro è lo patere che l'odirlo parlare; 43.38); similarly, "he who has felt it can't conjure its image for someone who hasn't" (A chi non l'à provato non lo pò emagenare; 43.50). Whereas the image is vicariously inaccessible, sound marks the very place of this vicarious sensation, which nonetheless remains rigorously other ("altro") to its object. The virtuous mean would then consist, also, of that space in which an unfigurable image and a disfiguring sound meet to sustain the commonly held singularity of mystical experience.

This paradox, with its spatial and sensory construal of what is restlessly communicable in a singular instance of "patere" or "provare," finds its most succinct expression in the final verses of the poem. Here Iacopone practically cries out:

> I abide between the scissors, each blade cuts me,
> I'll shorten my speech, to end in this place.
>
> [demoro entro le forfece, ciascun coltel m'affètta,
> abrevio mea ditta, en questo loco finare.] 43.61–62

Instead of lyric closure, Iacopone offers an abrupt, forced ending. This ending is tied, syntactically and semantically, to the place his speaker occupies: to cite the title of David Wojnarowicz's now classic queer narrative, Iacopone is close to the knives, his "mezzo" a way of wounds.[56] And yet it is, like the dynamically "permanable" life of the saints, a state paradoxically sustained: Iacopone dwells ("demoro") between the blades of opposing terms, lets the contradictions cut him as long as he can, until bringing this impossible place to a close, indeed, until marking it as the arbitrary but no less necessary place of closure.

This paradoxical place is not unlike that of a magician's assistant enclosed in a box stuck through with swords. It is bound up with a crucial speech act (the abbreviated "ditta" like an abracadabra) and rests upon a simultaneity of places—inside and outside, between the blades and pierced through by them—sustained by an optical illusion. For evidence of this mystical optics, we must look to the sixty-fifth laud in Mancini's edition, bound up as it is with the very technique of abbreviation that both marks the "loco" of contradiction and brings it to an end here. First, however, I would argue that, even if Ivos Margoni is right in suggesting that courtly *mezura* is to be understood "in its social, erotic, heroic, and aesthetic— not philosophical—resonance,"[57] Iacopone's emphasis upon such an unbearable "mezzo" is precisely the Bonaventurean, and thus philosophical, inflection of what will elsewhere appear as specifically anti-courtly "esmesuranza." Stated positively (as aporetic "mezzo") or negatively (as excessive "esmesuranza"), the place of spiritual ordeal remains, paradoxically, the contradictory house whose roof gets broken open by anagogic "consurgere," whose walls are torn by scissors. But does the place occupied by the virtuous, immoderately moderate soul exist prior to its occupation? And where does this poem's sharp closure cut into the enclosures suggested by the "houses" and "dwellings" where contradictions are brought together?

The *Laude*, even at a glance, pivot upon a crucial spatial contradiction: the simultaneity of enclosure and fugitive movement. In this way, they condense into a single, paradoxical state the alternation of wandering and enclosure that can be found, for example, in Bonaventure's life of Francis.[58] Iacopone's lyrics thus constitute to some extent the literary counterpart to the Assisi fresco of Saint Francis in ecstasy, where a cloud intervenes around the rapt saint to signal "both the radical discontinuity and—at the same time—the possibility of communication between the human world and the divine order."[59] Franciscan poetics in general seems drawn toward the interval between here and there, and specifically toward the ways in which what is out of place, or apparently placeless, might nonetheless be also dynamically engaged with its surroundings—indeed, more so than if it belonged to the same order of perspective or propriety.[60] For example, in laud 2, "Fugio la croce, cà mme devora," one of Iacopone's two speakers confesses to fleeing the internal cross that "devours" him, while finding no place in which to take refuge: "I find no place [to rest], for I carry it [the cross] in my heart" (non trovo loco, cà la porto en core; 2.5). Likewise, Iacopone's heart in laud 89 "Burns and blazes, finds no place; / It can't flee, bound as it is, / consumed thus like wax in the fire" (Arde et encende, nullo trova loco, / non pò fugir, però ched è legato, / sì sse consuma como cera a ffoco; 89.3–5). This simultaneity of interiority and dynamism pushes to new extremes the Bonaventurean synthesis that Denys Turner has neatly summarized as one of "interiorised hierarchy."[61] Iacopone offers, beyond the neoplatonic journey inward and upward, an account of enclosure as flight and fiery dissolution. I would call it a place-less place, but it may make more sense—i.e., it may be easier for the senses—to describe it as an enclosure whose very walls tremble: pierced, persecuted, burning.

Tongues and Tails

That there might be a restless atopia inscribed at the heart of enclosure (and in Iacopone's heart *as* enclosure) becomes still more evident in laud 53, "Que farai, fra' Iacovone?," Iacopone's detailed description of his imprisonment. He confesses to ten years of penitent wandering ("gir bezocone"; 53.130) before being confined by Boniface VIII to his monastic prison, "an underground house" (una casa sotterrata) where "a latrine flows" (arèscece una privata; 53.16–17). Just as wandering and incarceration find their place within a single poem, the poem itself is at once static and dynamic, composed within the underground prison and capable of transgressing its confines:

> O page of mine, go spread the word,
> Iacopone the prisoner sends you
> to the Roman court, that extends itself
> to every tribe, language, and nation:
> "In Todi I now lie underground,
> Imprisoned forevermore.
> In the Roman court I earned
> such a benefice!"
>
> [Carta mea, va' mitti banna,
> Iacovon preson te manna
> en cort'i Roma, che sse spanna
> en tribù lengua e nazione:
> "En Todo iaccio sotterrato,
> en perpetua encarcerato.
> En cort'i Roma ho guadagnato
> sì bon beneficïone!"] 147–54

The poetic page is, to be sure, a traditional metonymy, but it is one that nevertheless both *contains* the imprisoned body's relationship to its prison and *extends* this body beyond the prison's bounds in what can only be described as a kind of metonymic contamination. As in the life of Jehan Bouche d'Or, the written text flows from the enclosed body and thereby makes visible this body's boundaries, the places at which it touches upon building and page. Yet whereas Jehan's salivary script serves to vouchsafe his virtue by *containing* the repetitive impulse, which might otherwise wreak havoc upon his solitary body, Iacopone's page seeks precisely to *break through* the prison walls in order to show its virtue to the outside world. This jailbreak specifically mimics the expansion ("sse spanna") which is said to characterize the Roman, that is, papal, court. To what extent, then, does Iacopone's poetic production, which seeks to speak his enclosure (" 'En Todo iaccio sotterrato' ") by at once penetrating and extending the ecclesial wall, participate in just the kind of hole-making that is, for Peter Damian, the tell-tale sign of sanctity and sodomy?

My query may seem less random if an earlier passage of this poem is taken into consideration. In language consonant with the bitterly playful irony that underlies the rest of the poem (most famously the "new dance" [nova danza; 53.25] of his body as he beats it with chains) Iacopone critiques the worldly preoccupations of the papacy and the Franciscan order:

> The Order has such an opening
> That there is no obstacle to leaving through it;
> if that break were closed,
> they [the friars] would stay at the trough.
> I have been wandering around, speaking
> And licking [the ass of] the Roman court,
> So much that finally the punishment has arrived
> for my presumption.
>
> [L'Ordene sì à un pertuso
> c'a l'oscir non n'è confuso;
> se quel guado fusse arcluso,
> staran fissi al magnadone.
> Tanto so' gito parlanno,
> cort'i Roma gir leccanno,
> c'or è ionto alfin lo banno
> de la mea prosonzïone.] 53.87–94

Iacopone likens his fellow friars to animals who keep escaping through a hole in the barnyard fence. Mancini argues that Iacopone is speaking here of "the possibility of acceding, without reproach, to prelatures and places of worldly responsibility,"[62] and I'd argue that Iacopone's hole is thus first and foremost hermeneutic, that is, an opening in the Franciscan Rule through which less stalwart friars can escape into worldliness. What is especially curious about this passage, however, is how smoothly one enclosure gives way to another, the subterranean prison cell (perhaps in the monastery of San Fortunato in Todi) functioning as the transformed enclosure, the "pertuso arcluso," proper to the strictly observant friar. So too does one sort of orality give way to another: on the one hand, the ideally enclosed friars, eating in a fixed place; on the other, Iacopone's transgressive tongue. In fact, Iacopone's page, which penetrates the subterranean walls of his prison to become *coextensive* with the papal dominion, thus appears to respond to a punishment inflicted in response to the touch of a tongue ("gir leccanno"). The punishment (enclosure) doesn't so much fit the crime (traversing an opening) as invert it; but the prisoner subsequently *reverts* to his original crime (through his trangressive "carta") and thereby inverts again, or *reinverts*, the enclosive function of his prison. What is underscored, in all these versions or turnings, is the bare point at which language constitutes and dissolves the walls that enclose Iacopone's body. The poem establishes movement, "gire," as the basis of the speaking and licking tongue, flickering between "banna" as public speech and "banno" as punishment. Yet one question remains, upon which any attempt to trace this movement must rest: precisely what kind of lingual contact does Iacopone's initial, ironically phrased transgression consist of?

In many ways, the answer is obvious. Serge and Elizabeth Hughes translate Iacopone's act as "asslicking,"[63] inasmuch Iacopone's irony clearly alludes to his particularly unflattering speech acts against the Roman court. The touch of the tongue is doubly metonymic: inasmuch as tongues produce, and indeed literally are, speech; and inasmuch as the territory this tongue enters, which its shit-smelling confinement ("arèscece una privata") both responds to and provokes, is the ecclesial anus. The architectural opening ("guado") of the worldly friars is thereby displaced by, and redoubled as, the rimmed asshole of the worldly pope.[64] Yet is it possible that Iacopone, who here speaks with the most open irony, is actually keeping his tongue to himself? It is, first of all, worth recalling that Iacopone's "lengua" appears almost obsessively in the *Laude* as an organ whose powers are cut short by mystical experience. At 21.24 and 36.100, his tongue is "mozzata": blocked, suppressed, withdrawn. Is it therefore possible that Iacopone's irony here might in fact enact this withdrawal even as it proffers the transgressive tongue? Giovanni Pozzi has suggested that Iacopone's more polemical poems are not primarily satires, "as too often one thinks, nor polemics of a strictly political nature, but prophetic messages," prophecy here indicating the primacy of theophany, as the root of what passes for mystical "experience," over politics.[65] Irony would, then, inscribe a kind of mystical apophasis, an unsaying or untouching, at the heart of Iacopone's anilingus, thereby obscenely preserving the theological at the heart of institutional politics.

To insist upon this point is, I realize, to push Iacopone's text beyond even its own rather extreme borders. And yet the overlapping holes and crossings amidst this scene of toilet scribbling push me, as it were, to push.

Let me restate the interconnection of irony, the teasing tongue, and apophasis. Iacopone's imprisonment is, of course, the result of explicitly *refusing* to lick the pope's ass, forsaking the worldly hole through which his peers have escaped. Yet by sending forth his text, inscribed with the declaration of enclosure, to the "cort'i Roma," he insinuates his tongue, a wandering of words, into the ecclesial hole. This insinuation—which is not merely metaphorical flattery but a metonymically *extensive* penetration—is marked, by irony, also as a withdrawal, and thus is able to participate, as polemic, in the dialectic of saying and unsaying that lies at the heart of mystical discourse. One could thus also say, inversely, that Iacopone sends forth his asshole, the *site* of an offered withdrawal and the *sign* of the theological absence in secular church politics, into the circle of papal speech. In either case, he inscribes a break in the discursive or physical body of the church.

Moreover, Iacopone does this all from within a cell that smells like shit, the olfactory double of Boniface's "pertuso." Iacopone's prison has thus closed around him *as* the ecclesial opening he has refused to enter. If he has failed to lick Boniface's asshole, the poem suggests, it is because it already contains him. Irony is, so to speak, the only way out, inasmuch as its tongue flickers, withdrawing in every extension. Iacopone was not explicitly concerned with sodomy—he mentions Sodom only once, in passing, in all the lauds[66]—but he bears in this way all the prevalent marks of Damian's uncanny sodomite, always already inside the institution that closes him off (and thus closes him in). The church, however, or more explicitly the monastery, would function as Iacopone's prison, coextensive with the prison of language, the enclosure of worldliness. Such an enclosure, cannot, this side of death (I am thinking again of Santi's "al di qua"), be escaped but only, rather, teased and transgressed, by an apophatic tongue recoiling backward every time it licks.[67]

In Geoffrey Galt Harpham's reading of Sassetta's fifteenth-century painting of the meeting of Saint Anthony and Saint Paul the Hermit, anality is the sign of ascesis. Harpham has shown how the arch created by the saints' backs as they embrace, with their upper bodies joined, lower bodies at a distance, and hands on each other's buttocks, reproduces the shape of the hermit's cave figured in the painting and inflects it anally. Indeed, it is worth pointing out that contiguity, specifically the saints' mutual touch, discloses the anal enclosure. Harpham draws two conclusions from Sassetta: first, if ascetic deprivation "entails a repudiation of nature," then "ascetic restraint falls into the category of an unnatural act"; second, this unnatural ascesis inflects aesthetics, as summoned by the arch of the saints' bent backs and the anal cave's dark opening, the latter of which shows "the essence not only of asceticism but. . .of the aesthetic itself, the formless origin of form."[68] Iacopone thus seems to participate in a tradition of articulating ascetic self-denial as equivalent, in its risk and constitutive absence, to the impossible community of overlapping absences that Damian describes, and Sassetta depicts, as homoerotic.

Yet Iacopone also articulates what we might call a kind of anal *thrownness*, not unlike Harpham's description of anal aesthetics, in which the ascetic response to the world can only ever be a repeated recognition and bodily remembrance of its own implication in what it resists: the ascetic body or apophatic page as at once tongue and hole, making and unmaking its world. This latter phrase, borrowed from Elaine Scarry's study of bodies in pain, is meant to indicate the extent to which a radically self-negating linguistic practice both withdraws from the body's sensory imperatives by making sense of them and, through the constitutive absence of this sense-making, its supplementary will to nonsense, withdraws *into* them. Pain is not, as in Scarry's reading, necessarily alleviated by this articulation; indeed, it is perhaps reinforced. In fact, it is a question less of pleasure against pain than of sensory intensity against sensory attenuation. The papal anus, thus configured as both the spatialized aesthetic frame for Iacopone's discursive dissidence and the abject around which this dissidence takes shape, comes to inscribe the extent to which each refusal seizes, intensely, the risk of reproducing what it refuses. More than this, the more convex and penetrative the poetics, the more it withdraws into the concavities it delineates. The pope's hole is both the "formless origin of [mystical] form" and the retreat of sameness, of homoness, around which Iacopone constructs his discursive difference.[69]

Abbreviated Allegory

Just as Iacopone's prison poem retraces the participative relationship between tongue and hole, materiality and its withdrawal, erotics and abjection, so do his engagements with the Song of Songs tradition inscribe negation and retreat at the heart of mystical union.[70] Such engagements, most prevalent in but not limited to laud 65, also serve to reinforce, in terms resonant with Iacopone's lingual jailbreak, the specifically spatial dynamics that inhere within the border crossings of erotic language. Denys Turner, in his lucid exposition of apophasis and cataphasis, is careful to note that

> there is a very great difference between the strategy of *negative propositions* and the strategy of *negating the propositional*; between that of the *negative image* and that of the *negation of imagery*. The first of each of these pairs belongs to the cataphatic in theology, and only the second is the strategy of the apophatic.[71]

Evelyn Underhill, one of the first and most prolific modern scholars of mysticism, undertakes the former sort of negation in her 1911 "spiritual biography" of Iacopone. She notes that "Omo chi vòl parlare," laud 65 in Mancini's edition, "can hardly be offered to the modern reader," inasmuch as it contains "a peculiarly daring and detailed description of the Spiritual Marriage."[72] Her move is not unlike that of many medieval exegetes of the Song of Songs: one must be careful that these precariously theological erotic texts don't fall into the wrong hands.[73] Underhill says to her readers: look at what I'm *not* showing you; hear the thud of bedroom noises behind my "daring and detailed description." If Iacopone withdraws his tongue as he extends it within and across the papal hole, Underhill very primly lets hers slip through the alliterative gap in her denial, the cataphatic presence at the heart of her negation.

Iacopone's poem begins by asserting its own status as discourse, and specifically "brief" discourse. Brevity has a range of meanings for Iacopone, only some of them stylistic: "abrivïare" indicates sensory mortification in laud 19, for example,[74] whereas it serves a mnemonic purpose in laud 40[75] and designates the humility of the Incarnation in laud 44.[76] Here, however, Iacopone admits that "abbreviating what is long, / generally gives men pleasure" (el longo abrivïare / sòle l'om delettare; 65.7–8). It is just such "delettare" that abbreviation is supposed to *remedy* in laud 19's account of the senses. Abbreviation thus becomes the stylistic sign of apophasis: it at once produces and denies delight, foregrounding the sensory component of poetry (the mnemonic value, but also the humility, of rhythm and rhyme) while inscribing a negation at the heart of the sensible. In this way, the dialectic of length and brevity, delight and mortification, which abbreviation makes sensible rewrites more erotically the structure of withdrawal and extension in Iacopone's prison poem. Abbreviation is thus a companion to irony, while more explicitly concerned than the latter with an aporetic *recuperation* of what it denies, delight and length and sense.

Having thus situated his poetic practice in an apophatic theology, Iacopone announces that he will give an account "of the ordered man, / that place where God rests / in the soul which is his bride" (De l'omo ch'è ordenato / La 've Deo se reposa, / Ell'alma ch'è sua sposa; 65.14–16). Keeping in mind that order and measure are intimately connected both for Bonaventure and for Iacopone, and that the place of the rapt soul is precisely associated in laud 92 with what is *beyond* order and measure, it is curious to see Iacopone's description of the *ordered* man as this amalgam of bride and bridal bed, place and spouse, wherein God rests. It is as though Iacopone were spelling out here, in abbreviated form, the way in which metonymy draws participation (of body in place, place in God) from contiguity.[77] But something more is at work here, even at the level of tropes. Iacopone proceeds to elaborate the characteristics of this body/bed as though it were a traditional schematic *allegory*, thus radicalizing the allegorical through the participative contamination established by the poem's initial metonymies. The ordered mind, according to this metonymic allegory, is a bed with four feet ("la mente sì è 'l letto" at 65.17). Its frame is bound with rope; a blanket lies on top of its mattress, which itself lies on top of a coarser mattress ("saccone") laid directly upon the rope supports. The lower parts of the bed correspond to parts of the soul: the feet, for example, are the four cardinal virtues (prudence, justice, temperance, fortitude). Yet, as the description ascends, the soul's place in the allegorical tenor gives way to Christ: the mattress is "Christ crazy for me" (Cristo pro me pazzo; 65.46) and the headboard "Christ ascending the cross" (Cristo ch'en croce sale; 65.50). The bedsheets, however, are "contemplation in flight" (lo contemplar che vola; 65.54), a surface enclosure that comprehends both Christ's humanity and the virtuous soul. The allegory of the bed thus depends upon the cohesion of its contiguous components: they touch, and thus merge, into the contemplative flight where distinguishing subject from object is no easy task.

But this segue from contiguity to participation does not merely occur as something *transferred* from the allegorical vehicle (the sheet-swathed bed) to its tenor (the contemplatively enclosed God-and-soul). The allegorical tenor, in fact, *touches* its vehicle; Iacopone thus fills in the gap that separates them, inscribing metonymy at the heart of allegory:

[The bed] is covered with Hope,
to give me a firm certainty
of becoming a citizen
of that divine lodging.
Charity reaches [joins] it,
and joins me with God;
it joins my lowliness
with God's goodness.
Behold, a love is born,
which has [for charity has] impregnated the heart,
full of desire,
of inflamed mystery.
Thus filled it liquefies,
languishing it gives birth;
it gives birth to rapture
and is drawn up into the third heaven.

[Coperto è de speranza
A ddarme ferma certanza
de farme cittadino
en quell'abbergo devino.
La caritate 'l iogne

> e con Deo me coniogne;
> iogne la vilitate
> cun la divina bontate.
> Ecco nasce un amore,
> c'à emprenato el core,
> pleno de disiderio,
> d'enfocato misterio.
> Preno enliquedisce,
> languenno parturesce;
> e parturesce un ratto,
> nel terzo cel è tratto.] 57–72

Iacopone effectively *inflates* the space of the allegorical vehicle, allowing Charity, ostensibly part of the tenor, to touch it, and thus to be comprehended within it. The bed thereby exceeds the sterile and vaguely two-dimensional world of correspondence, entering into an active relation with a term that it would ordinarily be expected to *represent*. To spell this out: Charity reaches the bed, slips under the covers, but also *joins* it (this is the double meaning of "iogne") as a kind of acting-out, in the literally virtuous terms of the earlier correspondence-allegory, of that joining which is then made explicit as that which happens between "God" and "me." To be more precise, it is only through Charity's humping the bed that God and I can come together. In fact, Charity and the bed are joined just as God and I are joined, but this "just as" indicates not the gap of a comparison but the common border whereby one term, or pair of terms, *participates* in the other. One could almost say that allegory passes, through metonymy, into something like a new literalism, a spaced-out (and thus no longer immanent) immediacy.[78]

Iacopone's poem thus offers, among other things, a critique of Paul de Man's reading of symbol and allegory. According to de Man, the symbol's structure, in Romantic poetics, "is that of the synecdoche, for the symbol is always a part of the totality that it represents." In allegory, as in irony, "the sign points to something that differs from its literal meaning and has for its function the thematization of this difference," a difference articulated *temporally*.[79] Inasmuch as, for de Man, parts that ostensibly represent wholes more often than not reduce to the very totalities they claim to represent, they cannot accomodate temporality as the mark of internal difference. Allegory, according to this reading, not only accommodates such difference but knows it does so. In response to de Man, I would argue that metonymy offers a relationship of contiguity (indeed, contiguity as enclosure), which does not swallow part into whole but, rather, preserves each of its terms in the *surface* upon which they touch. Metonymy is thus the trope of borders, tact, and the very *spaciousness* of these.

The Birth of the Bedroom

To be sure, there are precedents for the bed's pivotal role in binding discrete terms, rhetorical and otherwise, into a participative relation. Indeed, one wonders whether the medieval ear would have been able to hear the proximity of *legare* (to bind) to *leggere* (to read), and from *letto* (read) to *letto* (bed). Bernard of Clairvaux allows spatial contiguity, spatial enclosure, and differential sameness to overlap in his classic exposition of nuptial union with God: "They [Bride and Bridegroom] share the same inheritance, the same table, the same home, the same marriage-bed, they are flesh of each other's flesh."[80] It is crucial to recognize that "same" does not necessarily mean reducible or identical, although the threat of solipsism, nearly always present in mystical discourse, is not to be taken lightly. In fact, I would argue that "flesh of flesh" introduces a signal difference into these apparent affirmations of identity, specifically a sense of borrowedness, derivation: this flesh (and with it this bed, this home) comes from elsewhere. In terms to be spelled out later in this book, it is dragged.

With the turn to Christ's passion in thirteenth-century devotion, it is inevitable that the shared, borrowed bed should become conflated with the cross. Angela of Foligno, Iacopone's contemporary, uses precisely this conflation to inscribe the crucifixion, and its material exhaustion, at the heart of the soul's ineffable union with God. This latter "darkness" enables Angela to see neither more nor less than Christ's humanity: "In short, what proceeds from those eyes and that face [of Christ] is what I said that I saw in that previous darkness which comes from within, and which delights me so that I can say nothing about it."[81] Indeed, Angela's reiteration of the "joy of the humanity of Christ" causes her to break into song:

> At this moment, my desire is to sing and praise:
>
> I praise you God my beloved;
> I have made your cross my bed.
> For a pillow or cushion,
> I have found poverty,
> and for other parts of the bed,
> suffering and contempt to rest on.
>
> When I, brother scribe, asked her for a better explanation of what she had said, Christ's faithful one added: This bed is my bed to rest on because on it Christ was born, lived and died...On this bed I believe I die and through this bed I believe I am saved. I cannot describe the joy which I expect from those hands and feet and the marks from the nails which pierced them on that bed.[82]

This is, fascinatingly, the only poem—strictly speaking, a *lauda*—in the entire text of the *Memorial*. Its structural symmetry to Iacopone's poem is striking: the bed's "parts" correspond to the various components of abjection, just as Iacopone's bed begins by corresponding to the various virtues. Yet the bed remains a *surface* here, a plane on which Angela can identify with Christ, suffer with Him; Angela does not become the bed, and Christ does not join it as he joins her. In this way, it stops short (though just barely, and perhaps with a sense of the participative abbreviation we've seen in Iacopone) of Iacopone's impregnating junction of space and time, divine and mortal bodies, tenor and vehicle, allegory and metonymy.

For Iacopone's bed of contiguous union is also a childbearing bed. Though theologically similar to Meister Eckhart's "birth of God in the soul," it nonetheless suggests, where Eckhart describes the "detachment" of the soul from materiality, the metonymic participation of the material in the strictly spiritual.[83] In a construction sandwiched between giving birth to love and giving birth to rapture (and it's unclear, and for Iacopone beside the point, whether this is really one birth or two), the heart becomes pregnant and liquefies, swells up and dissolves. Birth precedes and follows a dissolute pregnancy. Iacopone's contemporary Margaret of Oingt describes how Jesus, about to deliver the world salvifically and maternally (i.e., deliver *from* and deliver *to*), was "placed on the hard bed of the cross," where all his nerves and veins were "broken."[84] This maternal extenuation builds upon a lexicon of "stretching," which Margaret develops throughout her *Page of Meditations*:[85] such an intensification of (and challenge to) spatial boundaries is further intensified, and quite literally *inflated*, in Iacopone's scene of full liquefaction, the exhaustion and transcendence of the joint surfaces of body and bed. Specifically, when rapture is born, it drags the heart, as though by its umbilical cord, into the third, seraphic, heaven. If this is so, Iacopone is suggesting that mystical ascent is not a matter of levitating gracefully upward, toes flexed toward the earth; rather, if rapture is the child pulling its mother to heaven, it is pulling her by the womb, and she's ascending upside-down, her legs in the air.[86]

This inverted ascent, with its echoes of metonymy's "dragging" ("trahit") in the *Ad Herennium*, thus appears to participate quite literally in what Sarah Beckwith has called the "violently inverting tactics" of Franciscanism. These "tactics," namely "replacing health with sickness, embracing the leprous and the maimed, the high with the low, its embrace of filth and flesh, its emphatic fetishizing of Christ's torn and bleeding body as the object, indeed subject, of compassion and passion," are, in Iacopone, also *tactile*.[87] There is no doubt that Iacopone is playing here with gender as a kind of *coincidentia oppositorum*. True, Evelyn Underhill once swooned at the thought of Iacopone's masculine prowess: in the course of her study, she speaks of his "rough male brutality" and his "virile spirituality."[88] And every account of Iacopone's life is careful to give him a wife, usually named Vanna, who dies tragically when the balcony she's dancing on collapses, thus securing our hero's heterosexuality and observance of gender oppositions just in time to abbreviate them. Yet if Iacopone's "omo" is a manly man, he is pregnant in the way that too much testosterone can cause a weightlifter's breasts to swell: masculinity spills over, swells out, into the feminine. This wouldn't necessarily be surprising, if we consider a Franciscan faithfulness to the letter of scripture in light of Stephen Moore's reading, in *God's Gym*, of the ways in which the masculine excesses of the Old Testament God have distinctly (or actually indistinctly) feminizing consequences.[89] This would give new, or perhaps merely radical, meaning to Francesco Santi's observation of the "hermaphroditism" that underlies Iacopone's poems.[90] It would also, and more importantly, confirm Jennifer Fisk Rondeau's observation that "a kind of spiritual cross-dressing becomes almost required by the texts of many laude," a gender transgression made possible "precisely because lauda singing marks itself off as ritualized, liminal space."[91]

So let's return to this ritualized space, the *khora* of the choral voice, which is, at the same time, Iacopone's birthing bed. To sum up: love is born of the bed, and all of a sudden we're bounced right up to the third heaven. But something has come out of us in the meantime, pulling us by the womb (but let's say also, against an abiding prudishness about saints' bodies not shared by saints themselves: by the twat, by the balls) into that realm of "esmesuranza" which Iacopone elsewhere describes, and undescribes, in great detail. In fact, inasmuch as these paradoxes draw upon sensory language, we might ask how we know what we're seeing in this scene of rapture, birth and generative dry humping. The only time Iacopone calls attention to visual mechanics in the poem is when he announces that the bed has four feet to rest on, "just as I saw it in a figure" (como en figura el vidi; 65.20). Sight—which was seen, in laud 43, to resist representing singular experience and thus offering it for appropriation—is here linked to representation. The bed is based on another bed. Plato, curiously, gives a reading of the bed as object of representation (or the bed of representation) in *Republic* 10, to emphasize the aporia between Ideas and material imitations.[92] I nonetheless prefer to see Iacopone's bed as *conforming* to its model, its "as" ("como") participating in God's "measureless as" or "measureless how" (como esmesurato; 82.3): *leaning* imitatively, reaching out to touch its "figura" just as charity reaches it, joins it, engenders with a touch. A metonymic connection is inscribed at the heart of representation: in Plato's terms, the bed binds Idea, painter, and carpenter together, and with them the bouncing, ecstatic soul.

Furthermore, in laud 92, "Sopr'onne lengua amore," Iacopone radically deconstructs the notion of the figural or the representative. He asks God, "Light beyond all figures, / who can figure you?" (Enfigurabel luce, / chi te pò figurare?; 17–18). At greater length, later on, he adds:

If you go figuring for yourself
an image to look at,
and strive to know by sensory knowledge
what the measureless is,
you believe that by seeking
infinite power
you can possess it,
and that seems to me very deceived.

[Se te vai figurando
imagen' de vedere
e per sapor sapere
que è lo esmesurato,
cridi poter, cercando,
enfinito potere,
sì com'è, possedere,
multo parm'engannato.] 137–44

The poem is saturated with this kind of disfigured figuration, and develops a notion of visuality to support it: taken up and "trasformato" in God, the soul "feels what it had not felt, and sees what it had not known or sensed" (sente que non sentio, / que non conubbe vede; 73–74). *It even sees its own rapture*: the poem speaks of "là", there, that place, "where he sees himself rapt" (v'el se vede ratto; 96). The mystical bedroom has mirrors on the ceiling, outdoing even the self-consciousness of de Man's allegory. And yet this vision is neither immanent nor exhaustible nor, in the strongest sense, comprehensible. As if he hasn't been clear enough about this, Iacopone suggests that "All faith ceases, for now he is given sight...And seeing what he had previously thought, it was all blindness" (Onne fede se cessa, / ché lli è dato vedere /...Vedere ciò che pensava, tutt'era cechetate; 281–82, 289–90). I'd like to suggest that Iacopone is not, perhaps even in spite of himself, denying sensation but rather opening up new sensory and, as it were, trans-sensory possibilities.[93] This surplus of sight, and of the figuration that sight perceives and transmits to the refiguring powers of "volere" and "parlare," creates space: the "there," "là", where the soul's rapture is visible to itself, as in the *Phaedrus*, through its beloved. When the soul, in "Omo chi vòl parlare," gives birth to a rapture that pulls it (by the surplus) into the seraphic heaven, it gives birth to the bedroom, to the erotic interstices between where it is and where it is going.

The Threshold of Enclosure

Thus the Song of Songs' entreaty, "come into my bedroom" (intra in cubiculum meum), is reworked in the following way: the heart's body, the "cor" that shapes the "corpo," gives birth to, expels, even as it is drawn inside, the place of its rapture. It is this heart-shaped bedroom, like some visual or perhaps trans-visual equivalent of Satine's room in *Moulin Rouge*, which Iacopone invites us to see with eyes that no longer constitute points from which a glance is thrown but which themselves dilate and contract, contain and, dissolving, give birth to what they see and where they see it. And yet they do this because they have been touched.[94] The "inside" into which Iacopone's bed draws us, its contiguously generated enclosure, resonates thus with a stunning passage on space in Jean-Luc Nancy's *The Sense of the World*:

> In order to be understood as a world of sense—of "absent sense" or exscribed sense—the world must also be understood in accordance with the *cosmic* opening of space that is coming towards us: this constellation of constellations, this mass or mosaic comprising myriads of celestial bodies, their galaxies, and whirling systems, and deflagrations and conflagrations that propagate themselves with the sluggishness of lightning, the almost immobile speed of movements *that do not so much traverse space as open it and space it out* with their motives and motions, a universe in expansion and/or implosion, a network of attractors and negative masses, a spatial texture of spaces that are fleeing, curved back, invaginated, or exogastrulated, fractal catastrophes, signals with neither message nor destination, a universe of which the unity is nothing but unicity open, distended, distanced, diffracted, slowed down, differed, and deferred within itself.

> [Pour être compris en tant que monde du sens—du "sens absent" ou du sens excrit—, le monde doit aussi être compris selon l'ouverture *cosmique* de l'espace qui nous arrive: cette constellation de constellations, amas ou mosaïque de myriades de corps célestes et de leurs galaxies, systèmes tourbillonnaires, déflagrations et conflagrations qui se propagent avec la lenteur foudroyante, la vitesse comme immobile de mouvements *qui traversent moins l'espace qu'ils ne l'ouvrent et l'espacent lui-même* de leurs mobiles et de leurs motions, univers en expansion et/ou en implosion, réseau d'attracteurs et de masses négatives, spatio-texture d'espaces fuyants, recourbés, invaginés ou exo-gastrulés, catastrophes fractales, signaux sans messages ni destinations, univers dont l'unité n'est que l'unicité en soi ouverte, distendue, distanciée, diffractée, démultipliée, différée.][95]

Traversal as inflation: what Nancy maps out cosmologically could be said to resemble Iacopone's heart-shaped bedroom, and Nancy's non-immanently unitive "unicité ouverte" likewise echoes the "unione" in "trasformazione" that the bed of the heart engenders. Moreover, the notion of "spaces that are fleeing, curved back, invaginated, or exogastrulated" not only resonates with Iacopone's upside-down ascent to God but also dovetails nicely with his elliptical way of locating God in space. But what Nancy drives home, vis-à-vis Iacopone, is the fact that this is also, and at every moment, as much a cosmological question as a psychological one: that is to say, there is a world, or worlds, at stake in all these diffracted births.

It is just such an open, still-arriving cosmology that should haunt us as we watch how the first quatrain of "Sopr'onne lengua amore" hurls its oblique prepositions like boomerangs at their elusive object:

> Love above every tongue,
> Goodness without representation,
> Light outside all measure,
> shines in my heart.
>
> [Sopr'onne lengua amore,
> Bontà senza figura,
> Lume for de mesura,
> Resplende en lo mio core.] 1–4

Iacopone shows us the way back to the heart, but the *itinerarium* is one of going too far and coming up short, *sopra* and *senza*, outside and inside, *for* and *en*. Just as the miracle pushes the *contra naturam* into the *supra naturam*, or causes at least their friction and enfolding, the impression here is of a heart convulsing: this is the pulse, the throb, the engendering spasm of a bed that beats. Not just *my* bed, but *ours*.

This bed thus acquires, through the rhythm of this oscillation of paradoxes, exactly the sort of *temporality* that rescues it from de Man's critique of the symbol. What is more, it conforms to a Franciscan poetics "whereby," according to Sarah Beckwith, "through the medium of Christ's body, identities are restored, transformed, revived, absorbed and submerged."[96] Iacopone's radicalization of Franciscan thought consists precisely in his *collocation* of crossing, all the transformations of "trans," at the heart of the heart, the body, and the bed. When the soul's desire is "placed / within the measureless / Giver of every good" (collocato / en quello esmesurato / d'onne ben Donatore; 92.194–96), its enclosure is transitive, dynamic.

Gender, as well, metonymically touches upon and participates in space: it is a masculine subject who sees himself rapt, just as it is a masculine subject who is urged, in the laud praising Saint Francis, to "let yourself die / of love in that fountain" (largatece morire / <'n> la font'ennamorato; 40.187–88). If this masculine look, as subject, is in danger of a solipsistic vision in which it sees only itself, it is nonetheless, as object, always already touched, given, situated, spaced out. Looking at itself through God's specular place, the soul undergoes what might be called an "excorporative identification," right at the site, the mirror, which Lacan calls the "threshold of the visible world."[97] The soul does not assimilate what it sees; it is acted upon, it touches the seen, and is thereby drawn out of itself, across itself, into the edge of something new. The threshold stretches.[98]

So too, in Kaja Silverman's reading of Cindy Sherman's photo stills, "the pose is so representationally resonant that it can impart photographic significance to its surroundings and everything with which it comes into contact."[99] Iacopone's soul-bed, placed *within* the God it touches, not only "imparts significance" but, before and beyond significance, engenders the space of abbreviated, but metonymically recuperable, speech. This is how to read the farewells—"Vale, vale vale!"—with which the poem closes (65.85). They ascend and stand still, torn (in the way that farewells always are) between here and there. God's "reposarse" is, similarly, not only a question of resting but, more importantly, a question of replacement, re-placement, and posing again. Rest is thus coextensive with repetition: difference is inscribed at the heart of spatial and temporal immanence, like a dream in a sleeping body, and this immanence is shown to be just a pose. God, the "Giver of every good," gives himself to be photographed, but in the process he gives, metonymically, everything that he touches upon, everything that he encloses, to be photographed—seen, touched, sensed, aesthetically reproduced—as well. And this is all done from within the limited space, the confinement, of Iacopone's poem, itself a kind of prison. Where, in laud 53, the prison cell is provoked and transgressed by written discourse, here the poem is provoked and transgressed by the space between desire, close by, and its ultimate collocation, where God is and repeats himself. Such space and such words make both poem and cell vibrate. This point of vibration is the mystical bed, the threshold where contiguity becomes enclosure, vehicle becomes tenor, allegory becomes metonymy, and God becomes the soul, shaking. Like the hole in Damian's wall, and like the smelly aperture of laud 53, Iacopone's bed at once exposes its edge and elicits entry, through its very status as sensible trope ("como en figura e'l vidi"), into the threshold of enclosure: the strange place of the holy and the strange time of repose.

Claustrophilia, in this way, does not finally fetishize space. Rather, it embraces, tongues, and flaunts spatial delimitation in order to make room, within these limits, for something like temporal difference, for something like repetition. Enclosed space is, in Iacopone, Damian, and the other authors and authorities cited above, always something to which one erotically relates, and which in turn (or simultaneously) permits an erotic relation to something other than enclosure, but something that can become perceptible only through enclosure, only between its bindings. This relation makes itself felt, in every case, temporally: as the double bind of the already penetrated, impenetrable church wall in Damian or, in Iacopone, as the "ecco nasce," the sudden, deictic birth that occurs at the touch of a bed. There is no love of enclosure without this temporal spacing, without this tremulous touch.

CHAPTER 4

LYRIC ENCLOSURES

Dragging the Song

I have attempted to show how claustrophilia suspends itself between touch and temporality, between tact and traction. In what follows I want merely to intensify the boundaries, formal and phenomenal, of this suspense, this stuttering syncopation. After all, when Iacopone's soul is dragged into the third heaven, it is not straightforwardly launched there; it does not propel itself onward. It is dragged there, kicking and gasping.[1] I have argued that metonymy has a similar logic of drag: for the author of the *Ad Herennium*, metonymic speech is dragged from nearby terms ("quae ab rebus propinquis et finitimis *trahit* orationem").[2] Consider, then, the final verses of one of the earliest criticisms of stilnovist poetry, Bonagiunta da Lucca's famous sonnet to Guido Guinizzelli, "Voi che avete mutata la mainera":

> And you surpass everyone in subtlety,
> and there's no one to be found who can explain you,
> so obscure is your speech.
>
> And it is held as a great unlikeness,
> even if the sense comes from Bologna,
> to drag a song by force out of learned writing.
>
> [E voi passat'ogn'om di sottigliansa,
> e non si trov'alcun che ben ispogna,
> tant'è iscura vostra parlatura.
>
> Ed è tenuta gran dissimigliansa,
> anchor che 'l senno vegna da Bologna,
> traier canson per forsa di scrittura.][3] 9–14

Bonagiunta's sibilant lines accuse Guinizzelli of having dragged his "canson" by force, "traier. . .per forsa," out of a preexisting "scrittura."

Bonagiunta's accusation takes for granted the fundamentally metonymic nature of song-production: the lyric does not pop, Minerva-like, out of the poet's head; rather, it is contiguous to other texts: altogether too close, here, for Bonagiunta's comfort. Indeed, inasmuch as Guinizzelli drags lyric *forcibly* from scholarly script, there is something decadent about this drag. The accusation is not unlike that of Peter Damian against his sodomites, hell-bent as they are on forcing their way into the church they are always already within.[4] For "sottigliansa," subtlety, rhymes with "dissimigliansa," unlikeness: Guinizzelli's error is not, ultimately, pedantry so much as passing. He has forced lyric into a metonymic relationship with scholarly prose, passing off the latter as the former, and all of this under cover of darkness ("tant'è iscura vostra parlatura").

What would it mean, then, to speak of lyric drag? Drag as metonymic motion, bound up with what it touches, in this way touches upon drag as transvestism: the *OED* places the latter sense of drag under the subheading of "something that drags, or hangs heavily, so as to impede motion." Drag is motion in spite of itself: irony at the heart of the linear production of lyric and gender identities, always stickily attaching these identities to the very things they seek to move beyond. If it is tempting to invoke the arguments developed in the early 1990s in praise of performativity, such an invocation cannot take place without a more thorough appreciation of what the performance never leaves behind, the resistance with which one identity is (barely) dragged from another. Drag, in the sense of Bonagiunta's "trarre" as well as the gender performances of the twentieth-century stage, always has what contemporary culture might call "a lot of baggage." It never leaves behind what it's dragging; or, better, its "behind"—the belatedness of the materiality that its performance, its "canson," is inscribed upon—is never easily distinguishable from the "before" of its surface. (It is, of course, a contestable concession that surface should precede depth.) Fred Schneider sings, in an old record of the B-52s: "I need to leave my past behind; I need to leave my behind in the past." Bonagiunta's "anchor che," his "even if" or (better) "still, though," stages the temporal afterlife of drag: its status as belatedness made present, like the light from a dead star.

Assertions such as these are made possible by two texts that, fifteen years ago, changed the way we talk about gender. Judith Butler argues, in *Gender Trouble*, "if the inner truth of gender is a fabrication and if a true gender is a fantasy instituted and inscribed on the surface of bodies, then it seems that genders can be neither true nor false, but are only produced as the truth effects of a discourse of primary and stable identity."[5] And yet, as Butler has insisted repeatedly in the wake of her argument's success, the superficial fantasy of gender that drag foregrounds is not, however, a mere signifier with no relation or accountability to the materiality upon which it is inscribed:

"the point of this text," she writes in the preface to the new edition of *Gender Trouble*, "is not to celebrate drag as the expression of a true and model gender...but to show that the naturalized knowledge of gender operates as a preemptive and violent circumscription of reality."[6] This "naturalized knowledge" of gender is what thinks it has drag figured out: that it can cleanly distinguish between real and fake, background and foreground. In *Vested Interests*, Marjorie Garber cannily *spatializes* what she calls the category crisis that drag inaugurates (or, keeping in mind the behind in the past, a crisis followed, brought along, dragged). "Transvestism," she argues, is "a space of possibility structuring and confounding culture: the disruptive element that intervenes, not just a category crisis of male and female, but the crisis of category itself."[7] In the 1990s, drag attained a kind of radical chic, but the implications of these theories remain strong for Guinizzelli's song. To say that Guinizzelli opens up, through Bonagiunta's accusations, a "space of possibility" between scholarship and poetry is not to empty Garber's statement of its specificity. In fact, I would argue that a return to drag in this literal sense—which is not merely the sense of linguistic "performativity" cited by so many in Butler's wake—*intensifies* the gender effects of transvestism. Guinizzelli's sin, in *Purgatory*, is after all "hermaphrodite" ("Nostro peccato fu ermafrodito"; 26.82). But to insist upon this is to get ahead of ourselves, when drag would demand we stay behind.[8]

To return, then, to the literal sense that drags gender along with it, as the behind it can't leave in the past, Bonagiunta introduces in his few, dense lines two tropes crucial to drag in whatever sense: by positing Guinizzelli's "traier canson," he inscribes metonymy at the heart of poetic production; by judging this process to be nonetheless a "gran dissimigliansa," he turns metonymy into irony. And not just any irony: what is at stake here is, more precisely, antiphrasis. As Simon Gaunt observes, summarizing Donatus and Isidore, "*Antiphrasis* occurs then when one word is intended to designate the opposite of its literal meaning. It differs from *ironia* only in that with *ironia* the whole statement is intended to mean the opposite of what it says, while the irony of *antiphrasis* depends upon the meaning of just one word."[9] Here that word is song. On the one hand, Guinizzelli's lyric posits, between song and scholarship, clothes and body, an adherence or, more precisely, a *traherence*: precisely not an identity but something more like a smear or a snag. Drag, in this metonymic "traier," names lyric's dependence, its contingency, the *propinquitas* through which it comes to be, out of other forms to which it remains tenuously but participatively connected.[10] In the place of the primordial singing savages of Enlightenment mythology—as in Rousseau's observation that "the first discourses were the first songs" and "poetry was devised before prose"—here we have a borrowed song, a song rubbed off of something else, glistening with its residue: dragged.[11]

And yet, on the other hand, in the antiphrastic "canson," radical difference and insurmountable aporia are introduced into this very participative relation. Does scripture stick to the song, or is the song not even a song at all? Antiphrasis, it should be emphasized, is a trope with a certain genealogical resonance. Curtius writes that "one of the masters of the new poetics, Matthew of Vendôme, referring to a hardhearted father who lets his son starve, says that he could be called a father only 'per antiphrasin.'"[12] And yet the antiphrastic father is confirmed as such only belatedly: his son's death proves that he had never been a father, inaugurating not just a category crisis but an unsettling of filial relations: here the unfather is born of the unson. Christine de Pizan, 300 years later, makes clear the gender ramifications of such genealogical aporia when Lady Reason, appearing to Christine, announces that the *City of Ladies* will be built upon an antiphrastic interpretation of misogynist treatises:

> As far as the poets of whom you speak are concerned, do you not know that they spoke on many subjects in a fictional way and that often they meant the contrary of what their words openly say? One can interpret them according to the grammatical figure of *antiphrasis*, which means, as you know, that if you call something bad, in fact, it is good, and also vice versa.[13]
>
> [Et des poetes dont tu parles, ne scez tu pas bien que ilz ont parlé en plusieurs choses en maniere de fable et se veulent aucunefois entendre au contraire de ce que leurs diz demonstrent? Et les peut on prendre par une figure de grammaire qui se nomme *antifrasis* qui s'entent, si comme tu scez, si comme on diroit tel est mauvais, c'est a dire que il est bon, aussi a l'opposite.][14]

Antiphrasis, in Christine's use, posits a symmetrical relationship between one term and another, and in this way appears to inscribe rhetorically all those bad (or good) dualisms to which Garber's notion of category crisis alludes. And yet Christine's insistence upon opposition prompts the reader to look to Matthew for a way out: indeed, what is the opposite of "father"? The filial relationship can be figured in many ways—as one of temporal sequence, or cause and effect, for example—but not as one of sheer inversion.[15] Thus Matthew's "father" embodies antiphrasis not as a referent diametrically opposed to its sign but as a sign *belatedly starved* of that upon which its first-order signification and second-order reference depend: a son. The son, starving, starves the father. A name antiphrastically embodies an event of the flesh: materiality thus ecstatically and belatedly comes to inhere within the name, even as this name fades, like the body that possesses it ("possesses" in both senses: as ownership, in the case of the father's body; as overtaking, in the case of the son's, spoken through the father's name).[16]

Scholarly "scrittura" is, likewise, an unfit mother from which to drag a song. And yet it is the song that is named *per antiphrasin*—or, rather, the process of traherence through which the song comes to be. Does Bonagiunta's lyric, then, inscribe an antiphrastic fading at the heart of the metonymic act of poetic production that Guinizzelli has abused? Is metonymy, finally, just irony?

It should be clear by now that what is at stake here is less a matter of Bonagiunta's antiobscurantism and more a statement about the relationship of lyric to other literary genres, on the one hand, and to the particular conditions of lyric enunciation, on the other. Lyric drag, Bonagiunta suggests, is at once hyperbolic and unexposed: Guinizzelli has "surpassed every man in subtlety" (passat'ogn'om di sottigliansa), and no one, consequently, can be found to explain—literally to "expose" (ispogna)—him. But how would such an exposure of excess take place? Bonagiunta hints at one possibility when he suggests that dragging the song is literally *held* as unlikeness, "tenuta": you have to hold it there, not let it escape, in order to understand the poet's sleight of hand. What this entails, of course, is a manual maneuver of one's own, a hermeneutic laying on of hands. Antiphrasis is in this way enclosed. To state this dialectic as succinctly as possible; indeed, to overstate it, with a necessary hyperbole: the irony inscribed at the heart of metonymy is here metonymically held. Irony may be contagious, tearing away at the conditions of lyric utterance even as it seeks to preserve those conditions in some fictitiously unadulterated state, but metonymy is also catching, in both senses: grasping even the most rigorously exposed unlikeness and making of it, of that momentary contact with it, a new creature: a monster or a miracle.[17]

Thus Bonagiunta's handiwork, despite its intention to correct the metonymic manipulations of Guinizzelli, only exposes itself—even as it grasps, and reveals, Guinizzelli's sophistry—to the metonymic contact that has dragged lyric from scripture. This is in part why it is so tough to talk about this poem without falling prey to the very problems it performs: Bonagiunta is holding Guinizzelli's "dissimigliansa" in his hands, and with it the whole (metonymically traherent) world. Lyric drag articulates—in the strongest sense, as "the inscription of a meaning whose transcendence or presence is indefinitely and constitutively deferred"—the unlikeness that is necessarily held each time a script is rewritten.[18]

Moreover, lyric drag literally, if precariously, embodies this unlikeness. It challenges, with its belated, compromised body, the all too neat account of embodiment and lyric production given by Giorgio Agamben in *The End of the Poem*. In the middle of an essay in which bodies conveniently appear and disappear in the service of an argument about the self-reference of poetry, Agamben writes, "Bonagiunta's reproach of Guinizzelli accusing him of 'drawing song by the force of writing' (where 'by the force of writing' must be read, as Guglielmo Gorno has suggested, as a syntagma), must then be placed in the context of this transition from a strongly oral compositional canon to one in which writing has become completely autonomous."[19] Lyric drag flouts, flamboyantly and metonymically, Agamben's logic of the imperative. It is impossible, in what I'm calling the traherence of songs and bodies, to say that one "must" read—much less "be placed"—in a single, unequivocal way. It is equally impossible to ignore or disavow the multiplicity of hands that intervene between my body and this poem's. These hands occasionally need to get a grip; and occasionally they need to let go. Agamben seems to require a kind of purity from Bonagiunta's line, but he does this at the expense of the line's "forsa," its literal force. Impurity, one might argue, is drag's only necessity.

Scholarship and song are, moreover, spatially situated. Bologna, Guinizzelli's hometown as well as the seat of medieval Italy's largest university, names the place of this drag. What is more, if one considers Dante's collocation of Guinizzelli among the lustful in purgatory, it is not impossible to say that Bologna, in this sense, is burning. More precisely, the *excessively held exposure* through which the "canson" can be ironically divorced from and metonymically restored to "scrittura" is the kind of vision that takes place only in the midst of flames.

Burning Belatedly

Dante finds Guinizzelli, in Purgatorio 26, as a shade amongst such flames:

> and I with my shadow made the flames appear
> a deeper red, and I saw it was something
> that many shades noticed as we were passing.
>
> [e io facea con l'ombra più rovente
> parer la fiamma; e pur a tanto indizio
> vidi molt'ombre, andando, poner mente.][20] 26.7–9

Dante's shadow, evidence of his embodiment, intensifies the flames that mediate his vision of the purged. Likewise yet inversely, in Matthew of Vendome's anecdote, the son's bodily fading diminishes the name of the father that is revealed, belatedly but not surprisingly, to be mediated by precisely this body. Guinizzelli's shade, among the lecherous, observes that Dante's body is, indeed, a wall: "Tell us how you make of yourself a wall / to the sun" (Dinne com'è che fai di te parete / al sol; 26.22–23). And yet the body's architectural opacity is precisely the sign of its living quest to obtain "[experience] of our region" (de le nostre marche. . .esperïenza; 26.73–75).

The body as building is no rigid monument, no tomb. It is, rather, the material *risk* that causes shades to come to view. And this material risk, this enabling of vision, thus resonates—as *experience*—with both Lacoue-Labarthe and Silverman, as discussed in chapter 1: it names lyric's embodied gift of visibility, indeed of sensibility, to the always-mediated, shadowy world; it also names lyric's traversal of dangerous "marche," going out on a limb to rub against that world. Unlike Lacoue-Labarthe's Celan, however, despair is not, for Dante, the result of this exposure and this traversal: Guinizzelli speaks of paradise as "the cloister / in which Christ is the abbot of the college" ([i]l chiostro / nel quale è Cristo abate del collegio; 128–29). Heaven is an enclosure where Dante's wall will find its reinforcement, its materiality not lessened but redoubled, transfigured. Whereas flames, and the dialectic of hide-and-seek they suggest, separate one poet from another in purgatory, this opposition is already being metonymically negotiated, most signally when Dante "move(s) forward a little" (Io mi fei al mostrato innanzi un poco; 26.136), toward a tact, a touch, which is still suspended but inevitably transforming.

There is a risk in speech, in nearness: the risk of confounding generic distinctions, getting too close to the flames. Guinizzelli responds, in "Omo ch'è saggio non corre leggero," that in the hierarchical scheme of the cosmos everything has its place, including abstruse poetry. But what is less obvious about his response becomes clearer if, metonymically, we allow Bonagiunta's diction to touch and transform Guinizzelli's:

A man who's wise does not rush in lightly
but goes step by step, as measure warrants;
when he's done thinking he holds it back
until the truth becomes certain to him.

[Omo ch'è saggio non corre leggero,
ma a passo grada sì com vol misura:
quand'ha pensato riten su' pensero
infino a tanto che 'l ver l'asigura.][21] 1–4

Once this wise man has thought, he holds his thought back, "riten su' pensero": instead of excess, Guinizzelli advocates restraint. In fact, he invokes, of all terms, "misura" to characterize this cautious hermeneutics. What is classically unclear in this poem, however, is whether Guinizzelli is describing the poet's restraint in not offering more accessible accounts of things, or whether he is admonishing Bonagiunta to keep his ignorance to himself. The final verse affirms, "therefore, man shouldn't say what he thinks" (perzò ciò ch'omo pensa non de' dire), but "omo"—like enclosure, in my earlier account—is fundamentally ambivalent, both morphologically (as palindrome) and hermeneutically (as the point of contact between reader and writer).²² Therefore—to echo the almost syllogistic structure of this concluding verse—just as Bonagiunta's accusation of unlikeness is overcome by his hermeneutics of holding, here too the restraint of Guinizzelli's "omo" is overcome by its status *qua* restraint: for Guinizzelli's "omo" repeats his thought, "*ri*-ten su' pensero," every time he holds it back. Like Iacopone's dynamic repose, this restraint, which enables "omo" to overcome his constitutive ambivalence and pass for "saggio," is itself far from restrained. The priority of thought to retention (indicated here in the sequence of tenses) doesn't hold. Or, rather, it is held back, held again, bringing "omo" belatedly to being.

Thus it is not a question of Guinizzelli's hybrid triumph over Bonagiunta's cult of purity. What these poets offer, in contrast to Iacopone's third heaven where the soul, dragged, both exhausts and overcomes dualism, is a poetics of withholding. In such a poetics, the communal dimension of what is held—the "with" in "withholding"—emerges, in spite of what the poem purports to say, as the truth (" 'l ver") whose certainty arrives only too late, if it arrives at all: for the moment of Guinizzelli's enunciation is the moment of the retained thought, of the "infino a tanto," the *until* whose temporal incompletion is that of "dire" as speech and song. Jean-Luc Nancy speaks, in his essay on "literary communism," of a "literature of truth" whose communication "incompletes it instead of completing it, and suspends the completion of the heroic-mythic figure it cannot fail to propose."²³ Through their rhetorics of drag and restraint, Guinizzelli and Bonagiunta are both, in their only apparently opposed ways, incompleting the myth of early Italian poetry, indeed, of the birth of vernacular lyric in general.²⁴

Guinizzelli in fact sings, elsewhere, "My lady, I take and hold my worth from you" (Madonna, da voi tegno ed ho 'l valore), and "My lady, the words I speak to you / Show there is in me the overflow / Of every true feeling" (Madonna, le parole ch'eo vo dico / mostrano che 'n me sïa dismisura / d'ogni forfalsitade).²⁵ Here what is held (" 'l valore") is also what is derived from elsewhere: the poem exists ecstatically, as a function of its addressee.²⁶ And this ecstatic poetics corresponds to an excess, a "dismisura," which is explicitly and textually spectacular: Guinizzelli's words *show* the excess within him, write into their surface his interior overflowing. In this way, Guinizzelli is not far from Iacopone's own dialectics of *for* (here audible in the "forfalsitade," literally beyond-falsehood) and *en*, the love-spasms that project an interior beyond as a surface effect.²⁷ It is precisely this sense of poetic ecstasy that comes forth to disturb the more measured concerns of the debate with Bonagiunta. The song is derived, derivative, belated. But even if it were retained, held back, its constitutive "dismisura" would appear in the very fact of its being held and withheld. Restraint is not originary; silence, too, comes from elsewhere. The withheld words that pass for silence thus metonymically *incomplete* irony, dragging the purity of ironic opposition (e.g., silence/speech) into the impure place of suspended truth.[28] This place is, indeed, that which Dante occupies in Purgatorio 26 as he finds himself literally "suspended" (sospeso; 26.30) as he watches the two groups of the lustful approach each other:

for in the middle of the burning path,
people were coming facing the other
way so that I stared at them in wonder.

Then I see each shade going one way hurry
to kiss each shade going the other way,
not stopping, content with the brief greeting.

[ché per lo mezzo del cammino acceso
venne gente col viso incontro a questa,
la qual mi fece a rimirar sospeso.

Lì veggio d'ogne parte farsi presta
ciascun' ombra e basciarsi una con una
sanza restar, contente a brieve festa.][29] 26.28–33

The suspense is grammatically held between past and present, "fece" and "veggio." It must therefore be acknowledged, if only as a theoretical premise, that Dante's own mythological status is also incompleted in the lyric time and space of Guinizzelli's suspended truth. The spectacle of the convergence of purged souls suspends the pilgrim's gaze just as the spectacle of inner "dismisura" suspends the lady's distance, writing her at the heart of Guinizzelli's poem. Dante is written into the space between homo- and hetero-, a space that grows smaller as the two ranks draw close, and that maps onto the time—of suspense or belated presence—in which Dante sees and sings. The outcome of this drawing close is not, however, an assimilation, not a unity. It is, rather, a touch: the sensible affirmation of proximity within distance. More specifically, it is a kiss. The restless movement of these souls ("sanza restar"), their fleeting touch that borders on speech, is the counterpart to the pilgrim's supense (and its consummation). Dante thus names the restlessness of suspense, the belatedness of vision, but no more or less than Guinizzelli or Bonagiunta, who touch him, here, across the flames.[30]

If these poets can touch, "sanza restar," regardless of their status as *maggiori* or *minori*, what could be said of a touch across time?[31] Carolyn Dinshaw has written of such a touch as the basis for a queer engagement with medieval literature. "I speak of the tactile, 'touch,'" she explains, "because I feel queerness work by contiguity and displacement; like metonymy as distinct from metaphor, queerness knocks signifiers loose, ungrounding bodies, making them strange. . . ."[32] Queer history is informed by a poetics of contiguity, of bodies and other *corpora* rubbing against each other without any necessary continuity or identity among them. And yet this touch (and with it metonymy more generally) risks falling into utter *detachment*, the indifference of what Agamben might call *whatever* touch,[33] inasmuch as it does not account for the temporal and spatial present in which such a touch must occur. Texts do not, after all, randomly bump up against each other. An agency is needed to facilitate their touch: an intervention must be made. Queer history requires a queer historian. This is not to argue for a return to a subjectivist historical poetics, nor to substitute for Dinshaw's randomly touching texts a scholarly narcissism, which would amount to largely the same thing. Rather, it may be the case that one can do better than the rather vague characterization of contiguous temporality given by Homi Bhabha in Dinshaw's citation: "the contingent. . .is contiguity, metonymy. . .and, at the same time, the contingent is the temporality of the indeterminate and the undecidable."[34] Somehow an utter spatial proximity requires, for Dinshaw and Bhabha, an utter temporal disjunction. Especially given the desire for absoluteness, for intensity, in this opposition—Dinshaw seems to want, like the voice of the Lorenz Hart lyric, a nearness that is "nearer than the wind is to the willow"—it is surprising that one is made to settle for the merely "indeterminate" and "undecidable." That is to say, if metonymy can be understood as entailing the non-immanent participation of one adjacent term in (and out of) the other, what is the temporal mode of this participation? If its spatial mode is aligned with the deictic "here," singular yet not selfsame, might its temporal mode be similarly a specific, determinate "now" that is also "not yet" and "then," *this particular moment* of historical traherence? Metonymic temporality would show—again, in that deictic moment of "hey, look at this"—how every "veggio," each present act of seeing, entails a past making, or "fece," which is lost to it, distinct from it in time, but not irrevocably so: in fact, this past making or past-making is only apprehensible in its revocation, where *re-* designates a nonidentical repetition in which one voice is added to another, inexhaustibly. More than indeterminate or undecidable, this is a *choral* temporality: internally different yet shared; *and resonant, spectacularly sensible.*

In a recent poem, "Messiah (Christmas Portions)," Mark Doty hints at such a temporality and its relation to what Nancy might call the "offering of a presence in its own disappearance"—a characterization given, or offered, in an essay on laughter, another vocal phenomenon.[35] Listening to a rendition of *Messiah* by a felicitously named Choral Society, the lyric voice asks,

> Aren't we enlarged
> by the scale of what we're able

to desire? Everything,
the choir insists,

might flame;
inside these wrappings
burns another, brighter life,
quickened, now,

by song: hear how
it cascades, in overlapping
lapidary waves of praise? Still time.
Still time to change.[36]

Time's stillness here is also its flowing: lapidary cascades embodied in a voice that is not one but many. Still, in Doty's poem, is what endures and what suspends and what can become. Just as desire has spatial consequences—it "enlarges" us here—so too does its temporal "now" coincide with a "quickening": the deictic moment, what one might call presence, is a moment of intensification. In this moment, alterity is not subsumed into identity but allowed to flare up *within* the same: "another, brighter life" *burns* inside the "wrappings" that, enclosing it, catch on fire. Metonymic time, choral time, is not just queer but flaming; not undecidable but decided in countless and contaminating ways. It is "still time": not something atemporal or indeterminately temporal, but temporality's fixed flow, the lapidary overlappings out of which something else might come to be, all the while enduring.

"Still time" trumps the disembodied, indeterminate touch of Dinshaw's queer historiography by offering, in suspense, *these bodies, these voices*, in their never-self-identical moment of coming to the senses. Doty's speaker enjoins, "hear how / it cascades," and this sensed "how" echoes the "now" of the sensing: metonymic time is thus not discrete from the senses through which it is received; it is the mutual and irreducible imbrication of song and ear, through which desire—for Nancy, the nothing around which the flower blooms—enlarges the world, intensifies the finite precisely by exceeding it. "Still time to change": the closing infinitive here hints syntactically at the infinite, the eternal, as time's other, opening up in stillness, *to inform* and metonymically *to sustain* time's enduring and cascading.

Suspension and belatedness thus appear to be the modes according to which time stretches itself toward the eternal, which is to say toward its most extreme and finite temporality. Augustine is far more radical than queer theory in this respect. In "the vast cloisters of my memory" (in aula ingenti memoriae meae), Augustine posits a temporal enclosure in which are contained "the sky, the earth, and the sea" (caelum et terra et mare); "in it

I meet myself as well" (ibi mihi et ipse occurro).³⁷ And yet "the mind is too narrow to contain itself entirely" (ergo animus ad habendum se ipsum angustus est). ³⁸ The mind is more than it is, constitutively excessive inasmuch as it contains God, who (in a way that would not be lost on Augustine the rhetorician) metonymically contaminates and charges the narrow confines within which He is held. And yet the mind comes to an awareness of its excess only belatedly, if at all. In one of the most famous passages of *Confessions* X, Augustine elaborates this belatedness as the temporality of desire and sensation:

> I have learnt to love you late, Beauty at once so ancient and so new! I have learnt to love you late! You were within me, and I was in the world outside myself. . . . You called me; you cried aloud to me; you broke my barrier of defenses. You shone upon me; your radiance enveloped me; you put my blindness to flight. You shed your fragrance about me; I drew breath and now I gasp for your sweet odour. I tasted you, and now I hunger and thirst for you. You touched me, and I am inflamed with love of your peace.³⁹

> [Sero te amavi, pulchritudo tam antiqua et tam nova, sero te amavi! et ecce intus eras et ego foris, et ibi te quaerebam, et in ista formosa quae fecisti deformis inruebam. Mecum eras, et tecum non eram. Ea me tenebant longe a te, quae si in te non essent, non essent. Vocasti et clamasti et rupisti surditatem meam; coruscasti, splenduisti et fugasti caecitatem meam; fragrasti, et duxi spiritum et anhelo tibi; gustavi et esurio et sitio; tetigisti me, et exarsi in pacem tuam.]⁴⁰

Belatedness is at once the soul's shortcoming—its negligence of radical interiority for the false ecstasy of external quest—and, in characteristically Augustinian fashion, its means of redemption. "I have learnt to love you late" says, as well, that I have learnt to love you in lateness, in my own inevitable posteriority, my aftermath to you. Memory cannot contain itself; God's before exceeds and structures the soul's after. The senses can only receive God belatedly: their gasping preceded by his fragrance, their hunger by his taste. In this way, <u>the sensible is always prior to sensation</u>, a priority that inheres paradoxically within and excessively inflects the sensory "now." <u>Metonymic time, Augustine suggests, is that belated temporality in which "You touched me, and I am inflamed": a touch perceptible only through the present belatedness of my burning.</u> Belatedness thus names, beyond all nostalgia or decadence, the traherence of the eternal within time: the infinite in finitude's drag.

There is another blaze of belatedness in Mark Doty, one that brings out the extent to which the Augustinian soul might touch upon the Choral

Society and the converging kissers of Purgatorio 26. In his essay *Still Life with Oysters and Lemon*, Doty finds within seventeenth-century Dutch still lifes a temporality not unlike the still time of "Messiah":

> At first still life seems so entirely of this world—a clarification and celebration of what is—that it can have little to do with mortality. But in truth, the secret subject of these paintings is what they resist. What they deny is also the underlying force, more potent than lead or tin or orpiment, that makes these lemons glow with life.
> Everything in our field of vision is passing. And some of these things will be here just the briefest while; these opened oysters, this already-spotted quince are right at the edge of corruption even as we catch sight of them.
> And yet, in the suspension of these paintings, they will fade no more slowly than the hobnailed glass *roemer*, or this heap of rifled books; everything floats on this brink, suspended above the long tunnel of disappearance. Here intimacy seems to confront its opposite, which is the immensity of time. Everything—even a painting itself—is evanescent, but here, for now, these citizens of the great community of the disappearing hang, for a term, suspended.[41]

The temporality of these Dutch lemons is a suspended one, but the suspension is not absolute: rather, the fading to which materiality is inevitably subject slows down here. Indeed, the "here" and "now" of aesthetic reception name the space and time in which the "great community of the disappearing" is sensed as such. It can only be sensed in suspension, in that still time of which Doty speaks in "Messiah." Doty goes on to describe this community as "autumnal."[42] Autumnal community has particular resonance for the medievalist: it sums up Huizinga's impression that, in fifteenth-century northern Europe, "a high and strong culture is declining."[43] Yet Doty's ability to detect this decline in seventeenth-century Dutch painting, ostensibly the product of a renaissance, suggests *either* that decadence is a constitutive part of certain modes of aesthetic production and certain relationships to the sensible world, across historical periods; *or* that what autumn names is no decadence at all. Instead of spontaneity and passion—key elements of the "violent tenor of life" Huizinga describes— perhaps autumn marks the convergence of belatedness and suspension.[44] Autumnal community in this sense, as the suspension of a disappearance, would indicate that what is at stake is more than a great flourish before the curtain falls. It is also a question of a material belatedness, of a *sensory* sense of community that perforce (to echo Bonagiunta's "per forsa") arrives always too late.[45]

In an earlier poem, from *Atlantis*, Doty writes that "Autumn's a grand old drag / in torched and tumbled chiffon / striking her weary pose."[46] To strike a pose is to submit oneself to a certain temporal suspension. Autumn here, in her voluminous, voluptuous gown, interrupts and immortalizes the temporal process that has produced her weariness. And the mode of this interruption, this reprieve from linear temporality, is specifically *spectacular,* just as the lapidary overlappings of the voices in "Messiah" only come to the senses as a specifically choral *show.* One is late, but never too late, to receive, sensibly, what this painting and this choir offer: late, inasmuch as the quince is "already spotted"; but not too late, inasmuch as the community of the disappearing continues to hang, or hangs anew, "for a term," and we with it.

Moreover, Doty is radicalizing Bachelard's argument that "often it is from the very fact of concentration in the most restricted intimate space that the dialectics of inside and outside draws its strength."[47] That is to say, what is for Bachelard an argument about space becomes in Doty an argument about space *and* time. "Here intimacy seems to confront its opposite, which is the immensity of time": spatial "intimacy," the intimacy of small everyday objects, condenses and restricts temporal "immensity," which here seems to name precisely the suspended disappearance given, as belated appearance, to sight. Space thus metonymically encloses, suspends, and intensifies time, much as the "cloisters of memory" in Augustine prove through their very narrowness the infinite excess of what they hold. It is thus not primarily a question of space in relation to time, for or against time, but of space as metonymically bound up with time and time's other, eternity: of the participation of the "here" in the "now." And this participation is communal: it is the being-in-common of singular appearances as their disappearance, and the being-in-common of time and space as that which, apprehended and desired only belatedly, transcends and structures them. "The secret subject of these paintings" is the transcendence that burns in the "torched and tumbled chiffon" of autumnal community, of art as aftermath, held—and loved—singularly in common. Lest this last assertion appear unduly paradoxical, it is worth noting how Doty describes the birthday on which, among other things, he gorges himself on still lifes in Amsterdam: "I feel singled out, somehow, plucked out, lifted into a community of delight."[48] Singularity is not sublated or absorbed without remainder into this community; rather, singularity marks the difference that delight introduces into community: the ecstasy of the common.

Entering Community

Gillian Rose has observed that "we have given up communism—only to fall more deeply in love with the idea of community."[49] In the idea of community, she argues, "we hope for a collective life without inner or outer boundaries, without obstacles or occlusions, within and between

LYRIC ENCLOSURES 117

souls and within and between cities, without the perennial work which constantly legitimates and delegitimates the transformation of power into authority of different kinds."⁵⁰ This argument has something in common with Jean-Luc Nancy's critique of "the nostalgia for a more archaic community" in *The Inoperative Community*,⁵¹ and yet Nancy is also implicitly its target. For Nancy's literary community can, at most, interrupt:

> It is here, in this suspension, that the communionless communism of singular beings takes place. Here takes place the *taking place* (which is itself without a place, without a space reserved for or devoted to its presence) of community: not in a work that would bring it to completion, even less in itself as work (family, people, church, nation, party, literature, philosophy), but in the working and as the unworking of all works.⁵²
>
> [Ici, en ce suspense, a lieu le communisme sans communion des êtres singuliers. Ici a lieu l'*avoir-lieu*, lui-même sans lieu, sans espace réservé ni consacré pour sa présence, de la communauté: non dans une oeuvre qui l'accomplirait, et encore moins dans elle-même en tant qu'oeuvre (Famille, Peuple, Eglise, Nation, Parti, Littérature, Philosophie), mais dans le désoeuvrement de toutes ses oeuvres.]⁵³

Nancy's concern is, of course, to defuse the potentially totalitarian implications of a community reducible to a single work or a single essence. (That a totalitarian hermeneutics, a tyranny of transparent meaning, might go hand in hand with a totalitarian politics is one of the greatest insights of Nancy's essay.) And yet, Rose argues, to insist upon this kind of resistance to work—in Nancy's terms, to "retreat the political," deferring while constantly returning to it—is to capitulate to exactly the kind of totalitarianism one wishes to avoid. Writing of Poussin's painting in which Phocion's ashes, left outside the city walls by a tyrannical government, are gathered by his wife and her servant, Rose insists that what is at stake is not an opposition of "pure, individual love to the impure injustice of the world."⁵⁴ Instead, "the gathering of ashes is a protest against arbitrary power, it is not a protest against power and law as such."⁵⁵ Where Nancy would see an interruption of the myth of the city, Rose sees a "transcendent but mournable justice," framed—indeed, enclosed—by Athens.⁵⁶

This political argument is therefore also a spatial one. Nancy speaks, in a subsequent essay on community written after Rose's death, of the "with" that characterizes his sense of the "common": "The 'with' is dry, neutral: neither communion nor atomization, only the sharing of a place, at most a contact: a being-together without assembly" (L' "avec" est sec et neutre: ni communion ni atomisation, seulement le partage d'un lieu, tout au plus un contact: un être-ensemble sans assemblage).⁵⁷ Nancy's place-sharing, with its correlative ephemeral touch, inevitably seems tentative, if not washed out, next to the "magnificent, gleaming classical buildings" against whose background, for Rose, the bodies of Phocion's wife and her servant perform determinate political acts. Yet perhaps these thinkers are closer than they seem. For what if Nancy is elaborating a surface to complement Rose's depth? That is to say, what if a ritual act such as the gathering of ashes, and the classical background against which it takes place, were contaminated by that maximally evanescent contact of which Nancy speaks? Is there a contingency—that is to say, a singular and only differently repeatable contact—within even the most liturgically coded and politically framed of gestures?

There must be, I aver, if one is to escape the immanentist cult of family, state, and gleaming classicism. In this way, a politics of metonymy (which would be a politics not indifferent to the "architectural orders" that frame even the most fleeting touch) would not abandon work, as *opus* or *corpus*, but instead would expose the traherence of the unworked and unworkable within the work: as "scrittura" abides within "song," so too do a particular city, a particular architecture, and particular bodies abide within Nancy's shared space. Moreover, if time and space are not only themselves metonymic but metonymically related to one another (and, with one another, to the deictic here and now), there is no purity in the polis. It is as much a matter of a bent body (Phocion's wife huddled toward the ashes) as a matter of justice. The difficult work that Rose demands is thus precisely, in part, the fruitless thought of how a body's curve might be just: no facile politicization of aesthetics, this, but a coming to terms with metonymy's resistance to hypostasis. In the face of the "monstrosities" (monstruosités) of thought, politics, and profit, Nancy argues that "there is one task, which is to dare to think the unthinkable, the unassignable, the untreatable [aspects of] being-with without submitting it to any hypostasis" (il y a une tâche, qui est d'oser penser l'impensable, l'inassignable, l'intraitable de l'être-avec sans le soumettre à aucune hypostase).[58] Is that Athens in the distance—these thinkers prompt us to ask—or an already-spotted quince, a slice of lemon? Metonymy's muddle is in fact its exposure of the impossible traherence of bodies and things, not an indeterminacy but a confluence of determinacies: *this* body, *here*, *now*, gathering *these ashes*—and doing something with them that is beyond its grasp. How a touch is always more than it is (not more than it seems: this "more" inheres within the appearance): this is metonymy's ontological contribution, dragged (kicking and screaming: i.e., not without resistance) into politics as well as aesthetics.[59]

Why insist upon the political here, when time and space would suffice? Time and space, of course, are never self-sufficient, especially when what is at stake is a metonymic ontology of traherence. William Haver comes closest to expounding the political stakes of metonymy in *The Body of This*

Death, his engagement with theories of community vis-à-vis disaster. Reading Sue Golding, he observes that "the political is therefore not a public space into which pre- or reconstituted private beings enter, but that from which, and as which, every articulation emerges."[60] The political names, for Haver, an originary heterogeneity, only belatedly graspable. Is metonymic traherence, then, merely another inscription of the utterly heterogeneous? I find it necessary to think both with and against Haver here. For the emergence *from* the political has, in fact, much in common structurally with the logic of excorporation and immersion *out of* which, in the first chapter of this book, came to characterize a radically erotic ontology. Moreover, Haver is offering a critique of unproblematic disclosure: in his account, via Golding, being is not a private enclosure disclosed simply in "a public space"; rather, emergence entails deferral and resistance, indeed, takes place as an emergence *into* enclosure, an ontological spacing-out.

But this is also where it is necessary to think against Haver. For, just as Nancy can speak of "the intimate silence" (le silence intime) of the unavowable but not unspeakable community,[61] and just as Agamben argues that "truth manifests itself only. . .as the exposition of its own intimate impropriety" (la verità si manifesta solo. . .come esposizione della propria intima improprietà),[62] Haver similarly characterizes the erotic as "the passage from a monadic interiority to the radical nonintegration of alterity."[63] There is, in all three writers, something like an estranged solipsism. Intimacy and interiority are aligned with an articulate silence (the necessary "*askesis* of an unbearable silence," for Haver)[64] and an exposition of constitutive impropriety—and yet, self-emptying as these concepts are, they nonetheless offer no real outside to their inside, no adjacent zone between silence and speech, disclosure and enclosure, truth and falsehood: no threshold for metonymy to touch. No third heaven. If "the radical nonintegration of alterity" is the only alternative to "monadic interiority," then the erotic would seem to be relegated to a kind of frottage through cellophane: no trace, no drag, no imbrication of one term in the other. Haver's sensitive reading threatens here to become hyperbolically hygienic. In this way, aboriginal interiority, however opaque or diffracted, absorbs everything and becomes *immense intimacy*, an ironic inversion of *intimate immensity*, which, in Doty and Bachelard, is above all a sense of the ecstasy, literally the "delight," of boundedness. Such immense intimacy would also constitute, as inescapable origin and in its insistence upon radical exteriority as its only partner in (non)relation, a direct parody of the narrow mind that, in Augustine, only by virtue of belatedness could touch the transcendence within its limit.[65] Immense intimacy is thus the anti-enclosure.

And yet the logic of opposition itself is what enclosure and metonymy resist. Therefore, it will not do to speak of anti-enclosures. To put this otherwise: metonymy stages neither the emergence of an originary heterogeneity nor the extension of an ironic yet originary interiority. In fact, it resists the very opposition of interior to exterior, hetero- to homo-, before to after. And yet metonymy arrives at, or comes as, something other than indeterminacy. In its very structure as traherence, metonymy always drags a little: it is always too late to denote an origin, and just late enough to love. Its belatedness takes place, then, not in opposition to an origin, but as this origin's suspense. This is why it does not make sense to speak of an originary metonymy: like Augustine's late lover, metonymy discovers itself as the aftermath of something that pulses within it but is neither inside nor outside, strictly speaking, but impinging on all sides: in a word, close. A metonymic ontology is one of being surrounded.

These surroundings are, furthermore, erotically political. For just as Phocion's wife bends over her dead husband's ashes in an act both of love and of justice, and just as Dante suspends and confirms his *auctoritas* in the kiss of poets, and just as Mark Doty's Autumn slows down the disappearance of others in her pose, so too does metonymy *intervene*, across space and time, to show the excess of each appearance, the desire that pulls each determinate thing, not out of but within itself, toward another that is not utterly exterior but proximate and (how to say this otherwise?) *touchable*. I am aware that the particular crises to which Nancy, Agamben, and Haver address themselves—AIDS and fascism among them—do not compel a jubilant response. I do not wish to underestimate the work of mourning that inheres within the unworkings of their texts. And yet, as Gillian Rose would insist, mourning need not be interminable.[66] Metonymy alone awakens the mournful touch to the sensuousness with which it grasps, to the texture and warmth against which it brushes and out of which, to echo Bachelard again, it draws its strength. There is nothing facile about bumping up, in mourning, against joy, but there is a great deal about it that might give scandal. Kissable, touchable, fuckable: these adjectives name the gift metonymy bestows upon everything in its reach—which is to say, everything.

By rubbing up against another term, thing, or person, one does not just discover the desirability of this other but discovers it as semantically and sensibly overlapping, in its very discreteness, with oneself. This is, in other words, not too far from the truth. Keeping in mind that truth is precisely what is suspended and metonymically dragged in Guinizzelli, it may be possible to say that metonymy adheres to the not too far, the not too late. certainly far (otherwise it would collapse into monism); late, as well (otherwise it would collapse into myth); but just far enough, just late enough.[67]

This is not to say, however, that one doesn't sometimes feel the limits of metonymy. As I was beginning this project, I discovered the beautiful short novels and novellas of San Francisco–based writer Bo Huston, only to find out—too late—that he had been dead almost since their publication in the early 1990s. In a short story posthumously published in an anthology of writing about AIDS, Huston describes a trip to Zurich for an experimental therapy:

> The toilet is in its own closet, barely big enough for a person to fit inside. Indeed, when I sit on the john, the door won't close. That is disconcerting; I seem to desire privacy even in private.[68]

Enclosure is both a precondition and a desire: something one is ontologically stuck with (or thrown into) and something to which one is erotically inclined. It goes without saying that I arrived too late for Bo Huston, but thankfully just late enough for the books that bear his touch, which carry him metonymically beyond and into himself. I remember thinking what a shame it was that I had arrived in San Francisco in 1997, merely four years after his passing. But his enclosures persist, and metonymically inflame: I am thinking in particular, beyond the Zurich bathroom, of the reclusive burn victim with whom his HIV-positive protagonist shares a small provincial house in the 1991 novel *Remember Me*. Charlotte, covered in scars, "has arranged her life so as to have no choices": this is the root of her reclusiveness.[69] It is my wishful thinking, my metonymically inclined desire, to see in Charlotte's scars the traces of enclosure's flames: how material surroundings will alter a body, will not let what is close to them alone; in spite of this body's reluctance to decide, to choose, an intervention is made, and the body emerges, not unscathed, but more singular than before. The body can only emerge in this way, burned, just as the saint's body, as we have seen, can only emerge as determinately ambivalent, compromised, excessive. Metonymy materially and transformatively reinforces singularity in just this way. When the author is dead, this is a small consolation, but it is all we have: a trace neither utterly removed from its putative source nor synecdochically making this source wholly present (as in the medieval cult of relics), but metonymically dragging someone, something, momentarily close.

Mark Doty writes of such a contact in "Lilacs in NYC":

> You enter me and we are strangers
>   to ourselves but not
> to each other, I enter you
>
> (strange verb but what else
>   to call it—to penetrate
> to fuck to be inside of
>
> none of the accounts of the body
>   were ever really useful were they
> tell the truth none of them),

I enter you (strange verb,
    as if we were each an enclosure
a shelter, imagine actually

considering yourself a *temple*)[70]

    The enclosed community abides within Doty's "strange verb," inseparable from its syntactic elaboration: you enter me, I enter you. It is the community of entrance, of the metonymic threshold across which "you" and "I" participate, differently and deictically, in each other. Such a community is patently irreducible to a monism. Carol Muske-Dukes writes, in a voice directed toward fragments of written dialogue composed by a dead lover, "I want to enter every semblance of you—/ profile, ideogram, rainlight, zigzag kite, / shifting plinth."[71] Death relegates entry, here, to the realm of semblance, likeness, and symbol. Nonetheless, even in Doty's less somber verse, there is something similarly shifting or shifty about every amorous entry, every rippling reinflection of the boundary between your body and mine. Entering community is as much a work of language (of symbol) as a work of flesh.

    "Imagine actually / considering yourself a *temple*": the temple, Heidegger informs us, holds in protective heed even as it discloses. The materiality into which the temple retreats is marked here by the persistence of this strange verb: subject and object are reversed, but the entrance remains, newly determined each time. In the wake of all the failed "accounts of the body," accounts whose syntax would presumably be even more elaborate, even more prey to opposition and reversal, this entrance takes place—not undecidable but decided ever anew, nonidentically repeated. And it cannot be forgotten that the "accounts of the body," in such a lyric of corporeal entrance, have not been entirely left behind. Dragged into poetry, these discursive "accounts" function much like "scrittura" for Bonagiunta's critique of Guinizzelli—with one important exception: the "great unlikeness" of drag in Bonagiunta is replaced, here, by the strangeness of entrance, a strangeness that touches upon equally strange bodies. Metonymy thus binds lyric and lover together in a shared strangeness, and enclosure names the place of this binding: Bologna, New York, hermitage, bedroom, song.

CHAPTER 5

NOTHING BETWEEN

Enclosure and Immediacy

It is difficult to begin to gesture toward some kind of closure, especially when closure has been, in another sense, this book's gesture from its beginning. So let me say again what I have already said in other places and otherwise: to intensify a boundary in space can also be to stretch it out, to make room for other bodies and other desires. Closure becomes, in this way, a movement *within* enclosure, and not its terminus. The kind of enclosure I am describing is one in which it is impossible to be entirely alone. But if I am enclosed with you, enclosed by and as our touch, then what is there between us?

The twelfth-century poet Marie de France and the fourteenth-century English recluse Julian of Norwich are fascinated by this question. For both women, it is also a question of the relationship between this world and another, between the world of my body, which I seem to know and own, and the bodies, unknowable and beyond my grasp, that show just how far this semblance is from the truth, and just how close. Before turning to Julian's insistent, anaphoric construal of the reciprocal implication of God in man and man in God, I want first to turn to *Yonec*, one of Marie's most celebrated short narrative poems, or *lais*, where a jealously guarded enclosure becomes the site of a touch that at once marks the difference between two beloved bodies and breaks this difference down.

The story is, as these things go, relatively simple. A beautiful woman, locked up in a tower by her jealous old husband, asks God to send her a knight; God complies. A bird flies into her room, turns into a knight, and the affair begins. It will, of course, end badly: the jealous husband discovers the secret, sets a trap for the bird, and mortally wounds him. The bird, however, escapes, leaving a bloody trail for his lover to follow into a strange, silver city. Transformed back into a knight, he dies there, but not before telling his lady both that she is pregnant and that he will be avenged by Yonec, her unborn son. In the final lines of the lai, the son, upon hearing this story from his mother, kills his stepfather and assumes his father's vacant throne.

It is no secret that Marie is fond of enclosures. In *Guigemar*, another enclosed lady laments her state to the knight who, thanks to an enchanted boat, happens to have washed up on her shore:

"He [her lord] is painfully jealous,
by the faith I owe you.
He's locked me up inside this enclosure,
where there's only one entrance;
an old priest guards the door:
may God grant that an evil fire burn him!
Here I'm enclosed, night and day."

["Anguissusement est gelus,
par cele fei que jeo dei vus.
Dedenz cest clos m'a enserree.
N'i a fors une sule entree;
uns vielz prestre la porte guarde:
ceo doinse Deus que mals feus l'arde!
Ici sui nuit e jur enclose."][1] 343–39

Unlike Jehan Bouche d'Or's hermitage, with its "entree" redoubled and porously opened up as a "porte," here this redoubling emphasizes the extent to which the enclosure is, or wants to be, closed: its entrance is the exception that proves the rule. Marie's lexicon is telling: there is literally "nothing outside of one sole entrance" (n'i a fors une sule entree). The jealous husband's fantasy is one in which there is no outside, no possibility of communication with a world reduced to nothing. Of course, what this means, conversely, is that the entrance, or entrance *tout court*, is all there is. Entrance is inevitable, totalizing, irresistible. The husband's fantasy of absolute enclosure is, however, undermined not just by the grammar of exclusivity but also by the very circumstances of the lady's speech. She is, after all, describing her situation to a knight, Guigemar, who has somehow done the impossible: namely, to have gotten inside the room where she is, night and day, absolutely enclosed. Guigemar's body has been similarly and just as strangely troubled, his still-bleeding thigh pierced by a deflected arrow he had shot, earlier, at a hermaphrodite deer. Guigemar, in other words, can enter this enclosure only to the extent that he has been entered; in fact, to the extent that, bleeding and asleep on an enchanted ship that has brought him to the lady's entrance, he has been (to insist upon the felicitous ambiguity of this adjective) entranced.[2]

And yet, if Guigemar's own penetrability is the necessary precondition for his penetration of the impenetrable marital fortress, his body remains distinctly separate from that of his beloved. This is not the case in *Yonec*, where we discover that the wished-for knight's repertoire of metamorphosis is not limited to birds. To convince his locked-up lady that he is, after all, a good Christian boy, the knight offers to take communion:

> "Tell [the old crone who guards you] that you're overcome by illness
> and wish, accordingly, to receive the service
> that God established in the world
> on account of which sinners are healed.
> I'll take on your semblance:
> I'll receive the body of Our Lord
> and avow for you the entirety of my belief
> [or: say on your behalf the entirety of the creed].
> You will have no doubts about it."
> She responds that he has spoken well.
> Alongside her he lay down in the bed
> but he doesn't want to touch
> or embrace or kiss her.
>
> ["Dites que mals vus a suzprise,
> si volez aveir le servise
> que Deus a el mund establi,
> dunt li pecheür sunt guari.
> La semblance de vus prendrai:
> le cors Damedeu recevrai,
> ma creance vus dirai tute.
> Ja de ceo ne serez en dute!"
> El li respunt que bien a dit.
> Delez li s'est culchiez el lit;
> mes il ne volt a li tuchier
> ne d'acoler ne de baisier.] 161–72

Two things bear emphasis here. First, it is the lady's "semblance" that the knight will adopt. In fact, when subsequently confronted with the disbelief of the old crone at her avowal of sudden, mortal illness, she will take advantage of semblances in a different way: "she pretended she fainted" (*semblant* fist qu'ele se pasma; 185). The lady's appearance here is effective—the crone will run for the priest—but no less effective than the transformed "semblanz" by means of which her husband finally figures out that something is up: "On account of the great joy she experienced...her entire appearance had changed" (Pur la grant joie u ele fu...esteit tuz sis semblanz changiez; 229, 231). Appearances have consequences. They can be controlled (the feigned faint) or uncontrolled (the joyous transformation), but they are never *merely* phenomena. Appearances matter; appearances materialize.

Second, it is unclear where seeming (one body) and being (another) part ways. Take, for example, the enigmatic "vus" in line 167: when the knight says, "ma creance vus dirai tute," is he promising to make his statement of faith—whether a memorized *credo* or something more improvised—*to* his lady or *in her place*? He has just said that he will take on the lady's appearance and receive the host; it follows, then, that he would be speaking *as* the lady when he makes this profession. And yet the lady is also somehow the indirect object of the utterance: it is clear that the knight wishes to make this profession to and for her, so that any worries about his unusual way of entering her room (and, perhaps, now her body) might be assuaged. What would it mean to suggest that the knight can speak *as* someone and *to* that someone in the same breath, at once distinct and indistinct from her? Something analogous to this semantic ambiguity takes place in Marie's emphasis on the spatial contiguity of the lovers' bodies: the knight lies alongside the lady ("delez li") and yet he doesn't touch her; similarly, when the priest brings communion, we are informed that the lady lies reciprocally and symmetrically alongside her lover:

> The knight received [the host]
> and drank the wine from the chalice.
> The chaplain went away,
> and the old woman closed the doors.
> The lady lies alongside her lover:
> never have I seen such a handsome couple.
>
> [Li chevaliers l'a receü,
> le vin del chalice a beü.
> Li chapelains s'en est alez,
> e la vieille a les us fermez.
> La dame gist lez sun ami:
> unkes si bel cuple ne vi.] 191–96

This paratactic sequence shows us the knight, as the lady, taking communion; the priest leaving the room; and the lady lying alongside her beloved, to whom she is incomparably coupled. Stephen Nichols has argued that this coupling is actually quite comparable after all, and specifically comparable to the way in which "the mystery of the Eucharist itself subsumes alterity." In his reading of the poem, "the knight and the woman fuse into one and the same body which sometimes represents her and sometimes him."[3] Just as, for Nichols, the host is thoroughly Christ's body, so too would there be no distinction between the lady and the knight in this moment of commingled communion. Yet what must complicate such a reading is the crucial preposition "delez" or "lez," beside or alongside: on two occasions here it spatially configures the relationship between the knight and lady as one less of identity than of contiguity. Their adjacent, proximate bodies do somehow get inside each other—and they will get inside each other sexually as well, in the lines that follow—but not without Marie's insistence on their simultaneous separateness. When the knight is beside his lady or the lady beside her beloved, the "semblanz" they collaborate in creating is, in the terms of chapter 3, spaced out, their double contiguity written on the surface of what appears to be just one body.

This "semblanz" is, therefore, not something to which the knight and lady are univocally reduced but, rather, something in which they *participate*, at once beside and inside each other, touching without touching. They are not fused so much as immediate to one another in the strongest sense, the sense of *im*-mediacy, what is most internal to mediation, the simultaneously shared and continually negotiated difference according to which it is possible to speak of identity and alterity at all. There is between them only that fraught, tenuous "vus," opening up the space between *as* and *to*, articulating identity as address. It is the smallest, slightest, most crucial space. Whether this space, this difference, is ultimately anything at all, is what Julian of Norwich, asking the question of God and the soul, would like to know.

Julian's is perhaps the most famous, and most extensive, medieval elaboration of lived enclosure, "lived" only so to speak, given that a fourteenth-century anchoress was officially treated as entombed in her cell.[4] Julian uses enclosure to give an account not just of anchoritic life but of what might, in another era, have been called the human condition. Enclosure is not just the authorial situation of Julian's text: not just, that is to say, the environment of her text's production. It is her text's dominant trope. Frederick Bauerschmidt sums up a great deal of recent scholarship when he observes that "images of enclosure and envelopment run throughout Julian's writing, and indeed the very substance of her writing seems to fold back upon itself."[5] If much of the work of the preceding chapters has been oriented toward making visible the persistence or, if you will, the traherence of enclosures in moments of erotic exposure and discovery, Julian's enclosures, textual and historical, are almost *too* visible. In fact, precisely because it's so tempting to collapse the various kinds of enclosed practice on display in the *Revelation* into a complex but still unitary, self-evident concept—one too easily mapped onto the female or ecclesial body as this enclosure's deep truth—I want to resist speaking of enclosure here. Instead, I want to speak of mediation, of what it means to come or be between.

Mediation, like enclosure, is as much a phenomenological problem for Julian as an ontological one. Her text is, after all, a series of "shewyngs" or revelations, and none of these demonstrates the mutual implication of enclosure and mediation, specifically sensory mediation, better than the second revelation, in which Christ's face, one half at a time, becomes covered with blood:

> And one time I saw how halfe the face, begyning at the ere, overrede [was overrun] with drie blode til it beclosid to the mid face, and after that, the tuther halfe beclosyd on the same wise, and therewhiles [simultaneously] in this party even as it came. This saw I bodily, swemely [sorrowfully] and derkely, and I desired more bodily sight to have sene more clerely.[6] (10.14–15)

Christ's half-enclosed face brings home to Julian the limits of perception. Her sight, like Christ's skin, emerges and retreats from an ineradicable mediating term: an intervening layer of bodily opacity, whether in the sense of her eyes' inadequacy or Christ's crust of blood. What is more, it is signally Christ's "mid face" that gets underscored in this vision, the point at which enclosure and disclosure continually meet. At this "mid face," the face as fundamentally, dynamically in the middle, Julian desires *more* sight, more mediation; not less.

And yet if Christ's face, the object of Julian's vision, evokes the dynamics by which her vision operates, its play of enclosure and disclosure echoing Julian's play of darkness and clarity, is Julian herself ever anywhere other than in this middle? What would it mean to say that Julian is visually, and perhaps even ontologically, inside mediation? To suggest that, through her desire for more sight, she intensifies this middle to the point at which immediacy would start to sound like *im-mediacy*? It would not, in this case, be a question of a discrete subject drawn out into the interstices between herself and an object, but rather, in the first place, a reciprocal approach and withdrawal, a tracing out of a middle ground, anterior to these distinctions. Julian's eyes, like Christ's face, would be dynamically, and inexhaustibly, awash in blood. Immediate enclosure would locate each "halfe" of vision—the two sides of Christ's face, each of Julian's two eyes, and Julian and Christ facing each other—in a tremulous "mid face" excessive to, and constitutive of, all of them.

As early as the fifth chapter of the long text of her *Revelation* (ca. 1373), Julian juxtaposes enclosure and immediacy. On the one hand, there is the mutual enfolding of God and creation, in which each is precisely mediated through the other. On the other hand, there is "nothing between" God and the soul. This latter observation occurs, in its most direct form, much later in Julian's book: "And therefore it is that ther may, ne shall, be ryte nowte atwix God and mannys soule" (53.86). But in the fifth chapter, mediation comes first; the "atwix," between, takes precedence over the "ryte nowte." This is, after all, the moment in the *Revelation* when Julian introduces her comparison of creation to something like a hazelnut in the palm of God. Being is, in this way, being enclosed:

> In this same time our lord shewed to me a ghostly sight of his homely loveing. I saw that he is to us everything that is good and comfortable for us. He is our clotheing that for love wrappith us, [halseth {*embraces*}] us and all beclosyth us for tender love, that hee may never leave us, being to us althing that is gode, as to myne understondyng. (5.7)

God wraps us in his clothes, sartorially embraces us, and *entirely* encloses us—"all beclosyth us"—because of his love. Enclosure is textile, embodied, erotic. Yet we aren't just shrink-wrapped in God. When God "all beclosyth us," he leaves no part of us unenclosed; we've got God on all sides, as close as close can get. In this way, God preserves and cultivates our boundedness, in much the way that, in François Ozon's 2000 film *Under the sand* (*Sous le sable*), Charlotte Rampling's protagonist, in impossible mourning for a husband who may or may not be dead, offers herself to a dense array of hands that emerge from the darkness of her apartment to caress and delimit her body. When she is putatively most alone—masturbating, as it happens—she is surrounded.

Enclosure and Anaphora

But "all" is not just any word for Julian. Recall her famous mantra, the most succinct articulation of her alleged universalism: "all shall be well."[7] Whereas Barbara Newman eloquently characterizes this assertion as "unresolved and fraught with contradiction,"[8] it is fundamentally the contradiction—or, better, the paradox—that inheres within Julian's resolve, within this "all" as the sign of an eschatological *resolution*, that interests me here. For when God "all beclosyth us," the "all" is both the mode of his action—he *entirely* encloses us—and that *into which* we're enclosed. It is both dynamic and substantive. All takes no prisoners; or, rather, all takes them all. But is to be entirely enclosed—to be entirely enclosed, even, by entirety itself—ultimately to be reduced to or absorbed by this "all"? Is God's enclosive clothing like some kind of fabric that would dissolve into the skin, or, like the cloak Deianira gave Hercules, would cause the skin itself to dissolve?

Another way of asking this is to return to the terms of chapter 1: between "all" as that which can only be known in opposition to, or at best just to one side of, the inevitably limited here and now,[9] and "all" as that which, precisely in its totality, cannot be excluded from this here and now, is it merely a question of staging an intervention, deciding which side you're on? Either here (inside your skin) or there (outside it), *en-deçà* or *au-delà*? But how, if this is the case, to keep the logic of "us," here, and "all," there, from being reduced to a synecdoche whereby God would just name a bigger version of us, univocal in quality if not in quantity? How, in short, to keep enclosure from becoming sublation or, worse, collapse?

Julian soon adds: "I be so fastened to him that there is right nowte that is made betwix my God and me" (5.7). What later appears as merely "ryte nowte," as we've seen, here gets qualified as "nowte that is made." Nothing *created* comes between God and the soul. That is to say, if enclosure presupposes an intermediary—if only in the sense of a boundary, a threshold, a limit—this is nothing created. So even as porous a metaphor as human skin surrounded by divine cloth won't do. But is there, then, something *unmade* between God and me? Or is it, first and foremost, a question of that "between," and its attendant conjunction, "and," so crucial for Julian's poetics? What if, for a woman whose legacy in English prose is "all shall be well, and all shall be well, and all manner of thing shall be well," the crucial thing is not so much the future being-well as that anaphoric "and"? An "and" that, in order to describe the relation between God and me, must not be made, must somehow approximate or voice or participate in a distinction anterior to that between creator and creature?

Keeping in mind that the hazelnut as which Julian sees creation "might suddenly have fallen to nowte for littil" (5.7), I want to suggest that, in an account of creation where nothingness is always imminent, Julian's anaphoric "and" marks at once the mysterious parataxis of creation *ex nihilo*, as articulated in the repeated "and" of the first sentences of Genesis; and the equally paratactic, constantly imminent collapse of creation back into nothingness. But because God sustains it, and because God is strictly speaking no thing, there is a difference *within* nothingness: thus an uncreated difference. That by which creatures are sustained is God, no thing; that into which they would fall again, but for God, is nothing. To "fall to nowte" begins to sound suspiciously—or, perhaps, beautifully—like falling into God, but God as self-differing, as excessive and at least proto-relational.[10] That is to say, the "and" of "And then there was light" and the "and" of "And all shall be well" articulate the extent to which creation, in a sense, falls out of God and back into him; but also the extent to which God falls out of and back into himself. "And" names the simple paradox, hard and dense as a hazelnut, of being at once inside and between.

This is a little fast, and certainly more than a little "fastened" to an ontological problem that makes it difficult to speak in the hypotactic cadences of critical prose. (How can "thus," "thereby," or "whence" compare with this bare, mysterious "and" through which the world is made and unmade?) Julian will make ample use, as always, of this most banal and bizarre of conjunctions in her longest description of the mutual enclosure that obtains between God and man. In fact, it is precisely the relationship between the anaphoric "and," on the one hand, and the spatial prepositions ("between," "in") crucial to this enclosure, on the other, that Julian foregrounds in the fifty-fourth chapter of the *Revelation*:

> And I saw no difference atwix God and our substance, but as it were al God, and yet myn onderstondyng toke that our substance is in God: that is to sey, that God is God, and our substance is a creture in God; for the almyty truth of the Trinite is our fader, for he made us and kepith us in him; and the depe wisdam of the Trinite is our moder in whom we arn beclosid; the hey goodnes of the Trinite is our lord and in him we arn beclosid and he in us. We arn beclosid in the Fadir, and we arn beclosid in the Son, and we arn beclosid in the Holy Gost; and the Fader is beclosid in us, and the Son is beclosid in us, and the Holy Gost is beclosid in us...(54.87)

What initially appears to be a distinction between the Father's "making and keeping" and the enclosive function of the Son and Spirit turns out, instead, to be a mutual gloss: to enclose is, in some sense, to make and keep; perhaps even to say that keeping is its own kind of creation. This would reiterate the way in which creation's relation to God is in some way anaphoric; differentially, additively repetitive, just like Julian's "and." Anaphora, after all, functions primarily by means of "reference to a term already mentioned in discourse"[11] and therefore exists only inasmuch as it sustains or keeps this reference. And this reference itself, not unlike God with respect to creation, is at once inside and outside the repeated structure: inside, to the extent that the precise syntax of the anaphoric structure (e.g., "and X is beclosid") does not *necessarily* follow from external circumstances; outside, to the extent that the accumulation of nonidentical repetitions, here, avoids a kind of trance-like, tautological immanence (X is X is X is X) and, instead, creates a horizon, a limit, within which these individual anaphoric utterances can be understood. There is, in other words, an *analogous* relationship between Father, Son, and Holy Ghost as differential repetitions of a single God, on the one hand, and the anaphoric phrases as differential repetitions of a single syntactical structure, on the other. Within this analogous relationship, anaphora is *added to* trinitarian repetition, which obviously does not require anaphora, no more than it requires any figure of speech, for its being.[12] This addition, through which what is made is also minimally and superlatively kept, is that of the paratactically creative "and." In fact, even the decidedly non-theological account of figures of speech in the *Rhetorica ad Herennium* is beautifully precise about the extent to which anaphora accommodates difference within sameness: "Epanaphora occurs when one and the same word forms successive beginnings for phrases expressing *like and different* ideas" (Repetitio est cum continenter ad uno atque eodem verbo in rebus *similibus et diversis* principia sumuntur).[13] Julian's "and," in this way, bears a striking resemblance to the *Rhetorica*'s "et," that barest term of mediation between likeness and difference.

And yet an asymmetry must follow from this: for, Julian tells us, the relationship between the soul and the three persons of the Trinity is one of *reciprocal* enclosure, but God is neither made nor kept, in any strong sense, by the soul. Our substance is explicitly "a creature in God," and this cannot be true in reverse. That is, it is one thing to say that the soul is, first and foremost, uncreated; it is quite another to say that God is, first and foremost, a creature. How is it possible for Julian to set up this relationship of enclosive reciprocity, as though "in" God and "in" the soul were the same thing, and yet to preserve the creature's unique status, outside of God, *as* created?

Perhaps this is the wrong question, inasmuch as it rests upon a presumed univocity, not so much of being (as in the critique of a separate fourteenth-century theological tradition, that of Duns Scotus, by John Milbank and others), but of space and, precisely, this locative preposition: "in." After all, Julian remarks, just a few chapters earlier, that the Son sits at the Father's right hand in rest and stands at the Father's left hand in labor. And yet "it is not ment that the Son syttith on the ryte hond, syde be syde, as on man sittith be another in this lif" (51.81). Trinitarian space is analogous, not equivalent, to human space.[14] Likewise, in the passage cited above, Julian's beautifully chiastic anaphoras do not so much eclipse as precisely *depend upon* the strange presence, just before they begin, of the distinction, rhetorically slight but ontologically fundamental, between "God is God" and "our substance is a creature in God." To be specific: God *is*, while even that highest part of the soul *is in*. "In" names not a quality of the soul—as though the soul could be thought apart from its being in God—but that mark of its ontological distinctness from its divine source. If every "awtix," every interval posited as "between" God and the soul, serves as a way of keeping the divine "all" from collapsing into creation, then this creaturely "in" similarly, perhaps still more strongly, makes a case for spatial metaphor, and ultimately for space *tout court*, as that which vouchsafes the ontological difference.

But "in" is of course the thinnest of prepositions. If "and" articulates the most basic, fragile, yet fundamental joining, "in" likewise names not so much a *mode* of being in space but the bare ontological *fact* of being in space itself. What I'm getting at, here, is a sense of space analogous to what time is for Augustine, time which, according to *Confessions* X, is so evanescent it "has no space" (nullum habet spatium). Space would be, likewise, the sign—but not just the sign; more like the material inscription or practice—of createdness, in which the local difference between creatures (where it is impossible for two creatures to be in the same place at once) participates in and elaborates a more fundamental difference: that between creatures and their creator, who in this way is not a *transcendental*, not the greatest extremity or intensification of being-in-space, but precisely *transcendent*. So when Julian goes on to show, again in a thoroughly Augustinian fashion, the mutual enclosure of Trinity and soul, it is nonetheless with the explicit purpose of inscribing an ontological difference into seamless chiasmus. God is enclosed in me; I am enclosed in God: yes, but God's being is separate from this "in," whereas mine is not. If Julian sees "no difference between God and our substance," it is because this distinction is not, strictly speaking, visible. Sight, and the "between" across which sight reaches, stops just short of its object, just this side of what transcends it. Julian therefore stages the dialectical passage—I'm even tempted to say analogical passage—from mediation (sight) to apparent immediacy (no difference) to *im-mediacy*, that is, mediation again and otherwise (between as both *in* and *and*).

To say this again: I am implicated in what I see, but not just in Merleau-Ponty's sense of the body's inability to sever itself from the field of perception.[15] For what is "between" God and me is no ordinary object of perception. It is something I am *in*, but (or *and*) it is also my addition, my exteriority to God, inasmuch as I am *in* it at all. Julian underscores this when she records her inability to see the precise moment of Christ's death on the cross. "Betwix that one and that other," between the "last poynte" of his passion and his rejoicing beyond death, "shal be no tyme" (21.31). And this imperceptible, perhaps even nonexistent, "betwix" is in the future tense because it also names our mysterious participation in Christ's passing beyond passion. Thus I am *in* between, no matter how precious it sounds. But inasmuch as I do not dissolve into God, inasmuch as even this "into" would still keep me, in the strongest sense, within the confines of being (and therefore separate), "no difference" comes to name not an immediacy but the paradox of a mediation (*between*) to which I am at once immanent (*in*) and excessive (*and*). Moreover, this paradox, this im-mediacy, becomes perceptible as a crisis of perception.

To sum up: enclosure is, then, a relationship of *asymmetrical* reciprocity between God and the soul.[16] This reciprocity is structured like an anaphora: that is to say, each repeated articulation of being enclosed is analogous to, and slightly different from, the one before. To say I am enclosed in the Son and I am enclosed in the Spirit is to say not quite the same thing;

it is to inscribe a difference, or to reiterate the difference, at the heart of God. Likewise, to say I am enclosed in your mouth and I am enclosed in your hand is to inscribe a difference at the heart of you, to rearticulate you not as self-evident, not as unitary and transparent, but as differentially *coherent*. What is more, the anaphoric structure of this reciprocity—between God and me, between you and me, or between God and us—saves enclosure from collapse into absolute identity. It does this by making its mode of mediation at once, and barely, immanent and excessive, same and different (*similibus et diversis*). It doesn't say the same thing differently; it says the same thing *and* the different thing. They are held together only by their saying, only by their articulation.

Nothing Between

The next crucial moment, crucial for Julian's ontology as for the claustrophilic community elaborated in chapter 4, is the "our" in Julian's "our substance." It is this "we" that, as the being-in-common of creatures, names again the extent to which human being is always being *in*, and never alone. When Julian discusses the inevitability of sin in chapter 37, she hints at what might be at stake in this "we": "thowe our lord shewid me I should synne, by me alone is understode al" (37.51). She has just glossed "al" as "al my even cristen, al in general and nothing in special," that is, all her fellow Christians or all her fellow humans, depending on how far one is willing to stretch Christendom. Is Julian's "I," then, a synecdoche? Does she speak, in this way, as a representative Everywoman, ready to sacrifice her singularity to this representative function?

I want to suggest that Julian's "I" here actually *saves* her singularity by marking both its participation in a community (the "fellow Christians or humans" who thereby stretch "I" semantically into "we") and its irreducibility to this community. How? Julian's "all," even as "all my fellow Christians or humans," reproduces precisely that "all" which, in the passage from chapter 5 cited above, came not to obliterate the enclosed soul in its suffocating totality but, rather, to impart to this soul, asymmetrically, some of its internal difference. If "all" does not, then, just establish itself as utterly, ontologically different from the singular "I" but, moreover, *intervenes* between "I" and "we," *this side of the ontological difference*, then it is again a question of how what is *between* "I" and the "we" in which I participate places me *in* a community and, at the same time, asymmetrically but reciprocally produces both this community and myself as excessive to one another. I *as* we becomes, in this way, I *and* we. I cannot take place without a community; but I am added to this community, even as I participate in it. Not because there is an ontological difference between, or within, us; but because the ontological difference intervenes *as* the anaphoric relation internal to our taking place, *similibus et diversis*, irreducible to any transparent whole but yet, simultaneously, unable to mean, unable to be, in isolation.

Jean-Luc Nancy has proposed that " 'we' is always inevitably 'us all,' where no one of us can be 'all' and each one of us is, in turn (where all our turns are simultaneous as well as successive, in every sense), the other origin of the same world" ("nous," c'est forcément 'nous tous,' dont pas un n'est 'tout' et dont chacun est à son tour—des tours simultanés autant que successifs, des tours dans tous les sens—l'autre origine du même monde).[17] Though the logic of anaphora to which I've alluded bears a certain resemblance to Nancy's conflation of the "simultaneous" and the "successive," anaphoric relation in fact does something more. Nancy's "other origin of the same world" ultimately subsumes radical difference into a synecdoche according to which "each one" is to "other" what "us" is to "same." Singularity and alterity come, in this way, to reside within community and sameness as their internal difference; but only as their *internal* difference. If there is no external, ontological difference, no exteriority as such, in the strongest sense—*that is to say, if there is no mysterious, absurd "and" which has happened and will happen again*, then all we're left with is an aporetic betweenness, a suspension and a non-coincidence, within "us." Our "same world" collapses into a fireworks show of exploding origins. Where Julian's account might suggest that there is "nothing between" us to the extent that there is "nothing between" us and God, and to the extent that God names this very nothing, here there is, instead, *everything* between us. The "all" comes back and bites us in the ass. In this "same," putatively small world, the distance between you and me, let alone between either of us and the "us" in which we participate, is enormous.

In contrast to this, and in the spirit of Julian's *Revelation*, Graham Ward gives a helpful gloss on what "we" might instantiate in the Eucharistic fraction, the breaking of bread, that even now persists in some Anglican liturgies: "The priest holds the wafer over the chalice of wine and breaks it into two saying: 'We break this bread to share in the Body of Christ.' The congregation respond with: 'Though we are many we are one body because we all share in one bread.' "[18] The "we" is, Ward insists, first synecdochic, spoken by one person for many, then "antiphonal," taking up, re-citing, and literally fleshing out, across multiple bodies and voices, the first utterance. The priestly part does not, that is, ultimately *represent* the ecclesial whole, since the response of the congregants inscribes a difference at the heart of the "we," a difference that makes this "we" irreducible to any one utterance or summary moment—while at the same time saving the "we" from absolute incoherence and irredeemable dispersal. "Distinctions,"

Ward argues, "are affirmed within the 'we,' for the repetition of the rhythm 'we are' is not identical: 'we are many we are one.' "[19] Through nonidentical repetition, the Eucharistic fraction breaks up the "we" beyond reducibility to a knowable whole, either immanently present in itself or represented through priestly synecdoche. Still more crucially, it writes the paradox of being many and one as the effect, indeed perhaps even as the sign, of an "all" that transcends ordinary space while nonetheless informing it: an "all" articulated here, as in Julian, through that "we," which precisely cannot be absolutely or exclusively "all." For sharing "in the Body of Christ" and sharing "in one bread" constitute not a monistic self-devouring mass but, instead, a community of shared singularities, united in their very brokenness, whose irreducibility to one another is not just preserved but made possible by the mysterious "in" of their participation, beyond all identity, in that broken bread-as-body.

In other words, "one," "many," and "all," constituted across a handful of carnal crumbs, do not name successive moments in a progression toward a transparently holistic "we" but, rather, produce human difference as precisely a coincidence of delimitation, its being held in common, and the ontological enclosure wherein these delimited singularities are broken anew, differently and excessively: *one, many, all*. Which is to say, also: *in, between, and*. The broken bread is something we share *in*, something that stretches us *between* our singularities, out of isolation, into an embodied community and temporal moment to which we are nonetheless excessive— we do not entirely become this bread, or body, by ingesting it—and which is excessive to us, which breaks us again even as it is broken. Furthermore, if this recited "we" is, as Ward suggests, "antiphonal," we break almost as a voice breaks. That is, each voice is given back to itself, as more than itself and more, too, than its community, only at the limit of its self-articulation, only when it chorally comes undone.[20]

To repeat, almost anaphorically, a question from chapter 4: what would it mean to think of a community of lovers, or readers, along these lines? Catherine Brown has spoken to the latter of these concerns in her observation that "readers and the objects they read are, as long as reading happens, cotemporal and cospatial."[21] Against the background of so many well-intentioned injunctions to respect the radical alterity of texts from the distant past—and, really, of texts in general—it is refreshing to see Brown's refusal to concede that a text, however finally ungraspable it may in some way remain, does not also share a space and time with me in the moment of our encounter. Brown goes on to insist, "What matters for me, when I think about this coeval encounter, is not the search for some unmediated 'authenticity'; rather it's the conscious embrace of mediation, of the dynamics of relation and exchange."[22] I would like to suggest that Julian's fundamentally *immediate* mediation, her inscription of an enclosive "in" and an excessive "and" at the heart of the mediating "between," opens onto an account of textual encounter that would push Brown's binary understanding of "relation and exchange" between a reader and a text in a more tertiary direction. That is, for this kind of im-mediacy, there is not just me and my book; not even me, my book, and some other book (or reader). There is also the "we," separate from both, or all, of us, in which we participate and to which, nonetheless, we are *added* anaphorically and not reduced. Each individual textual encounter thus participates in a history of textual encounters and yet is more than these.

In *Purgatorio* 15, anticipating the enclosed, flaming touch we've seen amongst the lustful, Dante describes this "we" as specifically an effect of enclosure. "For the more they say 'ours' there, the more / good there is for each one, and the more / charity is burning in that cloister" (ché, per quanti si dice più lì 'nostro,' / tanto possiede più di ben ciascuno, / e più di caritate arde in quel chiostro).[23] Taking these lines by their ending—as a way of preparing for the ending of this chapter and the ending of this book—another tertiary relation becomes visible: "we" (literally, "our"); "each one"; and "cloister." It is the latter that keeps the singular "ciascuno" and communal "nostro" from collapsing into each other; the latter that marks the place of their intensification. But this intensification also breaks out of the quantitative ("more...more...more") into transformation: how? The cloister, the enclosure, *burns*.

Here again, as we saw in Bo Huston and Mark Doty, fire names the transformation of bodies not in spite of their spatial and material limits but precisely on account of and through these limits. The burning cloister, *erotically* burning, communicates to these bodies the nothing out of which they are continually recreated and in which they are miraculously held. To be held in the midst of fire, held in such close proximity to annihilation, and held not alone but together with other bodies, is a miracle as old as the story of Shadrach, Meshach, and Abednego, bound and thrown in the fiery furnace by Nebuchadnezzar.[24] But even in that oldest of stories, the three bodies surrounded by fire were suddenly joined by a fourth. Claustrophilia, the trope of the burning cloister, likewise gives voice to that sudden advent that makes every enclosed amorous community exceed its boundaries. We kiss, and between us someone else intervenes: in truth, a whole series of others, but also the very phenomenon of otherness, and the horizon against which they all take shape. Difference, created and uncreated, writes itself where we touch.

This is, finally, both metonymy and anaphora. That is to say, it is the drag, the traherence, of "I" and "you" in "we"; but it is also the barest resonant difference in each reiteration of "uno atque eodem verbo," one and the same word. Or, to return to *Yonec*, it is how I remain separate from you even as I speak in your place, how being *inside* you is always simultaneously being *beside* you, irreducibly. In this internal proximity, what comes between us is nothing; what comes between us is, in other words, no created thing but, instead, the ground of creation: the fact that creation happens, that there is creation; that there is anything at all. Between and within "I" and "I," or "we" and "we," or even "mouth" and "mouth," creation happens all over again. In this same word, which is not Nancy's same *world*, sameness and difference are joined by virtue of their common emergence from nothing: an emergence framed by the enclosure as at once *in and between*, immediate and excessive. I am tempted to put it this way: there is nothing between us but this fire. No, that's not right. There is nothing between us. And this fire.

IN CLOSING

Modes of Entry

Claustrophilia takes place, then, in and between us, as the erotics of our being together in space, which is to say, the erotics of our being together at all. The hermitages and bedrooms and hand-enfolded hazelnuts make it appear and drive it home. Still, claustrophilia—its promise and its threat—informs even our most distant, far-reaching constitutions of community. It is only through the erotics of enclosure, only through this desire to hold and be held, that any community whatsoever can take place or be spoken. This diffuse, erotically extensive enclosure is the opposite, or really the refutation, of the tramway in Albert Camus's plague novel, *La peste*, where "all the occupants, as far as possible, turn their backs to each other in order to avoid a mutual contagion" (tous les occupants, dans la mesure du possible, se tournent le dos pour éviter une contagion mutuelle).[1] That is to say, you can try to keep your distance in such a small space, but it is better—I would wager, infinitely better—to try to keep a small space in and between so much distance.

Scholars traditionally cross great distances and huddle in tiny rooms. We fear and court contagion. In the final pages of *Mimesis*, Erich Auerbach makes a series of admissions relevant to the metonymically bound community in which we take shape, singular and plural. "I see the possibility," he writes,

> of success and profit in a method which consists in letting myself be guided by a few motifs which I have worked out gradually and without a specific purpose, and in trying them out on a series of texts which have become familiar and vital to me in the course of my philological activity...[2]

This almost meandering model of scholarship is also one of contiguity:

> Furthermore, the great majority of the texts were chosen at random, on the basis of accidental acquaintance and personal preference rather than in view of a definite purpose.[3]

Whether or not this confession is sincere, it is ultimately its status as trope that matters. Auerbach is clearly interested in impressing upon us, "us" in the strongest sense, the strange mixture of randomness and proximity that have made these texts the object of his writing. Their closeness is translated into his enclosure: think of the long citations embedded in *Mimesis*, those "accidents" incorporated along the lines of the Thomist "proper accident," human hand or Christ's humanity. Likewise, if the contiguous can be thus enclosed, so might the enclosed remain contiguous, refusing to relinquish its infectious proximity to other books, other bindings.[4]

And yet randomness is opposed to memory: Harald Weinrich has shown the difficulty with which the characters of Corneille's *Menteur* can remember any of the utterly random details of the protagonist's lies: "In effect," he asks, "what would memory attach itself to, if everything in the text, absolutely everything, were only incidental, circumstantial, haphazard?"[5] Can Auerbach's remembering reader really be expected to trust his assertion of random choice? In other words, what binds a book together: method; discipline; authorial memory? Weinrich would suggest that it is, in fact, style that makes these readings both memorable and coherent: "To give style to a text is effectively to pose its candidacy for a certain survival, however brief this might be."[6] Might this gift of style be a matter of reading as much as writing? And yet what does style suggest, beyond a certain foregrounding of tropes and figures? Weinrich's account relies heavily upon futurity here: the most appropriate style, in ancient *elocutio*, "will be that which, in a given situation, will best guarantee the work of memory, at first the orator's memory, then that of his audience."[7] In fact, the afterlife of style, indicated by these verbs in the future, is also an afterlife in memory: a future perfect, then; a recollection from a point still to come.

Elsewhere, Weinrich suggests that the story of Paolo and Francesca in *Inferno* V is fundamentally about the time and embodiment of poetry. Here two lovers read a romance and imitate the adulterous kiss they find in those pages; they pay for their mimesis with their lives, dispatched by Francesca's jealous husband. In the "punto" when Lancelot's kiss inside the book merges into Paolo's outside it, eternity opens: the moment of reading consummates and suspends the temporal order, marking what Weinrich calls the "pregnancy of the instant."[8] This pregnant moment, in which the smallest interval of time contains temporal suspension, enables Francesca's narrative of the lovers' tryst, an account that is no Wordsworthian recollection at a distance but, rather, an act of bodily memory. Her body, itself less than corporeal—the lovers' punishment is, in Weinrich's words, "to be deprived of their bodies while being constrained to remain close to one another"[9]— contains the unbearable excess of memory, just as the literary "punto" contains the unbearable excess of eternity. What is more, enclosure is written eternally as contiguity: in the absence of her material body, Francesca has only Paolo's nearness; in the absence of the intensely temporal "punto," she has the everlasting gusts of lust. At first, these accounts of style and poetry seem all too clearly opposed. For if Francesca and Paolo had only been a bit more mindful of their future and its recollection of the past, they would perhaps not have been so quickly killed (nor thus so quickly damned). At the same time, a stylistics based on the mere "punto" of feverish textual recognition and imitation would be blatantly unsustainable. Yet I would maintain that it is precisely between the play of future and past, on the one hand, and momentary eternity, on the other, that the strongest lesson in the temporality of reading is to be had. The negotiation of citation and linear critical argument that occurs in the experience of even the most avant-garde of scholarly texts makes this abundantly clear: those blocks of quoted material are the pregnant moments that instill in us the desire to imitate and kiss; the surrounding critical argument both engages with them mnemonically and prepares them to be remembered. Nevertheless, there remains a way in which all scholarship is scholarship in hell: specifically, inasmuch as contiguity is more immediately apprehensible than enclosure; and inasmuch as the chafing of text against text at times cannot help seeming like a poor substitute for an absorbing, materialized moment forever lost.

Let me propose, in closing, two primary ways in which the readings I have assembled here—of French, Latin, English, and early Italian devotional literature; of contemporary philosophy and criticism; and of contemporary gay lyric—might be seen to make sensible, if not always tactile, the enclosures that contiguity both mourns and reawakens. Inasmuch as the lovers' Galeotto poetically, mnemonically, endures, there is no question of absolute loss, just as there is no question of absolute presence. Consider, then, these modes of entry into what must, as enclosed, resist disclosure.

First, my arguments have been, in a not entirely unambiguous way, a critique of the dialectic, still ongoing, between the sexual closet and its alleged outside. Both the impenetrably "in" and the transparently "out" remain objects of unabashed fetishism. Recent historicist work has shown how contingent this imagined and material space finally is; I have attempted to approach the issue from the other way round, namely, by intensifying rather than contextually diminishing the thickly enclosive/disclosive work through which a body is seen as such. In this respect, I am responding to Lee Edelman's injunction to "construct retroactively out of the various accidents that constitute 'our' history a difference from the heterosexual logic of identity"—an injunction that Edelman couches in the rhetorical terms of metonymy's resistance to metaphor.[10] And yet it is in acknowledgment of the untenability, not to mention the undesirability, of a "pure" metonymy, that claustrophilia has come to enclose this poetics of difference and accident: claustrophilia attempts to come as close as metaphor can to metonymy, or rather to show the metonymy that always inheres within the metaphorical; claustrophilia also resists even as thoughtful a critic as Edelman's association of the metonymic, via syntax, with linearity.[11] To sense the dynamism (of meaning as well as being) within apparent stasis, the touch of the enclosed, has been this project's fundamental challenge.

For John Paul Ricco's recent formulation of anonymous, itinerant erotics, this sensory intensification is plainly not radical enough. After Blanchot, he writes of a "trajectory towards the outside," which, "insofar as it slips toward wherever, whatever, whoever, whenever, will always be the betrayal of architecture, identity, the social, etc."[12] At most, Ricco offers an intense attenuation of all those determinations by means of which one might potentially be fixed, captured, fully seen.[13] Such an argument seems to presuppose that to be seen is necessarily to be seen in full: better, then, to evacuate the sensible, retreat into the dark alleys of an ontology of cruising. Yet what if full, exhaustive vision is a myth told by disciplinary institutions and tacitly accepted by even their staunchest critics? What if the more you look at something, the longer you feel its edges, the more mysterious it becomes; the more it starts to feel at once more singular, never more itself than now, and more like other things, opening onto a vast network of associated textures and colors and tastes?

Is a queer body just a body after all, one thing among many? I hope it is clear by now that what this argument calls for is a more thorough reevaluation of the ontological and phenomenological dimensions, and consequences, of not just what comes to pass for sexuality these days, but also what comes to be read, what offers itself to the labor of making meaning and giving joy. Ontological, inasmuch as what must be relinquished is the notion of an indifferent, immanent Being in which beings (or texts) are interchangeable (or random) on account of their identical use-value: one studies X instead of Y, but X and Y are identically and thus contentiously reducible to the worthy-of-study. This immanence has required the strictest policing of disciplinary boundaries, discursive registers, and stations in life, so that the fundamental indifference and exchange of things might not become too palpable. Queer being is thus neither merely one exchangeable being among many nor a fetishized, radical singularity. Bound up with other beings, other books, queer *corpora* beg to be read in light of what they touch upon: those texts and bodies that give them meaning and that they, in turn, illumine. But could this not potentially extend to all bodies, all texts? Of course it could, but then this is not a question fundamentally about *which* bodies, *which* texts are lit up by a lover's gaze; it is a question of *how* to orient this gaze, how to sense (which means also: to read, to love) differently.

Let me make clear, then, that these pages are not offered as an apology for randomness. Mark Doty is no more random, vis-à-vis Iacopone da Todi, than Bonagiunta, Julian, or Peter Krause. Instead, randomness is what haunts scholarship—even queer scholarship—in the traditional mode, as the threat of what is unmemorable and indifferent about its own territorial methods: the constant defensive posturing in the wake of the question, "why are you writing about *that*, and not *this*?" Instead, let us ask, with Auerbach, "*how* are you reading?" Any text can be at-hand. But in the moment of critical illumination, that perhaps occasional and ephemeral contiguity is transformed into the greatest possible *convenientia*: no object could be more fitting, provided one learns to see it properly—an apparent tautology which means only that the look of love transforms apparent indifference into deictic singularity—*this, now, here, yes*—and is thereby transformed.

All the same, I can't help feeling that the texts assembled here have a particular affinity for one another, inasmuch as they stage the reorientation of the senses as their primary work. Medieval religious writers and certain gay lyricists, as well as the philosophical tradition used to bring them close, share this commitment to the risk that, we have seen, inheres etymologically in experience. I am tempted to say that they are antidotes to complacency, the intensification of tradition (*traditio*) to the point of betrayal (*traditio*). At the same time, it cannot be denied that a certain biographical and mnemonic narrative also connects them. We do not learn to love objectively, at a critical distance; neither are we content with just any object. In his novel *Lawnboy*, Paul Lisicky articulates this beautifully:

> That thing called chemistry, that elusive connection and tension, what was that about? . . . In the year following the breakup, she'd coined something she called the boner test—"Does he give you a boner?"—and every time she'd dated she asked herself that question, even though, for obvious reasons, it was figurative.[14]

Likewise, one can ask of a reader: what excites you hermeneutically, mnemonically, rhetorically? That is, which texts produce that only partly willed moment of intensity (literal or, "for obvious reasons," figurative), felt at once inside and at the surface of the body? The question itself is designed to produce the effect about which it inquires. Specifically, within the apparent tautology is an articulation of how an aesthetic or erotic response, in the very act of contextualization, nonetheless senses only *that* body participating in *this* one. Therefore, if *convenientia* is a matter of transformatively restoring to apparently accidental, peripheral, or abject objects the beauty they have never ceased to embody, it is also true that such a convenient poetics depends less upon the objects themselves than upon the very act of transformative restoration: here, the sense of being ecstatically bounded and bound.

At the risk of repetition, I want to emphasize that the problem of an erotics—and specifically an ontologically inflected erotics of reading—is phenomenological inasmuch as the way out of an immanent/indifferent ontology is precisely through a reorientation of the senses. Seeing the gap between one promiscuous citation and another can perhaps enable us to perceive, in a way close to our bodies, the leap that words make across our hermeneutic and graphic barriers: a leap that engenders other leaps, metonymically, transcendently. This is not to say that, leaping, one ever hits the ceiling of a hypostasized transcendence; rather, in the place of the agon of reducible and competitive texts and bodies and disciplines, what intervenes is a new sense of the metonymic participation of these adjacent texts and bodies and disciplines in one another, an intervention intensified when this adjacency is not particularly obvious: when one must apparently leap across something, a determinate boundary or obstacle, only to discover, mid-leap, a new sense of boundedness, of the permeability of bindings. This is how enclosure redeems the closet: it shows that the closet's boundaries are always more than they seem, precisely inasmuch as they seem.

If it is not already obvious, let me briefly state that the second mode of entry into this project—or the third, if one insists on seeing the sexual and the philosophical as distinct—is a literary theoretical one. Geoffrey Galt Harpham has described the way in which reading is a paradox of stillness and movement: having stayed up all night with *Tess of the D'Urbervilles*, Harpham is, one undergraduate morning, "both elsewhere, an occupant of Hardy's world and not my own, and immobilized, sitting exhausted and bleary-eyed on the floor of my frat-house room." Harpham goes on to make explicit what has happened here: "We could think of the reader's experience as a kind of oscillation, an outward movement of imagination and affect not just accompanied by immobility but positively determined by it, and crowned by it as its necessary backlash."[15] It is tempting to linger over that frat-house dawn and its attendant exhaustion—an image whose erotic resonance would not be lost on Harpham—but it is still more important to emphasize that Harpham is both *inside* his "frat-house room" and *beyond* it, that enclosure does not preclude but precisely enables transcendence. What is more, Harpham *remembers* this simultaneous oscillation, this spatial paradox made temporal as well: here and beyond, now and then. It is fundamentally *not* a question of a "now here" that would also be a "nowhere," as in Ricco's provocative but misguiding formula.[16] Never has that frat-house room (or Wessex, for that matter) been so fully here; never has the past moment of reading been so present. Memory intensifies.

If a certain kind of still movement—not unlike Mark Doty's "still time"—structures the act of reading, so too does a spatial paradox inform the theoretical: "if a fact is to become theoretical, it must travel beyond its original context, suffering a decay or degradation in the process, losing something of its original context-specific solidity."[17] Memory is one such mode of travel, of theory. So too, I would argue, is the kind of approximate reading I have attempted to perform here, the bringing-close of distinct bodies and bodies of literature, which thus appear to have always been touching. In this way, claustrophilia could never have remained a purely historical descriptor. The site-specific desires of medieval saints do not, as it were, keep to themselves. To remain, exhausted and delighted, on the floor of the frat-house room or the mystical *cubiculum* is simultaneously to travel elsewhere, to experience one's erotically intensified limits as their beyond. The frat-house is still a frat-house, but it is also Hardy's rank garden; the saint's cell is still a cell, but it is also a room in the mansion of paradise.

Claustrophilia thus constitutes a theoretical gesture inasmuch as it manages to travel from an "original context-specific solidity"—through what mysterious medium? memory, yes, but also the sheer closeness of things—into a greater density, an alloy of the medieval and its countless others. This theoretical movement would be analogous to what Harpham describes as the "directionality" of literature, from culture (the "placing function" of literature, often aligned with fantasies of fixity and rootedness) toward society (the "outreach function," aligned with fantasies of hypermobility).[18] The enclosure (*claustro-*) frustrates the fantasy of hypermobility, of the endless proliferation of meanings, even as desire (*-philia*) insists upon stretching the boundaries of place, pushing against the walls of what would (rhetorically, professionally, or erotically) confine. It is my conviction that medieval studies, no more or less than queer studies, could benefit from more claustrophiles, in this sense, and fewer closet queens, content to sweep the corners of their historical huts.

The Joy of Anachronism

Claustrophilia, in this way, might offer a new understanding of what it means to read comparatively. Those of us who choose to belong in some fashion to Comparative Literature, that amorphous, renegade discipline whose hallmark is something called comparison, routinely find ourselves asked to respond to an excruciating and virtually invariable question: "So what exactly do you compare?" The question, usually posed far from innocently, bears with it a set of presuppositions. Specifically, to compare, in this account, is to do one of two things, or perhaps both at once: it is to assert the "I" who compares as the only possible link between two radically heterogeneous objects (as in "only *I* could think that Patty Griffin has anything to do with Julian of Norwich") or it is to assert the "I" as the merest empirical observer of a quantifiable difference that is laughably obvious and obviously "out there" (as in "of *course* octosyllabic lines are shorter than decasyllabic ones"). The comparatist, in either case, finds herself the butt of the joke. Of course, what gets taken for granted in either of these responses, and more importantly what gets taken for granted by the question that elicits them, is that what comparatists do is to look down, from within some kind of panoptical structure, at objects arbitrarily or naturally arranged in an immanent field, objects whose only relation to one another is as discrete carriers of relative value. To repeat, in a literary register, what I suggested earlier about beings and Being: Dante, in such an account, would be ten percent more X than Marie de France; Crashaw, just a little less X than Villon. The comparatist would be, in this account of things, she who ensures that the only difference is relative, circumscribable difference, and who thereby also vouchsafes her subject-position as the unitary, unifying horizon of this difference.[19]

In contrast to such a comparison, and in contrast to the historicism that could just as easily be substituted for it (with a similar commitment to controlled, indefinitely variable but strictly circumscribed difference), I'd like to propose that claustrophilia offers the joy of anachronism. Richard Miller translates *jouissance* in Roland Barthes's *Plaisir du texte* as bliss, but I prefer the inexact resonance of joy.[20] (Perhaps this is because I learned, in a long ago sanctuary, to have it "down in my heart.") Barthes poses the question of joy's relationship to history, and specifically to literary history, in the following way:

> Is pleasure only a minor bliss? Is bliss nothing but extreme pleasure? Is pleasure only a weakened, conformist bliss—a bliss deflected through a pattern of conciliations? Is bliss merely a brutal, immediate (without mediation) pleasure? On the answer (yes or no) depends the way in which we shall write the history of our modernity.
>
> [Le plaisir n'est-il qu'une petite jouissance? La jouissance n'est-elle qu'un plaisir extrême? Le plaisir n'est-il qu'une jouissance affaiblie, acceptée—et déviée à travers un échelonnement de conciliations? La jouissance n'est-elle qu'un plaisir brutal, immédiat (sans médiation)? De la réponse (oui ou non) dépend la manière dont nous raconterons l'histoire de notre modernité.][21]

He goes on to outline the two kinds of literary histories enabled by these answers: continuous (where joy extends pleasure) or discontinuous (where joy disrupts it). But the kind of surveying operation whereby bliss and pleasure become moments in a history of continuity or discontinuity, and specifically of the subject's own historical consistency or self-contradiction, is what lies outside the scope of Barthes's question: it is, in fact, the place from which that question issues.

Barthes will write, later in the *Plaisir du texte*, about the historicity of this organizing subject-position:

> Whenever I attempt to "analyze" a text which has given me pleasure, it is not my "subjectivity" I encounter but my "individuality," the given which makes my body separate from other bodies and appropriates its suffering or its pleasure: it is my body of bliss that I encounter. And this body of bliss is also *my historical subject*; for it is at the conclusion of a very complex process of biographical, historical, sociological, neurotic elements (education, social class, childhood configuration, etc.) that I control the contradictory interplay of (cultural) pleasure and (non-cultural) bliss, and that I write myself as a subject at present out of place, arriving too soon or too late. . .: anachronic subject, adrift.

> [Chaque fois que j'essaye d' "analyser" un texte qui m'a donné du plaisir, ce n'est pas ma "subjectivité" que je retrouve, c'est mon "individu," la donnée qui fait mon corps séparé des autres corps et lui approprie sa souffrance ou son plaisir: c'est mon corps de jouissance que je retrouve. Et ce corps de jouissance est aussi *mon sujet historique*; car c'est au terme d'une combinatoire très fine d'éléments biographiques, historiques, sociologiques, névrotiques (éducation, classe sociale, configuration infantile, etc.) que je règle le jeu contradictoire du plaisir (culturel) et de la jouissance (inculturelle), et que je m'écris comme un sujet actuellement mal placé, venu trop tard ou trop tôt. . .: sujet anachronique, en dérive.]²²

The anachronic subject here, adrift across time and space, nonetheless remains explicitly in control of its writing—in control, that is to say, of the contradictions by which it is constituted; in control of its joy and its pleasure. Moreover, its relationship to itself, as "encountered" in the texts it reads, is one of explicit appropriation. The anachronic subject, that is to say, ultimately grasps himself, and not, alas, in the erotically "bleary-eyed" way of Harpham's exhausted frat boy. Sure, the anachronic subject may lose himself periodically (in moments or texts of bliss), but he will ultimately *come to*, instead of merely *coming*. What would anachronism look like without this control, this poetics of appropriation?

Paul Zumthor articulates a similar impasse in the concluding paragraph of his *Parler du Moyen Age*, not long after he asserts that "the only thing that justifies the effort of our reading is the pleasure it gives us" (Ce qui seul justifie notre effort de lecture, c'est le plaisir qu'elle nous donne):

> Whatever we do, we will never possess anything. That much we know. What remains is the derisive freedom to trace signs on paper, a small thing, like the designs in the naked twigs on a maple tree under my window. They are pretending to have caught the whole winter sky in their net—and who knows? Perhaps they really have caught it.
>
> [Quoi qu'on fasse, on ne possédera jamais rien. Ça, on le sait. Reste le liberté dérisoire de tracer des signes sur le papier, si peu de chose, le dessin de ramilles nues à la branche de l'érable sous ma fenêtre, qui feignent d'avoir capturé dans leur filet le ciel entier de l'hiver—et, qui sait? l'ont peut-être vraiment pris.][23]

In this final, exquisite sentence, as the branches of the tree catch the sky, Zumthor substitutes the pretense of possession for possession itself; or, in other words, substitutes a nominalist understanding of possession for a realist one. But possession itself remains unaltered: it is still a question of an object seized and held unilaterally by a subject; and never, say, of that subject's possession *by* what it is alleged to possess, in the sense in which we might speak, and have spoken, of demonic or radically erotic possession. Barthes and Zumthor accordingly offer extremely sophisticated, but ultimately frustrating, versions of just that horizon I attempted to describe earlier as vouchsafing the relative values of quantifiably arranged objects—sky and branch, childhood beginnings and adult conclusions.

So if even Barthes, that consummate aesthete, invokes history here as precisely that structure which sets pleasure and bliss, the subject then and the subject now, in relation to each other within a given horizon—as, in short, that discursive mechanism which allows us to compare them—then what alternatives to this kind of history, this kind of comparison, might we begin to think and write? In Nietzsche's scathing polemic on the "utility and liability of history for life," the options aren't particularly attractive: if the historically inclined among us, Nietzsche suggests, venerate process, the suprahistorically inclined among us venerate the transparent, static unity of present and past.[24] It is something like this suprahistoricism that comes in for critique by Zumthor under the aegis of amateurism, with, he says, "its perpetual mystifications" (l'amateurisme, toujours mystificateur).[25] Zumthor goes on to say, "I am advocating instead a radicalization of specialized disciplines, self-renewed, critical of their content, ascetically riveted to their concrete object, while denying any totalizing pretension" (...une radicalisation des disciplines spécialisées, autorénovées, critique de leur contenu, ascétiquement rivées à leur objet concret, pourtant négatrices de toute prétention totalitaire).[26] Where Nietzsche will speak of a "hygiene of life" by which the ahistorical and suprahistorical regrettably but necessarily temper the historical "sickness" of his contemporaries, Zumthor here speaks in terms of an academic asceticism, a denial that, we may assume, is above all a self-denial.[27]

Both thinkers, I would wager, lose sight of the fact that hygienic practices and ascetic ones are nothing if not radical intensifiers of what Eve Sedgwick might call a fundamentally paranoid subject-position. The ascetic, not unlike Saint Anthony, asks of every object or body that appears to him, "Are you an angel or a devil?" The same phenomenological skepticism applies to disciplinary "content" in Zumthor's fomulation and historically abetted "life" for Nietzsche. I might ask: "Is that a twelfth-century Old French romance I'm seeing, or is it actually the Zizek I read last week? Or, worse, what if what I recognize as Guinevere in that scene with Lancelot's wound bleeding on her bedsheets isn't Guinevere—isn't even Francesca, now that I think of it—but instead, on second thought, *myself?*" In each of these accounts, *either* I practice a hygienic technique whereby the literary object is constituted as such for me through a process of continual, vigilant distinction from both other objects and myself, or I risk confusing these objects with each other, and myself with these objects. Either way, it's me against them.

But what if the problem here is the "against"? The "vs." that haunts this book, even in these closing pages: inside *vs.* outside; medieval *vs.* modern; joy *vs.* pleasure; anachronism *vs.* historicism; and so on? Is there room, within our thought as comparatists and claustrophiles but also within thought more generally, for a relationship of contiguity or juxtaposition that would not be reducible to *either* an antagonism, on the one hand, or simple collapse, on the other? And more crucially, would such a relationship of adjacency offer an alternative to the Barthesian/Zumthorian subject and the flat field he surveys, wherein absolutely discrete objects possess only relative, quantifiable value and can, at best, be merely arranged into ever more complicated patterns? I am going to hazard the suggestion that Eve Sedgwick has partially beaten me to the punchline: "*Beside,*" she writes,

> is an interesting preposition. . .because there's nothing very dualistic about it; a number of elements may lie alongside one another, though not an infinity of them. *Beside* permits a spacious agnosticism about several of the linear logics that enforce dualistic thinking: noncontradiction or the law of the excluded middle, cause versus effect, subject versus object.[28]

While I want to affirm, here, the gesture beyond (or perhaps *just to the side of*) the "versus" of those dualisms Sedgwick cites, and while I like the reminder that, before Chrétien de Troyes and Dennis Cooper were temporally adjacent—though not continuous—authors for me, they were first books touching each other in space on my shelves, I nonetheless want to ask whether it is absolutely necessary to assume that one object lying beside another might not somehow sneak inside this other object, or be snuck into. Within an economy of metonymy and anaphora, of dragging and differential repetition, might it be possible to speak of a comparative critical practice, or even a comparative mode of being-in-the-world, where being beside something or someone is not, first and foremost, a question of hierarchical, quantifiable ordering but, rather, a question of how bodies, and bodies of literature, that are allegedly outside but close to me also, again and again, get under my skin and go to my head?

There's a lot, I know, compressed into this "again and again." But what it marks the place of, at the very least, is the way in which a body never appears to me just once or in isolation: never appears, that is, as itself isolated, or to me as myself isolated from the world. Indeed, "not isolated" is a euphemism; perhaps the right word is indiscrete. Not entirely, of course; and not so that objects might be reduced to a knowable, homogeneous unity; but the respect for or responsibility toward an object's irrevocable particularity, as shaped by a million and one historical circumstances (of which Barthes has named four or five), has come, in recent and not so recent scholarship, to depend upon a logic wherein objects are univocally shaped much like stones are eroded by weather: the weather doesn't get inside the stone; much less do other stones get inside it. Are bodies, and especially those tenuous, signifying bodies that form the objects of this study, really so invulnerable? Is such a body really at once so radically contingent upon temporal circumstances and yet, paradoxically, radically impregnable to anything like affect, association, or, God forbid, the *ek-stasis* of those bodies contiguous to it, in whatever sense? Impregnable, in fact, to its own self-excess, *similis et diversus*?

Jean-Luc Nancy has this to say about history and historicism:

> But it is precisely the question of beginning, of inaugurating or entering history, that should constitute the core of the thinking of history. Historicism in general is the way of thinking that *presupposes* that history has always already begun, and that therefore it always merely continues. Historicism presupposes history, instead of taking it as what shall be thought.[29]

Presupposing history's own temporal unfolding, its conformity to a determinate sequence or shape, is, in this way, analogous to what I described earlier as presupposing an array of objects—or, we could say, an array of times—whose possibilities of reconfiguration would lie firmly within the grasp of the surveying subject, without the question of their being-objects, not to mention their being-beside-one-another, ever having been raised. In opposition to this historicism, Nancy offers the inaugural thought of a history that would also be community: in his words, "a certain spacing of time, which is the spacing of a 'we' " (156). Nancy's "we"—as we, so to speak, have seen—is less radical, less open to transcendence, than the anaphoric, antiphonal "we" of liturgy in which each "I" is added and not subsumed. If Nancy's notion of "entering history" is taken accordingly with this less immanent "we," it becomes possible to suggest that claustrophilia desires precisely this communal entrance, where corporately and corporeally we make room for time, and where time, simultaneously, is given us in and as space, in and as the "middle" of any age. This gift is inexhaustible. No labor of contextualization or so-called historicism could ever fill it up. It is, literally and irremediably, medieval.

In Sébastien Lifshitz's 2001 film *Presque rien*, distributed in the Anglophone world as *Come Undone*, two lovers whose history is told out of sequence walk through the ruins of a medieval castle in Brittany. For Matthieu, the castle at Ranrouët, built over several centuries, is a "summary of military architecture" (un résumé de l'architecture militaire); for Cédric, "it's just some rocks" (ce n'est que des pierres). Cédric leans in to kiss Matthieu, who resists, clutching his history book. A nice, more or less homogeneous historicist synthesis here rubs up against the barest material contiguity. Cédric, unsurprisingly, comes a lot closer than Matthieu to a sort of being singular plural of the architectural object, and not just because he sees it, singular, as stones, plural. While Matthieu wants to appropriate Ranrouët as a content of organized historical knowledge, Cédric wants to make it the space in which a kiss opens up, in which bodies touch. Despite his reductive observation, the stones are ultimately less important, for Cédric, than the open space they frame, an open space the camera never fails to emphasize, even when Cédric tries to abbreviate the distance between him and Matthieu with that historically rebuffed kiss. Anachronism—and comparison in general—might speak to exactly this spaciousness *within* objects, and within times, that only becomes sensible when we see them as at once singular and plural, discrete and imbricated somehow in one another; and, finally, when we submit ourselves to their frames by seeking to undo them, and still more crucially, by seeking ourselves, singularly in common, again and again, to come undone.

Claustrophilia, likewise, names the love that lights up a body, building, or book *from within*, acknowledging what is discrete and irreconcilable in the beloved as the effect of one's own appropriative, organizing gaze. Relinquishing that desire for appropriation, one sees each former object *in light of* another, and thus beyond the logic of objectification: a light, hermeneutic and mnemonic, always refracted, always coming from elsewhere. "Inside that narrow space," writes Federico García Lorca, "light took a step / and sang."[30] Enclosed light is a paradox, but for this step. Just as Paolo's unassimilable nearness abets Francesca's speech, so too does Lorca's boundary become eloquent when touched, illumined, by love. It is, once again and finally, a question of modes of entry: not a choice among competing entrances but, instead, the question of entry itself, the critical and amatory movement through which one finds oneself inside the beloved body, book, or building, while remaining at a distance, at the surface, waiting for Lorca's luminous song. To hold is, thus, not just to behold; it is to be held, even to be held in suspense. To say this otherwise: you can only enter me to the extent that I entrance you.

NOTES

Introduction

1. Augustine, *Confessions* 8.12, trans. R. S. Pine-Coffin (Harmondsworth: Penguin, 1961), p. 178.
2. María Rosa Menocal, in the "Prologue" to *Writing in Dante's Cult of Truth: From Borges to Boccaccio* (Durham: Duke University Press, 1991), provides one of the more eloquent expositions of the problem of scholarly introduction. Although "the material at the beginning neatly 'restores' the harmony of diachrony that the writing process itself radically undermines," nonetheless "literary history is itself not diachronic but rather synchronistic: time is all jumbled up everywhere, authors from different centuries and different universes sit one next to another and shape each others' work, both proleptically and retrospectively, as well as in the 'normal' diachronic ways we are used to expecting and analyzing" (pp. 2, 3).
3. This book has, accordingly, a lot in common with Timothy Bewes's eloquent exposition of the religious in Kierkegaard: "Only the religious is both spiritual *and* material, worldly *and* otherworldly, timeless *and* rooted in the historical moment." See *Reification, or The Anxiety of Late Capitalism* (London: Verso, 2002), p. 233.
4. Gerard Loughlin, *Alien Sex: The Body and Desire in Cinema and Theology* (Oxford: Blackwell, 2004), p. 54.
5. Mieke Bal, *Louise Bourgeois' Spider: The Architecture of Art-Writing* (Chicago: University of Chicago Press, 2001), p. 44.
6. Bonaventure's metaphor can be found in the second chapter of *On the Perfection of Life, Addressed to Sisters*, as cited by Jeryldene M. Wood in *Women, Art, and Spirituality: The Poor Clares of Early Modern Italy* (Cambridge: Cambridge University Press, 1996), pp. 23–24.
7. Sarah Spence, *Rhetorics of Reason and Desire: Vergil, Augustine, and the Troubadours* (Ithaca: Cornell University Press, 1988), p. 86.
8. Anne Carson, *Eros the Bittersweet* (1986; repr. Normal, IL: Dalkey Archive Press, 1998), p. 73.
9. Slavoj Zizek, *Did Somebody Say Totalitarianism? Five Interventions in the (Mis)use of a Notion* (London and New York: Verso, 2001), p. 1.
10. Anne Carson emphasizes the edginess of eros in several chapters of *Eros the Bittersweet*, where she notes its connection to writing: "As eros insists upon

the edges of human beings and of the spaces between them, the written consonant imposes edge on the sounds of human speech and insists on the reality of that edge, although it has its origin in the reading and writing imagination" (p. 55). The implications of this can be extended to larger syntactic acts, most importantly (here) literary history.

11. See *Phaedrus* 255D, where the new lover is described, in the translation of Alexander Nehamas and Paul Woodruff (Indianapolis: Hackett, 1995) as follows: "It is as if he had caught an eye disease from someone else, but could not identify the cause..." (p. 46).
12. For a more extended discussion of why it is important to stress this affective response, see my essay, "Rude Theory: The Rough Trade of the Fabliaux," in Holly A. Crocker, ed., *Comic Provocations: Exposing the Corpus of Old French Fabliaux* (New York: Palgrave Macmillan, 2006).
13. Shari Horner, *The Discourse of Enclosure* (Albany: SUNY Press, 2001), p. 140.
14. Sarah Beckwith, "Passionate Regulation: Enclosure, Ascesis, and the Feminist Imaginary," *South Atlantic Quarterly* 93.4 (Fall 1994): 819 [803–24].
15. Richard Rambuss, *Closet Devotions* (Durham: Duke University Press, 1998), pp. 134–135.
16. See "Participation: Here," the penultimate section of chapter 1, for the "greater density, beyond all contrasts of density and lightness," to which a poetics of participation is fundamentally committed.
17. Anne Carson, "Just for the Thrill: An Essay on the Difference between Women and Men," *Plainwater* (New York: Knopf, 1995), p. 239.
18. Francisco X. Alarcón, "Eros," *From the Other Side of Night = Del Otro Lado de la noche* (Tucson: University of Arizona Press, 2002).
19. Adam Phillips, *Houdini's Box* (London: Faber and Faber, 2001), p. 48.
20. Thomas of Celano, as summarized by Jerydene M. Wood, describes Clare's escape from her family to the Porziuncula with attention to "her miraculous exit through an unused, sealed-up, and very heavy door" whose genital resonance, particularly given the Marian tone of this *vita*, could hardly be stronger (Wood, *Women, Art, and Spirituality*, p. 20).

Chapter 1   The Edge of Enclosure

1. Stacey D'Erasmo, *A Seahorse Year* (New York: Houghton Mifflin, 2004), p. 148.
2. Martin Heidegger, "The Origin of the Work of Art," in ed. and trans. David Farrell Krell, *Basic Writings* (San Francisco: HarperSanFrancisco, 1993), p. 181.
3. See *De doctrina christiana* III.10–12. Indeed, Augustine is not of one mind on the issue, arguing against believers who seek to explain away disturbing bits of Scripture while simultaneously urging a stringent contextualization of such upsetting phenomena as nakedness. In the translation of D. W. Robertson, Jr., *On Christian Doctrine* (Upper Saddle River, NJ: Macmillan, 1958), Augustine notes, "If it is shameful to strip

the body of clothing at the banquets of the drunken and lascivious, it is not on this account shameful to be naked in the baths. Careful attention is therefore to be paid to what is proper to places, times, and persons lest we condemn the shameful too hastily" (III.12.18–19; pp. 90–91). The baths are far from innocent, as amply demonstrated by Augustine's own experience in *Confessions* 2.3, trans. Pine-Coffin, p. 45: "One day at the public baths he [Augustine's father] saw the signs of active virility coming to life in me."

4. Allen J. Frantzen, *Before the Closet: Same-Sex Love from Beowulf to Angels in America* (Chicago: University of Chicago Press, 1998), pp. 9, 25.
5. Frantzen, *Before the Closet*, p. 20.
6. Hans Ulrich Gumbrecht, *In 1926: Living at the Edge of Time* (Cambridge, MA: Harvard University Press, 1997), p. 424.
7. Louise Fradenburg and Carla Freccero, "Introduction," *Premodern Sexualities* (New York: Routledge, 1996), p. xxi.
8. This is Betty Radice's translation. See *The Letters of Abelard and Heloise* (Harmondsworth: Penguin, 1974), p. 75.
9. Rafael Campo, "The Failure of Empathy on Center Street," in *Diva* (Durham: Duke University Press, 1999), p. 53 [51–53]. The italics are his.
10. In the preface to his exposé of the restaurant business, *Kitchen Confidential* (New York: The Ecco Press, 2000), Anthony Bourdain writes, "I wanted my little memoir/rant to reflect the somewhat claustrophobic worldview of the professional cook—that slightly paranoid, fiercely territorial mix of pride and resignation that allows so many of us to get up every morning and do the things we do" (p. xii). Here too claustrophobia is "territorial," and thus implicitly desirous of the enclosure it fears.
11. This is a gross simplification of the thrust of early queer theory, especially in the vein of Eve Sedgwick's *Between Men* (New York: Columbia University Press, 1985) and *The Epistemology of the Closet* (Berkeley: University of California Press, 1990).
12. Michael P. Brown writes, in *Closet Space: Geographies of Metaphor from the Body to the Globe* (London: Routledge, 2000), that "gay venues actively participate in the production of the closet because it is economically rational to do so" (p. 80).
13. Geoffrey Galt Harpham, *Shadows of Ethics: Criticism and the Just Society* (Durham: Duke University Press, 1999), p. 230. The critics Harpham discusses here are J. Hillis Miller and Martha Nussbaum.
14. These are described, in relation to Franciscan scholasticism, by Scott Matthews in *Reason, Community and Religious Tradition: Anselm's Argument and the Friars* (Aldershot: Ashgate, 2001), p. 69.
15. See, on this note, my discussion of Catherine Brown's delicate assessment of the middles of medievalism at the end of chapter 5.
16. This ambivalence, and its attendant anxiety, is staged in a 2001 video installation by the artist Andrea Contin "consisting of a model house inside of which has been placed a closed-circuit videocamera transmitting to a TV positioned next to it. The model room is empty. But it is the realistic effect of

the video, in contrast with the dimensions of the room (those of a guinea pig's cage), that transforms the game into a test of the anxiety produced by the two together, useful for measuring our index of claustrophilia."'(My translation from Raffaele Gavarro's Italian at http://www.colomboarte.com/it/artisti/enolaplay/cataloghi/cataloghi.htm.)

17. "Desfoutue," as Simon Gaunt points out in his chapter on the fabliau in *Gender and genre* (Cambridge: Cambridge University Press, 1995), would more literally be rendered "unfucked" (p. 258), but the reversal here doesn't undo so much as do damage: to be unfucked is to be fucked over. See "Celle qui fu foutue et desfoutue por une grue," in Luciano Rossi and Richard Straub, eds., *Fabliaux érotiques* (Paris: Livre de Poche, 1992), pp. 185–97. All line references are to this edition.

18. All references are to Maria Jolas's translation, *The Poetics of Space* (New York: Orion Press, 1964), followed by the French text of *La poétique de l'espace*, fifth edition (Paris: Presses Universitaires de France, 1967).

19. Bachelard, *Poetics*, p. 219; *Poétique*, p. 197.

20. For the notion of "shelter" as opposed to a (presumably Heideggerian) understanding of thrownness, see the first chapter of *Poetics*.

21. Bachelard, *Poetics*, p. xxxi; *Poétique*, p. 17.

22. Bachelard, *Poetics*, p. xxxii; *Poétique*, pp. 17–18.

23. Bachelard, *Poetics*, p. 229; *Poétique*, p. 205: "Often it is from the very fact of concentration in the most restricted intimate space that the dialectics of inside and outside draws its strength" (C'est souvent par la concentration même dans l'espace intime le plus réduit que la dialectique du dedans et du dehors prend toute sa force).

24. Bachelard, *Poetics*, p. 85; *Poétique*, p. 88.

25. Bachelard, *Poetics*, p. 227; *Poétique*, p. 203.

26. Bachelard, *Poetics*, p. 161; *Poétique*, p. 150.

27. In *Gaston Bachelard: Critic of Science and the Imagination* (London: Routledge, 2001), Christina Chimisso observes that "for Bachelard, knowledge gained in solitude had no scientific value. When Bachelard's rationalist retreats into solitude, he is no longer a rationalist, but rather a dreamer, a poet, or a human being on holiday" (p. 41).

28. Bachelard, *Poetics*, p. 214; *Poétique*, p. 193.

29. Bachelard, *Poetics*, p. 222; *Poétique*, p. 200.

30. Bachelard, *Poetics*, p. 32; *Poétique*, p. 46.

31. See Philippe Lacoue-Labarthe, *Poetry as Experience*, trans. Andrea Tarnowski (Stanford: Stanford University Press, 1999), p. 34. All citations are made in reference to this translation, followed by the French text as it appears in *La poésie comme expérience* (Paris: Christian Bourgois, 1986).

32. Lacoue-Labarthe, *Poetry*, p. 35–36; *Poésie*, p. 53.

33. Lacoue-Labarthe, *Poetry*, p. 38; *Poésie*, p. 57.

34. Bachelard, *Poetics*, p. 229; *Poétique*, p. 205.

35. The hermit-saint's refusal is indeed a topos of the hagiographic tradition. Abba Arsenius, in Abelard's citation from the *Lives of the Desert Fathers*, responds to a woman who has come to visit him, "I pray God to wipe the

NOTES   157

memory of you from my heart." See Letter 7 in *The Letters of Abelard and Heloise*, trans. Betty Radice (Harmondsworth: Penguin, 1974), p. 193.
36. Lacoue-Labarthe, *Poetry*, p. 92; *Poésie*, p. 131.
37. Lacoue-Labarthe, *Poetry*, p. 94; *Poésie*, p. 133.
38. Lacoue-Labarthe, *Poetry*, p. 94; *Poésie*, p. 133.
39. Bachelard, *Poetics*, p. 222; *Poétique*, p. 199.
40. All references are to the edition by Louis Allen in Charles Allyn Williams, *The German Legends of the Hairy Anchorite* (Champaign: University of Illinois Press, 1935), pp. 83–133. Jehan's life is discussed at length in Brigitte Cazelles, *Le corps de sainteté* (Geneva: Droz, 1982).
41. See Michel de Certeau's account of wandering mad saints in "The Monastery and the Public Square," the first chapter of *The Mystic Fable*, vol. 1, trans. Michael B. Smith (Chicago: University of Chicago Press, 1992), pp. 31–48.
42. See, however, the discussion of hands as quintessentially human, and their relationship to genitalia, in "Hand to Mouth," the third section of chapter 2.
43. Giorgio Agamben, *L'aperto: L'uomo e l'animale* (Torino: Bollati Boringhieri, 2002), p. 77.
44. Agamben, *L'aperto*, p. 58: "L'ente, per l'animale, è aperto ma non accessibile."
45. Agamben, *L'aperto*, p. 77.
46. In "The Sublime Body of the Martyr: Violence in Early Romance Saints' Lives," in Richard W. Kaeuper, ed., *Violence in Medieval Society* (Woodbridge: Boydell, 2000), Sarah Kay describes a parallel structure in the medieval lives of virgin martyrs, where the ambivalence in question has to do not with ethics but with embodiment. "The martyred philosophers [in the Old French life of St. Catherine] have 'sublime bodies' through which the violence addressed to them might become capable of indefinite prolongation (they could remain in their perfect state for ever, apparently) but which also 'embody' their belief in an immortality against which mere physical violence is powerless; the 'sublime body' both expresses, and resists, the destructive urge to which it is subject" (pp. 8–9). I would add merely that, in Jehan's life, this "destructive urge" is not so much independent of, or external to, the saint as constitutive of, and internal to, him—a question that again sets in motion the disclosive/enclosive intensification discussed above.
47. See Edith Wyschogrod, *Saints and Postmodernism: Revisioning Moral Philosophy* (Chicago: University of Chicago Press, 1990), p. xxiii.
48. Wyschogrod, *Saints*, p. xx.
49. Jean Genet, *Funeral Rites*, trans. Bernard Frechtman (New York: Grove, 1969), pp. 17–18. The French text is from Jean Genet, *Oeuvres complètes*, vol. 3 (Paris: Gallimard, 1953).
50. For Zizek, in *Totalitarianism*, "the properly modern post- or meta-tragic situation occurs when a higher necessity compels me to betray the very ethical substance of my being" (p. 14). Yet the examples he

gives—Abraham's sacrifice of Isaac, and an enigmatic "Christian" who sacrifices his soul for "God's glory"—suggest that "modern" does not primarily designate a specific historical moment so much as a resistance to the inexorable logic of classical fatalism and its fetishism of the unknown crime. See the related discussion of fatalistic circularity in chapter 2.

51. Heidegger, "Origin," p. 171.
52. Heidegger, "Origin," p. 172.
53. Euripides, *Iphigeneia in Tauris*, trans. Richmond Lattimore (New York: Oxford University Press, 1973), p. 14.
54. Euripides, *Tauris*, p. 15.
55. Euripides, *Tauris*, p. 15.
56. Euripides, *Tauris*, p. 16.
57. Euripides, *Tauris*, p. 53.
58. Euripides, *Tauris*, pp. 54, 56.
59. For the distinction between "presence effects" and "meaning effects," see Hans Ulrich Gumbrecht, *The Production of Presence* (Stanford: Stanford University Press, 2003).
60. Heidegger, "Origin," p. 180.
61. Euripides, *Tauris*, p. 56.
62. Phillips, *Houdini's Box*, p. 149.
63. Phillips, *Houdini's Box*, pp. 45–46.
64. Heidegger, "Origin," p. 194.
65. Heidegger, "Origin," p. 181.
66. Euripides, *Iphigeneia at Aulis*, trans. W. S. Merwin and George E. Dimock, Jr. (New York: Oxford University Press, 1978), pp. 95, 94.
67. Kaja Silverman, *World Spectators* (Stanford: Stanford University Press, 2000), p. 17.
68. Silverman, "Total Visibility: Rethinking Jeff Wall's Early Work," lecture given at Stanford University, March 2003.
69. Nora Gallagher, *Things Seen and Unseen: A Year Lived in Faith* (New York: Knopf, 1998), p. 125.
70. "A moment arrives when one can no longer feel anything but anger, an absolute anger, against so many discourses, so many texts that have no other care than to make a little more sense, to redo or to perfect delicate works of signification." See Jean-Luc Nancy, *The Birth to Presence* (Stanford: Stanford University Press, 1993), p. 6.
71. Slavoj Zizek, *The Sublime Object of Ideology* (London: Verso, 1989), p. 53.
72. Slavoj Zizek, *The Fragile Absolute* (London: Verso, 2000), p. 24.
73. Sigmund Freud, "Fetishism," in the *Standard Edition of the Complete Psychological Works of Sigmund Freud*, trans. James Strachey (London: Hogarth, 1961), vol. 21, p. 154. This particular mode of the fetish radicalizes, as well, its historicity: whereas for William Pietz, the fetish "is above all a 'historical' object, the enduring material form and force of an unrepeatable event," I would add that the fetishized *objet petit a* endures only inasmuch as it defers, or, in more spatial terms, takes up the intervening space that it

never ceases to open. See Emily Apter's introduction in Emily Apter and William Pietz, eds., *Fetishism as Cultural Discourse* (Ithaca: Cornell University Press, 1993), p. 3.

74. Indeed, the story of Medusa's head is fundamentally about a look that *will not let go*. This is what I take to be the insight of Zizek's observation that "the object that fascinates [the spectator] becomes the gaze itself" (*Totalitarianism*, p. 80). The spectacle of the Gorgon is petrifying, in other words, because there is something petrifying about the way she is looked *at*: phallic immobility, hypostasized in the appropriative gaze, produces only itself. To drop one's eyes, here, would be to refuse to freeze the Gorgon into the knowable embodiment of the unknowable, the (disclosed) masculine frame around an (enclosed) feminized absence. It would be to ask, what does the Gorgon see? Thus, it would be to assent, first and foremost, to being seen; and thereby to emerge continually from this gaze, instead of freezing it with one's own. This would amount to a new, dynamic dialectic of disclosure and enclosure, beyond the stasis imposed by fetishism.

75. Silverman, *World Spectators*, p. 55.

76. Silverman, *World Spectators*, p. 48.

77. John Milbank, Catherine Pickstock, and Graham Ward, "Introduction," *Radical Orthodoxy* (London: Routledge, 2000), p. 4.

78. Catherine Pickstock, *After Writing: On the Liturgical Consummation of Philosophy* (Oxford: Blackwell, 1998), p. 122.

79. Pickstock, *After Writing*, p. 49: "Without eternity, space must be made absolute and the uncertainty of time's source and end must be suppressed." See also p. 123: "The abandonment of participation in Being encouraged the establishment of *contractual* relations between the creature and God. . . This was combined with an increased emphasis upon the sovereignty of God's will."

80. André Vauchez, *Saints, prophètes et visionnaires: Le pouvoir surnaturel au Moyen Age* (Paris: Albin Michel, 1999), p. 52.

81. Jean-Luc Nancy, "Corpus," *The Birth to Presence* (Stanford: Stanford University Press, 1993), p. 203.

Chapter 2 The Verge of the Visible

1. Lynne Tillman, *Haunted Houses* (1987; repr. New York and London: Serpent's Tail, 1995), p. 64.

2. For example, in the 1995 "Retrospect" to *The Sexuality of Christ in Renaissance Art and in Modern Oblivion*, second edition (Chicago: University of Chicago Press, 1996), Steinberg shows how for the Greek tradition, the life of Adam and Eve before the fall (i.e., before desire) was also pregenital: "Had disobedience not intervened, they would have lived out their days in untroubled virginity, neither female nor male" (p. 230). For Augustine, however, and for the Latin tradition after him, "the First Couple were

indeed sexed," and procreation would have occurred as it does for postlapsarian life, except without desire (p. 231).
3. Steinberg, *Sexuality*, pp. 24, 18.
4. For "formal austerity," see Steinberg, *Sexuality*, p. 41; for "licentiousness," Steinberg, *Sexuality*, p. 17.
5. *The Rule of Saint Benedict*, trans. Abbot Parry OSB (Leominster: Gracewing, 1995), pp. 7–8.
6. Henry Chadwick finds the wandering monk "an irresponsible, disturbing element" as early as the fourth century: see *The Early Church* (Harmondsworth: Penguin, 1967), p. 178.
7. Virginia Burrus observes, in *"Begotten, Not Made": Conceiving Manhood in Late Antiquity* (Stanford: Stanford University Press, 2000), that in Athanasius of Alexandria's fourth-century life of Antony, "*topos*—place itself—mediates between the cultivated body and civic culture of man" (p. 77). Benedict's anxieties are to be understood within this tradition.
8. Aelred of Rievaulx, *Rule of Life for a Recluse*, trans. Mary Paul MacPherson, in *Aelred of Rievaulx: Treatises and Pastoral Prayer* (Kalamazoo: Cistercian, 1971), p. 45.
9. Aelred, *Rule*, p. 46.
10. John Cassian, *De institutis coenobiorum* 10.2; in Giorgio Agamben, *Stanzas*, trans. Ronald L. Martinez (Minneapolis: University of Minnesota Press, 1993), p. 4. Compare E. M. Cioran's assertion in *Tears and Saints*, trans. Ilinca Zarifopol-Johnston (Chicago: University of Chicago Press, 1995) that "the dull sadness of monasteries wore an emptiness into the soul of the monks, known in the Middle Ages as *acedia*. . .It is a loathing not *of* God but *in* him" (p. 86).
11. Bonaventure, *Breviloquium* 3.9; see Morton W. Bloomfield, *The Seven Deadly Sins* (Lansing: Michigan State University Press, 1967), p. 89.
12. The citation is from Ezekiel 16:49. See Bella Millet and Jocelyn Wogan-Browne eds., *Medieval English Prose for Women* (Oxford: Oxford University Press, 1990), p. 141.
13. Peter F. Dembowski, *La vie de Sainte Marie l'Egyptienne: Versions en ancien et en moyen français* (Geneva: Droz, 1977), p. 21. All references within my text will be to the line numbers of version T, pp. 33–66; the translations (and all errors therein) are entirely mine.
14. The description of Mary's pre-repentance life of prostitution as "hyperbolique" and "perverse" is from Brigitte Cazelles, "Modèle ou mirage: Marie l'Egyptienne," *The French Review* 53.1 (October 1979): 16.
15. Notice, too, how Marie is the *object* of luxuria, which grabs her: she is, as it were, the vice's passive agent. On the use of *luxuria* in a homoerotic context, with an emphasis on the difficulty of defining it, see Mark D. Jordan's *The Invention of Sodomy in Christian Theology* (Chicago: University of Chicago Press, 1997). Albert the Great, according to Jordan's reading, argues that *luxuria* consists in the misuse of the "generative power" (p. 128); though a restriction of most twelfth-century notions of the vice, it resonates

deeply with the argument I develop about Jehan Bouche d'Or later in this chapter.

16. Simon Gaunt, *Gender and Genre in Medieval French Literature* (Cambridge: Cambridge University Press, 1995), p. 216.

17. See Duncan Robertson, "Authority and Anonymity: The Twelfth-Century French Life of St. Mary the Egyptian," in Renate Blumenfeld-Kosinski, Kevin Brownlee, Mary B. Speer and Lori J. Walters, eds., *Translatio Studii: Essays by His Students in Honor of Karl D. Uitti for His Sixty-Fifth Birthday* (Amsterdam and Atlanta: Rodopi, 2000), p. 251.

18. Gaunt, "Saints," p. 219.

19. See on a related note the fabliau-like account of Saint Caquette, whose vaginal reliquary is the object of some discussion in Bruno Roy, "Getting to the Bottom of St. Caquette's Cult," in Jan M. Ziolkowski, ed., *Obscenity: Social Control and Artistic Creation in the European Middle Ages* (Leiden: Brill, 1998), pp. 308–18.

20. Karl D. Uitti, "The Clerkly Narrator Figure in Old French Hagiography and Romance," *Medioevo romanzo* 2.3 (1975): 397.

21. It is possible, however, to conceive of a less charitable version of this community, one in which heteronormative masculinity would take shape through the shared spectacle of the female body. Such a reading might find echoes in Linda Williams's eloquent reading of stag film in *Hard Core: Power, Pleasure, and the Frenzy of the Visible*, second edition (Berkeley: University of California Press, 1999), pp. 58–92. In a characteristic passage, Williams writes, "The visual pleasure of the stag film might thus be described as a prolonged oscillation between two poles of pleasure. The first is inherited from, but more extensive than, the striptease: it is the pleasure of the collective male group expressing its heterosexual desire for the bodies of women on display. In this pleasure the woman's body mediates the achievement of masculine identity. The second pole of pleasure [sic] consists in moving toward, but never fully achieving, identification with a male protagonist who performs sexual acts with the female body that shows itself to the viewer" (p. 80).

22. Uitti, "Clerkly Narrator," p. 396.

23. Here I want to mark my appreciation for Virginia Burrus' recent eroticized engagement (of a very different order from Uitti's) with the corpus of late antique lives of "holy harlots." At one point in *The Sex Lives of Saints* (Philadelphia: University of Pennsylvania Press, 2003), Burrus observes, "We have, perhaps, been unwilling to surrender to the power of the unabashed (possibly even unrepentant) pleasure that inheres in these texts. For what is conversion itself, if not a form of seduction—a conquest matched by an acquiescence to conquest, whether by a man or a God? Are the asymmetrical relations of power effected by seduction not, furthermore, peculiarly reversible? (Is the saint not marked equally by her seductiveness and her seducibility?)" (p. 131). My comments, in what follows, are merely

intended to flesh out phenomenologically and spatially the account of seduction that Burrus begins to give in her book.

24. Michel de Certeau, "Une variante: l'édification hagio-graphique," in *L'Écriture de l'histoire* (Paris: Gallimard, 1975), p. 282. Certeau's thesis also seems to articulate in narrative terms something akin to the way in which, in Leo Steinberg's reading, Christ's infant body is "at all times the Incarnation—very man, very God" (p. 10), as well as the repeated visual connections between the first and last wounds of the Circumcision and Passion. (These connections are corroborated textually in the *Legenda Aurea* and elsewhere: see Steinberg, *Sexuality*, p. 57.) There is no real process of becoming between Circumcision and Passion, unless it is a becoming-apparent.

25. Brigitte Cazelles and Phyllis Johnson, *Le Vain Siecle Guerpir* (Chapel Hill: University of North Carolina Press, 1979), p. 153.

26. Cazelles and Johnson, *Le Vain Siecle Guerpir*, p. 107.

27. That a bodily turn might mark a new mode of saintly visibility is also suggested by Hubert Damisch's account of the frescoes attributed to Giotto in the church of San Francesco at Assisi, in *A Theory of /Cloud/: Toward a History of Painting*, trans. Janet Lloyd (Stanford: Stanford University Press, 2002). We know that Francis appears to the monks in the Arles chapter house in an extraordinary way (i.e., as an apparition, an inflection of the sensible beyond conventional materiality) because he enters the frame from the right, when the entire narrative sequence of the frescoes has been oriented from the left: "When he does turn back in this fashion, thereby contradicting the general orientation of the cycle, the movement is clearly designed to signify a break with the past: the march of history proceeds from left to right" (p. 96).

28. Certeau, *The Mystic Fable*, p. 35; *La fable mystique* (Paris: Gallimard, 1982), p. 53. See, too, the bodily inflection of the "riche théâtre d'entrées et sorties" in Certeau, "Une variante," p. 285.

29. Cazelles, "Modèle," p. 19.

30. Cazelles, *Le corps*, pp. 27–28.

31. Cazelles, *Le corps*, p. 27.

32. Robertson, "Authority," p. 247.

33. All references here are made to Paris MS Arsenal 3516, as transcribed by Brigitte Cazelles.

34. Ellen Swanberg, "*Oraisons* and Liaisons: Romanesque Didacticism in *La Vie de Sainte Marie l'Egyptienne*," *Romance Notes* 23.1 (Fall 1982): 70.

35. Cazelles, *Le corps*, p. 124.

36. Cazelles, *Le corps*, p. 63.

37. A similar link between repetition and idleness can be found in the closing lines of the thirteenth-century Italian poet Iacopone da Todi's laud 21, "La Bontat'enfinita vòl enfinito amore," in which the lyric voice practically stutters, "O time, time, time, in how much evil is he submerged who does not govern you wisely, spending you in idleness!" (O tempo, tempo, tempo, en quanto mal sumerge / a chi non te correge, passanno te oziato;

NOTES 163

41–42). See *Laude*, ed. Franco Mancini (Bari: Laterza, 1974), p. 60, and my discussion of Iacopone in chapter 3.
38. See, too, the discussion of Iacopone's tongue, the papal anus, and the intervening page in chapter 3, "Tongues and Tails."
39. Cazelles, *Le corps*, p. 199.
40. Seth Lerer, "*Transgressio Studii*: Writing and Sexuality in Guibert of Nogent," *Stanford French Review* 14.1–2 (Spring–Fall 1990): 263 [243–66].
41. John Milbank and Catherine Pickstock write, citing *Summa contra Gentiles* IV.41 (7), (11), (12), that "a hand [as opposed to an axe, which would be an 'entirely accidental instrument of the soul'] is rather an 'organic' instrument of the soul," and " 'the tongue is the intellect's *own* organ.' " See *Truth in Aquinas* (London: Routledge, 2001), p. 71.
42. Milbank and Pickstock, *Truth*, p. 83: "There are certain hints that the ontological reversal accomplished by the Incarnation pivots about touch. We have already seen that the absolutely new ontological possibility realized by the hypostatic union is compared by [Aquinas] to the conjoining of a hand to a person as his 'proper instrument' of touch and formation. As a 'proper accident', this hand is involved in the event and events of touching, which are contingent and yet fully belong to the person who touches. Likewise the human nature comes, in time, to inhere in the *Logos*, yet now existentially belongs to it, in the most absolute sense."
43. Milbank and Pickstock, *Truth*, p. 71.
44. For Aquinas all sensation is a kind of touch. See Milbank and Pickstock, *Truth*, p. 77.
45. Duby, *A History of Private Life*, vol. 2, trans. Arthur Goldhammer (Cambridge MA: Belknap, 1988), pp. 51, 63.
46. Duby, *Private Life*, p. 520.
47. Duby, *Private Life*, pp. 523–24.
48. Duby, *Private Life*, p. 528.
49. Certeau, *Mystic Fable*, p. 70; *Fable mystique*, p. 97. His emphasis.
50. Enders is here especially concerned with the status of pain in the midst of all these permeable architectural bodies: see "The Architecture of the Body in Pain," pp. 96–111 of the second chapter of *The Medieval Theater of Cruelty* (Ithaca: Cornell University Press, 1999).
51. Certeau, *Mystic Fable* 82; *Fable mystique*, p. 110.
52. Duby remarks, cursorily but significantly, that "idleness was particularly dangerous for such feeble creatures [as women]" (*Private Life*, p. 79).
53. Indeed, what is "retraite" here is as much (etymologically, as "re-trahere") a drawing as a drag, not just the hinge between the obscene and the sacred, but the point at which they smear. See chapter 4.
54. The translation is from the Douay-Rheims version (Rockford: Tan Books, 1971). The Vulgate can be found at http://www.lib.uchicago.edu/efts/ARTFL/public/bibles/vulgate.search.html.
55. All the same, its enclosed and enclosive dimension distinguishes this extension from what Catherine Pickstock describes as the "new [Cartesian] construal of material reality as *extensio*, an homogeneous quantity divided into degrees

of motion and mechanical causes, and grasped fully in its givenness" (*After Writing*, p. 63). The pregnant princess amply demonstrates the fallacy of any attempt to grasp fully and immediately an only quantitatively differentiated given.

56. Emma Campbell, "Separating the Saints from the Boys: Sainthood and Masculinity in the Old French *Vie de Saint Alexis*," *French Studies* 57.4 (2003): 455 [447–62].
57. "Vie de Saint Marine," ed. Léon Clugnet, *Revue de l'Orient Chrétien* 8 (1903), p. 298.
58. In contrast, in the Old French life of Saint Euphrosine, another transvestite monk, it is the (female) saint's masculinity—as the product of "clothes, language, gestures"—which is desired by the monastic community. In Simon Gaunt's reading, "It is less her body that is desired, than an image of masculinity that turns out to be performative. Not only is the monks' desire homosexual, but for Euphrosine's body to be desirable to them, it needs to be dressed in men's clothes." If Euphrosine's fellow monks are content to look *at* her, not *through* her, the same could be said of Marina; and yet it is precisely the surface which is so troubling (and so temporally and spatially ambivalent) here. It is not a question of stripping off the masculine accident to arrive at a (temporally lost but eternally recuperated) feminine substance; rather, Marina's genital 'e' marks her femininity as between accident and substance, utterly contingent yet integral to her bodily specificity. Her genital display, this complex superficial show, is thus far more radical than queer performativity. See Gaunt, "Straight Minds / 'Queer Wishes' in Old French Hagiography: *La vie de Sainte Euphrosine*," in Carla Freccero and Louise Fradenburg, eds., *Premodern Sexualities* (New York: Routledge, 1996), p. 165 [155–73].
59. See my discussion of Nancy's *Sense of the World* at the end of chapter 3.
60. Lacoue-Labarthe, *Poetry*, p. 18; *Poésie*, pp. 30–31.
61. Jean-Luc Nancy, "Introduction: The Birth to Presence," in *The Birth to Presence*, trans. Brian Holmes et al. (Stanford: Stanford University Press, 1993), p. 5.
62. "Une théologie est toujours investie dans le discours hagiographique" ("Une variante," p. 284).
63. Lacoue-Labarthe, *Poetry*, p. 96; *Poésie*, p. 136.
64. Thom Gunn, "Touch," *Collected Poems* (New York: Farrar, Straus and Giroux, 1994), p. 169.
65. Thom Gunn, "Here Come the Saints," *Collected Poems*, p. 4.
66. See my discussion of intimate immensity in the final section of chapter 4.
67. This occurs, for example, at line 869 in Jehan's life.
68. "The threshold of the visible" famously names the moment of identification with specular wholeness which Jacques Lacan describes in his essay on the mirror stage, "Le stade du miroir comme formateur de la fonction du Je," *Écrits*, vol. 1 (Paris: Seuil, 1966), p. 91, where the "specular image" seen by the baby in the mirror "seems to be the threshold of the visible world," a visibility characterized by its fictive wholeness and propriety: "Pour les *imagos*

en effet. . .l'image spéculaire semble être le seuil du monde visible, si nous nous fions à la disposition en miroir que présente dans l'hallucination et dans le rêve l'*imago du corps propre*. . ."

Chapter 3 Spaced Out

1. Experience, however, also invokes the distinctly sensory and embodied notion of *experientia* current in affective piety since the Cistercians. Caroline Walker Bynum observes, in "The Cistercian Conception of Community," *Jesus as Mother: Studies in the Spirituality of the High Middle Ages* (Berkeley: University of California Press, 1982), pp. 59–81, "to Cistercians, learning by experience becomes deeply affective and sensual: experience means 'tasting,' 'embracing,' an almost tactile meeting with God" (p. 79).
2. For Ernesto Menestò, also the editor of the existing medieval lives of Iacopone, he is a "uomo emblematico del suo secolo"; see "La figura di Iacopone da Todi," in *Iacopone da Todi: Atti del XXXVII Convegno storico internazionale, Todi, 8–11 ottobre 2000* (Spoleto: Centro italiano di studi sull'alto medioevo, 2001), p. 3 [3–19].
3. Almost every study of Iacopone contains some small summary of his life. See, for example, George T. Peck, *The Fool of God: Jacopone da Todi* (University, AL: University of Alabama Press, 1980).
4. Paolo Canettieri, "*Laude* di Iacopone da Todi," in Alberto Asor Rosa, ed., vol. 1 *Letteratura italiana: le opere*, 8 vols. (Turin: Einaudi, 1992), p. 126 [121–52].
5. Jennifer Fisk Rondeau, "Conducting Gender: Theories and Practices in Italian Confraternity Literature," in Kathleen Ashley and Robert L. A. Clark, eds., *Medieval Conduct* (Minneapolis: University of Minnesota Press, 2001), p. 203.
6. Lino Leonardi and Francesco Santi, "La letteratura religiosa," in Enrico Malato, ed., vol. 1 *Storia della letteratura italiana*, 10 vols. (Rome: Salerno, 1995), p. 369 [339–404].
7. Aelred of Rievaulx, *Mirror of Charity* 3.110.11, as cited in John Boswell, *Christianity, Social Tolerance, and Homosexuality* (Chicago: University of Chicago Press, 1980), p. 225. See also Frederick S. Roden, "Aelred of Rievaulx, Same-Sex Desire and the Victorian Monastery," in Andrew Bradstock, Sean Gill, Anne Hogan, and Sue Morgan, eds., *Masculinity and Spirituality in Victorian Culture* (New York: St. Martin's, 2000), pp. 85–99.
8. Peter of the Morrone (Celestine V), *Autobiography*, trans. George Ferzoco, in Thomas Head, ed., *Medieval Hagiography: An Anthology* (New York: Garland, 2000), p. 735.
9. Peter of the Morrone, *Autobiography*, p. 740.
10. "L'Autobiografia di Pietro Celestino," in Arsenio Frugoni, *Celestiniana* (Rome: Istituto storico italiano per il medio evo, 1954/1991) 64.36–65.5.
11. This symmetry of the senses is in marked contrast to the way in which Iacopone inscribes a conflict between vision and sound at the heart of mystical sensation: see "Close to the Knives," later in this chapter.

12. See Dyan Elliott, "Pollution, Illusion and Masculine Disarray," in *Karma Lochrie, Peggy McCracken, and James A. Schultz, eds., Constructing Medieval Sexuality* (Minneapolis: University of Minnesota Press, 1997), pp. 1–23.
13. Iacopone, in fact, speaks of mortifying his body as "marcerar meo aseno" at 43.40, according to the numbering of Franco Mancini, ed., *Laude* (Bari: Laterza, 1974).
14. See Elliott, "Pollution," p. 11. The incident occurs on pp. 738–39 of Ferzoco's translation.
15. Jean Leclercq notes, in the context of Romuald's importance for Damian, that "As in the times of the Desert Fathers and the companions of St Francis, and each time that a powerful movement of religious fervor appears, an array of unexpected, paradoxical situations present themselves, which couldn't have been imagined if they hadn't been born of the [saint's] life itself. Those which Peter Damian brings out are marked by the austerities proper to the milieu to which he testifies. [Comme au temps des Pères du désert et des compagnons de saint François, et chaque fois qu'apparaît un puissant mouvement de ferveur, une foule de situations inattendues, paradoxales, se présentent, qu'on n'aurait pu imaginer si la vie même ne les avait fait naître. Celles que rapporte Pierre Damien sont marquées par les austérités propres au milieu dont il est le témoin.]" See *Saint Pierre Damien: Hermite et Homme d'Église* (Rome: Edizioni di Storia e Letteratura, 1960), p. 204.
16. "*Inurbamento* et observance érémitique ne sont compatibles que dès lors que l'érémitisme est vécu et conçu davantage comme 'un état d'esprit qu'une forme de vie,' pour reprendre l'expression d'André Vauchez." Cécile Caby, *De l'érémitisme rural au monachisme urbain: Les camaldules en Italie à la fin du Moyen Âge* (Rome: École française de Rome, 1999), pp. 792–93.
17. Caby, *Érémitisme*, p. 232: "Si l'érémitisme des XIe et XIIe siècles fuit la ville et cherche les déserts, celui de la fin du Moyen Âge, sur les traces de l'expérience décisive de saint François d'Assise, est toujours davantage marqué par l'urbanocentrisme."
18. On the extent to which speech and (at times sexual) violence were intertwined in medieval pedagogy, see the essays by Jody Enders and Marjorie Curry Woods, in Rita Copeland, ed., *Criticism and Dissent in the Middle Ages* (Cambridge, UK: Cambridge University Press, 1996).
19. Peter Damian, *Life of St. Romuald of Ravenna* 49, trans. Henrietta Leyser, in Head, *Hagiography*, pp. 309–10.
20. Although Leyser is translating from Tabacco's 1957 critical edition, I am citing (given its relative accessibility) the Latin of *PL* 144: 469 (O995A-0995B).
21. The variant can be found in C. W. Aspland, ed., *A Medieval French Reader* (Oxford: Clarendon, 1979), p. 32. Interestingly, "hermites" rhymes with both of these, and immediately precedes the declaration of sodomy/heresy in Lecoy's accepted edition: "Leres, leres, fait li hermites, / tu es pires que sodomites." These lines (63–64 in Aspland) can be found at 771–72 in Franco Romanelli's bilingual edition of Lecoy, *Il cavaliere e l'eremita* (Milano: Luni Editrice, 1987), pp. 66–67.

22. Mark D. Jordan, *The Invention of Sodomy in Christian Theology* (Chicago: University of Chicago Press, 1997), p. 29; see also pp. 45–66.
23. 31.6.71–72 and 31.9.123 in G. I. Gargano and N. D'Acunto, eds., *Opere di Pier Damiani: Lettere 22–40* (Rome: Città Nuova, 2001). All translations of the *Liber* are mine, with the help of the Italian edition.
24. Damian, *Lettere*, 31.16.272–81.
25. The church as body and building thus bears a strong resemblance to the park landscape enclosed by sky in Tillman's *Haunted Houses*: "Everything in the park seemed sharp, crisp, enclosed by the cold blue sky. The landscape was a jigsaw puzzle whose pieces could all break apart if touched" (p. 36). The difference lies, of course, in Damian's disavowal: the enclosure is abject inasmuch as it is thought to be unbroken.
26. *Rhetorica ad Herennium* 4.32.43, trans. Harry Caplan for Loeb Classical Library (Cambridge, MA: Harvard University Press, 1989), p. 335.
27. Damian thus provides a striking premodern example of what Lee Edelman describes, in *Homographesis: Essays in Gay Literary and Cultural Theory* (New York: Routledge, 1994), as the "double operation" (or what I would call the ambivalence) of homographesis as both a regulatory inscription of sexuality and the difference internal to this inscription. "Invoking, in this way, the aleatory collocations of metonymy to call into question metaphor's claim for the correspondence of essences or positive qualities present in themselves, homographesis (as it articulates the [differential] logic of the homograph) works to deconstruct homographesis (as it designates the marking of a distinct and legible homosexual identity)" (p. 13).
28. Bill Burgwinkle summarizes Peter's obsession with total visibility as follows: "Peter claims the ability to see what cannot be seen (omnia visibilia et invisibilia), to see what others must wait until death to see, even to see what the sinner cannot see in himself." See his essay, "Visible and Invisible Bodies and Subjects in Peter Damian," in Emma Campbell and Robert Mills, eds., *Troubled Vision* (New York: Palgrave, 2004), p. 48 [47–62].
29. Despite their radically different aims, Damian's logic here is similar to that of Alarcón's "cerradura," as described at the end of chapter 1.
30. Bruno Roy alleges, provocatively if ambiguously, that for medieval culture "obscenity was not moral, but rhetorical" (p. 317).
31. Damian, *Lettere*, 31.23.371.
32. See Carolyn Dinshaw on kissing and the disavowed homoerotics of the gift in *Sir Gawain and the Green Knight*: "A Kiss Is Just a Kiss," *Diacritics* 24.2–3 (Summer/Fall 1994): 205–26. Michael Camille similarly writes, in "Gothic Signs and the Surplus: The Kiss on the Cathedral," in Daniel Poirion and Nancy Freeman Regalado, eds., *Contexts: Style and Values in Medieval Art and Literature*, special edition of *Yale French Studies* (New Haven: Yale University Press, 1991), p. 151 [151–70], "During the Middle Ages the kiss was paradigmatic of the rich potentiality of the sign since it always led directly to something else." Damian's mouth-to-mouth metonymy shows that what the kiss leads *to* is always mixed up in where it is led *from*: in the

kiss, my mouth is dragged into yours. See the exposition of this sense of drag in the first section of chapter 4, "Dragging the Song."
33. See Jordan, *Sodomy*, pp. 60–61.
34. See *Phaedrus*, trans. Alexander Nehamas and Paul Woodruff (Indianapolis: Hackett, 1995). At 255d, Socrates announces, "Then the boy is in love, but has no idea what he loves. He does not understand, and cannot explain, what has happened to him. It is as if he had caught an eye disease from someone else, but could not identify the cause; he does not realize that he is seeing himself in the lover as in a mirror" (p. 46). So too does Damian's cleric risk seeing his reflection in the ostensible object of vision.
35. See Jehan's "hand and mouth" problem in chapter 2.
36. Indeed, he *saw* it in flames ("vidit"): Damian, *Life*, p. 310; Damian, *Vita*, PL 49.470.0995C.
37. Benedict, *Rule*, p. 7.
38. Benedict, *Regula*, PL 66.38.245B–46A.
39. These four versions can be found side by side in *The Complete Parallel Bible* (Oxford and New York: Oxford University Press, 1993).
40. Mark D. Jordan, *The Ethics of Sex* (Oxford: Blackwell, 2002), p. 96.
41. The translation is mine, inasmuch as this episode is not included in the published version of Leyser's translation.
42. Chapter 61 of Damian, *Vita*, PL 49.476.1001C-D.
43. *Rhetorica* 4.32.43, trans. Caplan, p. 337. The examples given are, first, calling Italians "Italy" and Greeks "Greece"; second, calling wealth "gold or silver or ivory."
44. Dalibor Vesely, "The Architectonics of Embodiment," in George Dodds and Robert Tavernor, eds., *Body and Building: Essays on the Changing Relation of Body and Architecture* (Cambridge, MA: MIT Press, 2002), p. 32 [28–43].
45. See Milbank and Pickstock, *Truth*, pp. 61–63.
46. Patricia Parker, "Metaphor and Catachresis," in John Bender and David Wellbery, eds., *The Ends of Rhetoric* (Stanford: Stanford University Press, 1989).
47. What I am suggesting here is not far from Denys Turner's claim, in *The Darkness of God: Negativity in Christian Mysticism* (Cambridge, UK: Cambridge University Press, 1995), p. 7, that "in the classical period of medieval theology, the *metaphors* of negativity are interpenetrated by a high Neoplatonic *dialectics* of negativity." Metonymy, in my analysis, functions as the point at which metaphor and neoplatonic dialectics (of participation) meet.
48. All references to Iacopone's poems cite laud and verse according to Mancini's edition. The translations are mine. An English version of the *Laude* nonetheless exists (trans. Serge and Elizabeth Hughes; New York: Paulist, 1982), which captures Iacopone's spirit while remaining too free for close textual scrutiny.
49. *Inferno* 31.97–31.99, 103–05, trans. Allen Mandelbaum (Berkeley: University of California Press, 1980), p. 273.
50. After all, Briareus's "volto," literally *what has been turned*, is the specific locus of the ferocity denied here to the pilgrim's vision.

51. This is also an anti-dualistic gesture, and thus fully in the Augustinian tradition from which Bonaventure also draws heavily.
52. Francesco Santi, "La mistica di Iacopone da Todi," in *Iacopone da Todi: Atti del XXXVII Convegno storico internazionale, Todi, 8–11 ottobre 2000* (Spoleto: Centro italiano di studi sull'alto medioevo, 2001) p. 66 [47–70].
53. Bonaventure, *Itinerarium Mentis in Deum* 1.11, trans. Philotheus Boehner, O.F.M. (Saint Bonaventure, NY: Franciscan Institute, 1956), p. 45.
54. "La stupenda descrizione del 'mezzo virtuoso,' in 43, chiarisce in modo inequivocabile che il faticoso raggiungimento di tale 'mezzo' passa attraverso un coinvolgimento senza riserve negli opposti estremi dell'amore e dell'odio...eccetera: rovesciamento radicale dell'aristocratica e ragionevole *mezura*." Elena Landoni, *Il "libro" e la "sentenzia." Scrittura e significato nella poesia medievale: Iacopone da Todi, Dante, Cecco Angiolieri* (Milan: Vita e Pensiero, 1990), p. 40.
55. Guilhem de Montanhagol, *Les poésies de Guilhem de Montanhagol*, 11.28, 30, ed. Peter T. Ricketts (Toronto: Pontifical Institute, 1964), p. 111.
56. See the discussion of Wojnarowicz at the end of this chapter.
57. "Quindi, se *mezura* è senza dubbio un elemento direttivo del sistema cortese, essa va presa in quel che ha di sociale, di erotico, di etico, di estetico, non di filosofico." Among other things, he is warning here against taking too strictly the vaguely Augustinian provenance of this love of moderation. Ivos Margoni, *Fin'amors, mezura e cortezia: Saggio sulla lirica provenzale del XII secolo* (Milan: Cisalpino, 1965), p. 141.
58. Francis, in Bonaventure's account, is almost always seen either on the road or in a monastic enclosure. The importance of unexpected movement across the enclosure's threshold, akin to what we see in the French hagiographies discussed above, becomes evident in an episode from Chapter 11 of the *Legenda Maior*: "Another time it happened that two friars came from a distance to the hermitage of Greccio to see the man of God and to receive his blessing which they had desired for a long time. When they came and did not find him, because he had already withdrawn and gone to his cell, they went away quite desolate. And behold, as they were leaving, although he could not have known anything of their arrival or departure through any human perception, he came out of his cell contrary to his custom, shouted after them and blessed them in Christ's name with the sign of the cross, just as they had desired." *The Life of St. Francis*, in Bonaventure, *The Soul's Journey into God, The Tree of Life, The Life of St. Francis*, trans. Ewert Cousins (New York: Paulist, 1982), pp. 288–89 [177–327].
59. Damisch, *Cloud*, p. 108.
60. Indeed, Damisch's argument hinges upon the extent to which Renaissance perspectivism would reduce "both the forms distributed within that [pictorial] space and the intervals between them to an interplay of identifiable and substitutable elements" (p. 123). The discontinuity that enclosure—or, here, cloud—introduces would thus make room for what defies representation, for the singularity of an event that linear perspective would seek to fix in an infinitely and indifferently replicable matrix. See my remarks on the

NOTES

implications of this for contemporary literary studies in the afterword, "In Closing."
61. See Turner, *The Darkness of God*, pp. 102–34.
    Hierarchy here is understood in its Dionysian sense, as a *dynamic* chain of degrees of participation in created reality.
62. ". . .si alluderà alla possibilità di accedere, senza riprovazione, a prelature e a posti di mondana responsabilità." See the entry under "pertuso" in the glossary to the critical edition (p. 786).
63. See Laud 55 (p. 176) in their translation: "With all my asslicking around the Roman Court, / I've gotten myself thrown into prison."
64. I cannot resist pointing out that, to this day, the anus and surrounding flesh of a turkey can be referred to as the "pope's nose." I am indebted to my grandmother, Winifred Pounds, for this insight.
65. Giovanni Pozzi, "Iacopone poeta?," in *Alternatim* (Milan: Adelphi, 1996), p. 85 [73–92].
66. The reference appears amid a list of vicious loves in laud 66: "O submerged land, Sodom and Gomorrah, let he who accepts your friendship run to your side!" (o somersa contrata, Sogdoma e Gomorra, / en tua schera se 'n curra chi prende tua amistate!; 66.13–14).
67. See, in this light, Ross Chambers's discussion of the extended, cancerous tongue on the cover of Eric Michaels's AIDS diary in *Facing It: AIDS Diaries and the Death of the Author* (Ann Arbor: University of Michigan Press, 1998). Iacopone's irony similarly seeks to spur his readers to action through its inscription of ambivalence at the heart of the apparently nonproblematic, disclosive text.
68. Geoffrey Galt Harpham, "Ascetics, Aesthetics, and the Management of Desire," in Susan L. Mizruchi, ed., *Religion and Cultural Studies* (Princeton: Princeton University Press, 2001), pp. 103, 104 [95–109].
69. "Homo-ness" alludes to Leo Bersani's assertion, in *Homos* (Cambridge, MA: Harvard University Press, 1995), that "Lack, then, may not be inherent in desire; desire in homo-ness is desire to repeat, to expand, to intensify the same" (p. 149). In this way, Iacopone's anal poetics does not seek to incorporate what it lacks; rather, it repeats, expands, and intensifies what it has, but what it never has purely or alone. The papal hole abides in and is intensified by Iacopone's speech, much like Paolo's body next to Francesca (see afterword, "In Closing").
70. In *Eros and Allegory* (Kalamazoo: Cistercian, 1995), Denys Turner has described some of the precedents for Iacopone's account of negativity in mystical eros, among them the association of affectivity with negation by Thomas Gallus in his thirteenth-century commentary on the Song of Songs (p. 54).
71. Turner, *Darkness*, p. 35.
72. Evelyn Underhill, *Jacopone da Todi: A Spiritual Biography* (London: Dent, 1911), p. 84.
73. For a detailed philosophical account of eros and monastic anxiety vis-à-vis the Song, see Turner's *Eros and Allegory*. Also useful is E. Ann Matter, *The Voice of My Beloved* (Philadelphia: University of Pennsylvania Press, 1990).

NOTES 171

74. The five senses here compete to see which of them can most thoroughly renounce itself: "their frivolous delight / each one must abbreviate" (la loro delettanza leve / ciascheun brig' abriviare; 19.3–19.4).
75. Iacopone declares that he has "abbreviated" the seven "figures" of the cross shown to Saint Francis "in order to count them": ".iole abbreviate / per poterle contare" (40.9–40.10).
76. "O Measureless one, reduced to such brevity; / to see all of heaven and earth in one little vessel!" (O esmesuranza en breve redutta, / cel, terra tutta veder 'nn un vasello; 44.57–44.58).
77. In this light, the explicitly *abbreviating* effect of dwelling close to the knives in laud 43 could be read as the knives' own entrance into discourse, participating in the speaking soul.
78. See, in this regard, the account of immediacy in chapter 5.
79. Paul de Man, "The Rhetoric of Temporality," in *Blindness and Insight: Essays in the Rhetoric of Contemporary Criticism* (Minneapolis: University of Minnesota Press, 1983), pp. 191, 209.
80. Bernard of Clairvaux, *On the Song of Songs* 7.2, trans. Killian Walsh and Irene Edmonds (Kalamazoo: Cistercian, 1971). Stephen D. Moore's provocative reading of this passage, and the Song of Songs commentaries in general, shares my sense of the queerness of mystical erotics, while concentrating on earlier material and diverging significantly from my rhetorical concerns. See *God's Beauty Parlor, and Other Queer Spaces in and around the Bible* (Stanford: Stanford University Press, 2001), pp. 21–89.
81. Angela of Foligno, *Memorial*, in *Angela of Foligno: Complete Works*, translated by Paul LaChance, O.F.M. (New York: Paulist, 1993), p. 205.
82. Angela, *Memorial*, pp. 205–06.
83. See Oliver Davies's account of Eckhart in "Later Medieval Mystics," *The Medieval Theologians*, ed. G. R. Evans (Oxford: Blackwell, 2001), pp. 226–27 [221–32]. Iacopone may not be unique among male mystics in using the language of childbirth to speak of mystical union, but his emphasis on ecstatic generation does break with what Caroline Bynum has described as the Cistercian preference for the nurturing aspect of motherhood (see "The Cistercian Conception of Community," p. 150). Bynum's reading remains useful in mapping the differences between the Cistercian tradition and the later affective literature, especially Franciscan, inspired by it. On the Franciscan debt to the white monks, specifically in their "devotion to the person of Jesus," see R.W. Southern, *Western Society and the Church in the Middle Ages* (Harmondsworth: Penguin, 1970), p. 273.
84. As cited in Caroline Walker Bynum, "The Body of Christ in the Later Middle Ages: A Reply to Leo Steinberg," *Fragmentation and Redemption: Essays on Gender and the Human Body in Medieval Religion* (New York: Zone, 1991), p. 97 [79–117]. A new translation of Margaret's works has appeared since Bynum's essay, and the passage to which Bynum alludes can be found in chapter 33 of *The Writings of Margaret of Oingt: Medieval Prioress and Mystic*, trans. Renate Blumenfeld-Kosinski (Newburyport, MA: Focus Library of Medieval Women, 1990).

85. Jesus is "stretched out" at the column to which he is bound when beaten, and then again at the cross, in chapters 35–37 of Margaret's *Page of Meditations*.
86. Jennifer Fisk Rondeau cites a fourteenth-century *lauda* that reproduces many of these connections, even to the point of rhyming "parturisco" with "rapisco." See "Conducting Gender," p. 200.
87. Sarah Beckwith, *Christ's Body: Identity, Culture and Society in Late Medieval Writings* (London: Routledge, 1993), p. 52.
88. Underhill, *Jacopone*, pp. 89, 113.
89. Moore offers a disturbing complement to Bynum's account of Jesus as mother in his study of Yahweh as bodybuilder. "So hypermasculine did he become that his body ceased to be merely male, and began to sprout female parts. Far from being assuaged, his insecurities about this masculinity now had something new to feed on—a pair of female breasts." Stephen D. Moore, *God's Gym: Divine Male Bodies of the Bible* (New York and London: Routledge, 1996), p. 100.
90. Santi has, of course, a more conservative notion of gender complementarity in mind: see pp. 58–59 of "La mistica di Iacopone da Todi."
91. Rondeau, *Memorial*, p. 195.
92. See Plato, *Republic* 596b–598d. In the translation of Desmond Lee (Harmondsworth: Penguin, 1974), this falls on pp. 422–26.
93. Similarly, Cioran argues, "The saints are not a-sexual but trans-sexual" (p. 19).
94. If, for Kaja Silverman ("Total Visibility"), we are fundamentally and irreconcilably "four, not two: seer, seen, touching, being touched," Iacopone shows the extent to which these ontological modes may nonetheless miraculously participate in one another.
95. Jean-Luc Nancy, *The Sense of the World*, trans. Jeffrey S. Librett (Minneapolis: University of Minnesota press, 1997), p. 37. The French text is from *Le sens du monde* (Paris: Galilée, 1993), p. 61. My emphasis.
96. Beckwith, *Christ's Body*, p. 52.
97. See Kaja Silverman, *The Threshold of the Visible World* (New York: Routledge, 1996), pp. 10–37, as well as the last section of Chapter two, "The Threshold of the Visible."
98. David Wojnarowicz demonstrates how such a spaced-out look mitigates against solipsism in *Close to the Knives: A Memoir of Disintegration* (New York: Serpent's Tail, 1991), pp. 109–10: "These days I see the edge of mortality. The edge of death and dying is around everything like a warm halo of light sometimes dim sometimes irradiated. I see myself seeing death. It's like a transparent celluloid image of myself is accompanying me everywhere I go. I see my friends and I see myself and I see breath coming from my lips and the plants are drinking it and I see breath coming from my chest and everything is fading, becoming a shadow that may disappear as the sun goes down." We cannot forget that it is death, not God, that prompts Wojnarowicz to see and stretch this ontological threshold; nonetheless, there is no nihilism here. Death participates in life, frames it for view: to see, however dimly and incompletely, with the eyes and words of the dead

(among them Wojnarowicz himself) is the properly political challenge Wojnarowicz poses against the (homophobic, AIDS-collusive) cult of pure, unborrowed vision and transparency.
99. Silverman, *Threshold*, p. 213.

Chapter 4   Lyric Enclosures

1. It is also worth noting that the miraculous oral ink of Jehan Bouche d'Or's life appears in an instance of dragging, first of the pen from the saint's mouth, and then of the saint's hand before his eyes. See "Hand to Mouth," the third section of chapter 2.
2. See chapter 3 for a more detailed engagement with *Ad Herennium* 4.32.43.
3. My translation. The Italian text is from Frederick Goldin, *German and Italian Lyrics of the Middle Ages* (Garden City, NY: Anchor, 1973), pp. 270–71.
4. See chapter 3, especially "Holes in the Wall: Peter Damian."
5. Judith Butler, *Gender Trouble*, second edition (New York: Routledge, 1999), p. 174.
6. Butler, "Preface (1999)," *Gender Trouble*, p. xxiii.
7. Marjorie Garber, *Vested Interests: Cross-Dressing and Cultural Anxiety* (New York: Routledge, 1992), p. 17.
8. Similarly, drag requires the revision, in hermeneutic practice, of Peter Dronke's assertion that in stilnovist poetics—and particularly in Guinizzelli and Cavalcanti—the goal is "to make style organically one with content." See Dronke, *The Medieval Lyric*, third edition (Cambridge: D.S. Brewer, 1996), p. 157.
9. Simon Gaunt, *Troubadours and Irony* (Cambridge: University of Cambridge Press, 1989), p. 16.
10. See my discussion of participation in the final pages of chapter 1, especially "Participation: here."
11. Jean-Jacques Rousseau, "Essay on the Origin of Languages," trans. John H. Moran, in *On the Origin of Language* (Chicago: University of Chicago Press, 1966), pp. 50, 51. In "Touch and Transport in the Middle Ages," an unpublished essay, Jeffrey Schnapp observes that "touching, seizing, and lifting figure among the central attributes of Dante's intercessors and guides." He cites specifically the description of Beatrice as she who "carried [tratto]" the Dante-pilgrim to freedom in *Paradiso* 21.85. Beatrice has, in fact, quite literally dragged Dante upward: such drag, in the sense of my remarks here, would render this pilgrimage (and this pilgrim) less pure, at once more compromised and more material.
12. Ernst Robert Curtius, *European Literature and the Latin Middle Ages*, trans. Willard R. Trask (New York: Pantheon/Bollingen, 1953), pp. 414–15.
13. Christine de Pizan, *The Book of the City of Ladies*, trans. Earl Jeffrey Richards (New York: Persea, 1982), p. 7.
14. Christine de Pizan, *La Città delle Dame*, ed. Earl Jeffrey Richards, a cura di Patrizia Caraffi (Milan: Luni Editrice, 1997), p. 48.

15. For a further discussion of opposition, this time in relation to metonymy, see the final section of this chapter, "Entering Community."
16. Likewise, in *Fear and Trembling*, one sees an antiphrastic fatherhood, which emerges (and fades) in the wake of the son's disappearance. Kierkegaard speaks, as Johannes de Silentio, to Abraham: "you had to draw the knife before you kept Isaac," but the point is not the keeping of Isaac but precisely the drawing of the knife. See the translation of Howard V. Hong and Edna H. Hong (Princeton: Princeton University Press, 1983), p. 23.
17. See chapter 1, especially "The Miracle and the Fetish" and "Against and Above," for a fuller discussion of how metonymic participation undoes the distinction between the monstrous and the miraculous, against (and above) fetishism.
18. " 'Articulation' means, in some way, 'writing,' which is to say, the inscription of a meaning whose transcendence or presence is indefinitely and constitutively deferred." See Jean-Luc Nancy, "Literary Communism," trans. Peter Connor, in *The Inoperative Community* (Minneapolis: University of Minnesota Press, 1991), p. 80.
19. Giorgio Agamben, "*Corn*: From Anatomy to Poetics," *The End of the Poem*, trans. Daniel Heller-Roazen (Stanford: Stanford University Press, 1999), pp. 33–34 [23–42].
20. Dante, *Purgatorio*, trans. W. S. Merwin (New York: Knopf, 2000), p. 253.
21. My translation; Italian text from Goldin, *German and Italian Lyrics*, pp. 294–95.
22. See chapter 1, "Ambivalence."
23. Nancy, *Inoperative Community*, p. 79.
24. Seth Lerer similarly finds, in his "survey of enclosed spaces" in early English lyric, a mourning *before loss*: belatedness is, in this way, the trope of emerging lyric subjectivity. See "The Genre of the Grave and the Origins of the Middle English Lyric," in *Modern Language Quarterly* 58.2 (June 1997): 127–61.
25. Guinizzelli, "Madonna, il fino amor ched eo vo porto," 4.37 and 7.73–7.75, in Robert Edwards, ed. and trans., *The Poetry of Guido Guinizzelli* (New York: Garland, 1987).
26. It is in this spirit that Sarah Spence describes troubadour lyric as "sing[ing] of the frustration of an orator who is not in control of his audience" in *Rhetorics of Reason and Desire*, p. 130. Indeed, in Guinizzelli, the audience sings ecstatically through the singer.
27. See chapter 3, "The Threshold of Enclosure."
28. In a sensitive recent study on Guinizzelli's "restlessness," *Guido Guinizzelli: Stilnovo inquieto* (Naples: Liguori, 2000), Pietro Pelosi reads Guinizzelli's response to Bonagiunta as an elaboration, beyond a merely analogical neoplatonic hierarchy, of an "isomorphism" which connects various elements in this hierarchy into a homogeneous whole. Let me insist that this is not what I am proposing here. The metonymic dimension of restraint and drag does not reduce its constituent terms to what Pelosi calls "a constant,

homogeneous whole" (un tutto costante, omogeneo; p. 64). In fact, what I am calling belatedness is precisely what preserves aporia within the relation and saves it from immanence.

29. Dante, *Purgatorio*, pp. 254–55.

30. I want to insist upon the "no more or less" in Dante's relationship to so-called minor authors, particularly inasmuch as I share Mark Doty's discomfort with "masterpieces of a grand scale, the heroic gesture, the cosmological scheme." See "Rooting for the Damned," in Peter S. Hawkins and Rachel Jacoff, eds., *The Poets' Dante* (New York: Farrar, Straus and Giroux, 2001), p. 370. Yet whereas Doty chooses the quotidian Dante over the monumental Dante (although, to his credit, it's as if he'd rather not have to choose Dante at all), I am more inclined to see the productivity of subordinating Dante to other texts, other arguments, negating the obviousness, the inevitability, which has come to be granted him: not to erase Dante altogether (thus effaced, his myth would only be reinforced) but basically to make him a footnote, an afterthought. In the process, it may become clear just what is at stake ideologically in his unquestioned and singular position for Italian medieval studies and Italian literary history more generally. After all, "the idea of the possible end of ideology," in Zizek's summary of Althusser, "is an ideological idea par excellence" (*Sublime Object* 2). It is precisely Dante's obviousness that makes him ideologically suspect in this way. One clue to the ideological underpinnings of Dante's status may lie in Curtius's observation of the unprecedented number of scholars Dante assigns to heaven (p. 371). Perhaps contemporary academics are merely seeking to return the favor; perhaps, too, the very (fantastic) pleasure of an evaluation whose consequences are eternal is the dirty secret they and Dante share.

31. I am not unaware of the methodological implications of these readings, whose departure from the philological puritanism of much Italian medieval scholarship is prompted by a conviction along the lines of William Haver's recent assertion that "if thinking accepts the 'practical' constraints of its institution and institutions, then thought is nothing more than the administration, or policing, of its disciplines; and in that case, we shall have not even begun to think what it is imperative to think in this time of AIDS." My response to this imperative is much less rigorous than Haver's, but a similar spirit animates it. See *The Body of This Death: Historicity and Sociality in the Time of AIDS* (Stanford: Stanford University Press, 1996), p. 180.

32. Carolyn Dinshaw, *Getting Medieval: Sexualities and Communities, Pre- and Post-Modern* (Durham: Duke University Press, 1999), p. 151.

33. "Whatever" designates, for Agamben, "singularity. . .such as it is [la singolarità. . .tale qual'è]." See especially the first chapter of *La comunità che viene*, new edition (Torino: Bollati Boringhieri, 2001), pp. 9–10.

34. Bhabha, "Postcolonial Criticism," in Stephen Greenblatt and Giles Gunn, eds., *Redrawing the Boundaries: The Transformation of English and American Literary Studies* (New York: MLA, 1992), p. 452, as cited in Dinshaw, *Getting Medieval*, p. 39.

35. Jean-Luc Nancy, *Birth to Presence*, p. 383: "Laughter is thus neither a presence nor an absence. It is the offering of a presence in its own disappearance. It is not given but offered: suspended on the limit of its own presentation." Such suspense is saved from a Bhabha-esque "indeterminacy" by its own embeddedness in time: "laughter 'itself' is nothing—nothing at the center of the flower, and nothing but the blooming of the flower." This blooming should be understood, in the context of the paragraphs that follow, as a precisely autumnal blooming: belated flower, emergence within fading.
36. Mark Doty, "Messiah (Christmas Portions)," in *Sweet Machine* (New York: Harper Flamingo, 1998), p. 32.
37. Augustine, *Confessions* 10.8.14, trans. Pine-Coffin, p. 215. The Latin can be found in James J. O'Donnell, ed., *Augustine: Confessions*, vol. 1 (Oxford: Oxford University Press, 1991), p. 124.
38. Augustine, *Confessions* 10.8.15, trans. Pine-Coffin, p. 216; Augustine, *Confessions*, ed. O'Donnell, p. 124.
39. Augustine, *Confessions* 10.27.38, trans. Pine-Coffin, pp. 231–32.
40. Augustine, *Confessions*, ed. O'Donnell, p. 134.
41. Mark Doty, *Still Life with Oysters and Lemon* (Boston: Beacon, 2001), p. 21.
42. In *Still Life*, pp. 21–22, Doty writes, of another still life, that "some lamp-shine of intimacy fires the whole thing, some sense of autumnal community, harvest-ripe and complete, the season moving to an ending."
43. Johan Huizinga, *The Waning of the Middle Ages* (New York: Doubleday Anchor, 1956), p. 335.
44. Huizinga speaks of the "spontaneous and passionate character" of political loyalty in the fifteenth century (*Waning*, p. 22).
45. Hans Ulrich Gumbrecht, in an essay on fifteenth-century *cancioneros*, observes that literary historiography must "consider whether it wants to see—as Huizinga does—the context of 'reception of the Middle Ages' in Western Europe in the fourteenth and fifteenth centuries as *still* late-medieval or *already* the beginning of the modern history of reception of medieval literature." That the "still" (premodern) overlaps with the "already" (modern) is one particularly strong point of resonance between Gumbrecht's argument and Doty's autumnal poetics, challenging both linear historicism and sharp distinction between secondary 'reception' and primary textual generation, as well as (more importantly) dragging scholarship once more into song. See "Intertextuality and Autumn / Autumn and the Modern Reception of the Middle Ages," in Marina S. Brownlee, Kevin Brownlee, and Stephen G. Nichols, eds., *The New Medievalism* (Baltimore: Johns Hopkins University Press, 1991), p. 303 [301–30].
46. Doty, "Couture," in *Atlantis* (London: Jonathan Cape, 1996), p. 16.
47. Bachelard, *Poetics*, p. 229.
48. Doty, *Still Life*, p. 58.
49. Gillian Rose, *Mourning Becomes the Law: Philosophy and Representation* (Cambridge: Cambridge University Press, 1996), p. 15.
50. Rose, *Mourning*, p. 16.

51. Nancy, *Inoperative Community*, p. 10.
52. Nancy, *Inoperative Community*, p. 72.
53. Nancy, *La communauté désoeuvrée* (Paris: Christian Bourgois, 1986), p. 180.
54. Rose, *Mourning*, p. 25.
55. Rose, *Mourning*, p. 26.
56. Rose, *Mourning*, p. 26.
57. Jean-Luc Nancy, *La communauté affrontée* (Paris: Galilée, 2002), p. 43. My translation.
58. Nancy, *La communauté affrontée*, p. 50.
59. Tim Dean's article, "Strange Paradise: An Essay on Mark Doty," http://www.english.uiuc.edu/maps/poets/a_f/doty/strange.htm, reminded me of Doty's defiant manifesto from *Atlantis*, "Homo Will Not Inherit," in which the speaker announces to the anonymous culprit of a homophobic poster, "...This city's inescapable / gorgeous, and on fire. I have my kingdom."
60. Haver, *Body*, p. 198. "Articulation" is to be understood, here, in Nancy's sense: see footnote 18 to this chapter.
61. Nancy, *La communauté affrontée*, p. 40.
62. Agamben, *La comunità che viene*, p. 15.
63. Haver, *Body*, p. 140.
64. Haver, *Body*, p. 201.
65. See Catherine Pickstock's account of the "radical solipsism of the Cartesian subject," characterized by a "written interiority," in *After Writing*, p. 72.
66. Similarly, Ross Chambers describes how AIDS diaries "want their own insertion in a process that is open-ended and transformative." See *Facing It*, p. 32.
67. Kaja Silverman speaks of the "good enough" as "a paradigm through which ideals can be simultaneously lived and deconstructed. To live an ideal in the mode of the 'good enough' is, first of all, to dissolve it into its tropes—to grasp its fundamentally figural status. Equally important, it is to understand that those tropes are only ever partially fulfillable. Finally, to embrace the principle of the 'good enough' is to realize that one's partial and tropological approximation of the ideal counts most when circumstances most conspire against it." Metonymic drag—just far enough, just late enough—is in this way just good enough. See *The Threshold of the Visible World*, pp. 4–5.
68. Bo Huston, "Meditations in Zurich," in Thomas Avena, ed., *Life Sentences: Writers, Artists and AIDS* (San Francisco: Mercury House, 1994), p. 75 [73–106].
69. Bo Huston, *Remember Me* (New York: Amethyst, 1991), p. 13.
70. Mark Doty, "Lilacs in NYC," *Sweet Machine*, p. 104. Similarly, when Doty sings, a few lines later, "You enter me / and it's Macy's, // some available version of infinity," he spatializes "the infinite in finitude's drag" as described earlier in this chapter.
71. Carol Muske-Dukes, "A Private Matter," *The New Yorker* (December 23–30, 2002): 126–27.

Chapter 5 Nothing Between

1. Marie de France, *Lais*, ed. Karl Warnke (Paris: Poche, 1990). All line references are to this edition.
2. For an extended queer reading of *Guigemar*, and particularly of Marie's use of the word "surplus" to account for the discursive, social, and ultimately heteronormative nature of what happens when Guigemar has sex with his lady, see Bill Burgwinkle's chapter on Marie de France in *Sodomy, Masculinity, and Law in Medieval Literature* (Cambridge: Cambridge University Press, 2004), pp. 138–69.
3. Stephen G. Nichols, "Deflections of the Body in the Old French Lay," *Stanford French Review* 14.1–14.2 (Spring–Fall 1990): 38, 37.
4. For a vivid description of anchoritic life, pieced together from Julian's text, the thirteenth-century English *Ancrene Riwle*, and Aelred of Rievaulx's twelfth-century rule for recluses, see Grace Jantzen's account in "The Life of an Anchoress," the third chapter of *Julian of Norwich* (Mahwah, NJ: Paulist, 2000 [1987]), pp. 28–50. In the broadest possible terms, an anchoress (or anchorite, if a man) lived a solitary life of prayer in a room or series of rooms, often attached to a church, which she never left. Jantzen stresses that an anchoress was not, however, entirely alone: "The solitude of the anchoress...was not absolute, for besides giving counsel to those who consulted her she had a domestic or two in her care. Nevertheless, her special hallmark was her strict enclosure. She never left her cell, and was regularly referred to as dead to the world, shut up with Christ in his tomb" (p. 33).
5. Frederick Christian Bauerschmidt, *Julian of Norwich and the Mystical Body Politic of Christ* (Notre Dame: University of Notre Dame Press, 1999), p. 107. I want to acknowledge, as well, the debt my argument owes to the particularly felicitous phrasing of Bauerschmidt's observation, earlier in his book, that "to be embodied is to have boundaries, but to have boundaries is also to have thresholds, points of opening into which others may enter and from which new things may proceed. It is this possibility that Julian highlights" (p. 64). This chapter is a kind of meditation on how exactly "new things may proceed" from enclosed, spatially delimited bodies.
6. All references are to chapter and page in Marion Glasscoe's edition of the long text: Julian of Norwich, *A Revelation of Love* (Exeter: University of Exeter Press, 1993 [1986]).
7. Jesus speaks in chapter 27 to remind Julian that "Synne is behovabil [Sin is necessary], but al shal be wel, and al shal be wel, and al manner of thyng shal be wele" (p. 38).
8. Barbara Newman, *From Virile Woman to WomanChrist: Studies in Medieval Religion and Literature* (Philadelphia: University of Pennsylvania Press, 1995), p. 130.
9. The notion that what exceeds our singular and singularly delimited bodies might be better thought of in terms of "beside" than "beyond" owes a great deal to Eve Sedgwick's introductory remarks in *Touching Feeling* (Durham: Duke

NOTES 179

University Press, 2003). See my discussion of this passage toward the end of "In Closing."
10. Julian, in this way, offers a radical theological critique of Jean-Luc Nancy's observation, in *Being Singular Plural*, trans. Robert D. Richardson (Stanford: Stanford University Press, 2000), that creation *ex nihilo* "signifies two things: on the one hand, it signifies that the 'creator' itself is the *nihil*; on the other, it signifies that this *nihil* is...the very origin [*provenance*], and destination, of some thing in general and of everything" (p. 16). The French text, from *Être singulier pluriel* (Paris: Galilée, 1996), reads as follows: "Cela signifie bien plutôt...d'une part que le 'créateur' lui-même est le *nihil*, d'autre part que ce *nihil* n'est pas, logiquement, quelque chose 'd'où' le créé pourrait provenir, mais la provenance elle-même, et la destination, de quelque chose en général et de toute chose" (p. 35). That is, Nancy remains invested in a logic of synecdochic reduction *to and from a univocal nothing*, "ce *nihil*," where Julian inscribes difference in the heart of this nothing.
11. This is Giorgio Agamben's summary, as found in *The Coming Community*, trans. Michael Hardt (Minneapolis: University of Minnesota Press, 1993), p. 94.
12. For an eloquent articulation of addition as a mode of the Incarnation, see Catherine Pickstock's chapter on "Truth and touch" in Pickstock and Milbank, *Truth in Aquinas*, especially pp. 86–87: "Through the Incarnation, it is revealed that divine goodness is not simply subjective self-giving as displayed in creation..., not just the substantive relational gathering of the *Logos* which is the ground of creation, but also the constitution of the *Logos* through 'assumed additions' which are neither logically essential according to a given nature nor merely willed accidents."
13. *Rhetorica ad Herennium*, trans. Caplan, 4.13.19, pp. 276–77.
14. Thomas Aquinas makes a similar claim about the eucharist. At *Summa Theologiae* IIIa.75.1, he notes, "Christ's body is not in this sacrament in the same way as a body is in a place, which by its dimensions is commensurate with the place; but in a special manner which is proper to this sacrament."
15. See, for example, his observation that "there is an immediate equivalence between the orientation of the visual field and the awareness of one's own body as the potentiality of that field," in Maurice Merleau-Ponty, *Phenomenology of Perception*, trans. Colin Smith (1958; repr. New York and London: Routledge, 2002), p. 239.
16. I owe the rhetoric of asymmetrical reciprocity to John Milbank's discussion of the gift in "Grace: The Midwinter Sacrifice," *Being Reconciled: Ontology and Pardon* (New York and London: Routledge, 2003), pp. 138–61, and especially p. 156.
17. Nancy, *Singular*, p. 11; *Singulier*, p. 30.
18. Graham Ward, *Cities of God* (London and New York: Routledge, 2000), p. 152.
19. Ward, *Cities*, p. 153.
20. See also the discussion of Mark Doty's Choral Society in chapter 4, "Burning, belatedly."

21. Catherine Brown, "In the Middle," *Journal of Medieval and Early Modern Studies* 30.3 (Fall 2000), p. 554 [547–74].
22. Brown, "In the Middle," p. 554.
23. Dante, *Purgatorio* 15.55–15.57, trans. W. S. Merwin (New York: Knopf, 2000), p. 145.
24. See Daniel 3.19–3.30 for the entire story.

In Closing

1. Albert Camus, *La peste* (1947; repr. Paris: Gallimard, 2005), p. 113.
2. Erich Auerbach, *Mimesis*, trans. Willard R. Trask (Princeton: Princeton University Press, 1953), p. 548.
3. Auerbach, *Mimesis*, p. 556.
4. In "Medieval/Postmodern: HIV/AIDS and the Temporality of Crisis," in Steven F. Kruger and Glenn Burger, eds., *Queering the Middle Ages* (Minneapolis: University of Minnesota Press, 2001), pp. 252–83, Kruger employs the rhetoric of both contiguity and enclosure in his exposition of the temporal crisis provoked and embodied by HIV/AIDS and its implications for historicism: "What is needed is a different sort of historicism...where...phenomena in the present might be connected to both the past and the future without being thereby projected into a wholly alien moment" (p. 276); "doing history can mean a commitment not just to excavating the past but to considering how the past inheres in the present in such a way as to demand that the present, and thus the future, be thought otherwise" (p. 278).
5. "En effet, à quoi la mémoire s'attacherait-elle si tout, absolument tout dans le texte n'était qu'incident, circonstance et hasard?" Harald Weinrich, "Le style et la mémoire," in Georges Molinié and Pierre Cahné, eds., *Qu'est-ce que le style?* (Paris: Presses Universitaires de France, 1994), p. 349 [339–54].
6. "...donner du style à un texte équivaut à poser sa candidature à une certaine survie, si brève soit-elle." Weinrich, "Le style," p. 354.
7. "...sera donc celui qui, dans une situation donnée, garantira au mieux le fonctionnement de la mémoire, d'abord de l'orateur lui-même, puis de son auditoire."
8. "Ce 'point' dans le temps où coïncident les événements lus et vécus est donc un instant extrêmement prégnant pour Francesca et Paolo,...Dante apprend ici que, dans la balance de la justice divine, une action poctuelle, un seul événement fatal peut avoir le même poids qu'une peine éternelle puisqu'elle détermine à jamais le destin humain." Weinrich, "La poésie en enfer," *Cahiers d'Histoire des Littératures Romanes / Romanistische Zeitschrift für Literaturgeschichte* 19.3–19.34 (1995), p. 391 [387–94].
9. "...ils sont condamnés à être privés de leurs corps tout en étant contraints à rester proche l'un de l'autre." Weinrich, "La poésie en enfer," p. 392.
10. Edelman, *Homographesis*, p. 23.

11. Edelman, *Homographesis*, p. 13: "Bearing no singular identity, the homograph. . .precipitates into meaning by virtue of its linear, its metonymic, relation to a context that seems to validate, which is to say, 'naturalize,' one denotation over another."
12. John Paul Ricco, *The Logic of the Lure* (Chicago: University of Chicago Press, 2002), p. 8.
13. Intense attenuation seems the best way of paraphrasing Ricco's argument, itself a kind of Foucauldian reading of Nancy and Agamben, that "this attenuation [*ascesis*] is not a reduction or a suicidal renunciation of self, but rather an intense desubjectification, in which notions of individuality in the form of a subject, of intersubjectivity in the form of intimacy, and of collectivity in the form of community are rendered impossible" (p. 21). It should be clear from my reading of Augustine in chapter 4 that intimacy may have a mode beyond both intersubjectivity and nomadic anonymity: this mode would be that of the *intimior intimo meo*, one's own excess of oneself.
14. Paul Lisicky, *Lawnboy* (New York: Turtle Point Press, 1998), p. 351.
15. Geoffrey Galt Harpham, *Shadows of Ethics*, p. 3.
16. See, for example, Ricco, *Lure*, p. 3.
17. Harpham, "Inertia" 11.
18. Harpham, "Inertia" 13–16.
19. This description of the immanent, quantifiable field owes a great deal to Frances Ferguson's *Pornography, the Theory: What Utilitarianism Did to Action* (Chicago: University of Chicago Press, 2004), which nonetheless does not just describe but, in its rigorously historicist method, enacts the kind of comparison I've sketched out here.
20. Roland Barthes, *The Pleasure of the Text*, trans. Richard Miller (New York: Hill and Wang, 1975).
21. Barthes, *Pleasure*, p. 20. The French is from vol. 2 of Barthes, *Oeuvres complètes*, ed. Éric Marty (Paris: Seuil, 1994), p. 1504. Subsequent references are to these editions.
22. Barthes, *Pleasure*, p. 63; *Plaisir*, p. 1526.
23. Paul Zumthor, *Speaking of the Middle Ages*, trans. Sarah White (Lincoln: University of Nebraska Press, 1986), p. 93. The French text is from *Parler du Moyen Age* (Paris: Minuit, 1980), p. 103.
24. See, for example, "On the Utility and Liability of History for Life," in Friedrich Nietzsche, *Unfashionable Observations*, trans. Richard T. Gray (Stanford: Stanford University Press, 1995), p. 93 [83–167].
25. Zumthor, *Speaking*, p. 85; *Parler*, p. 93.
26. Zumthor, *Speaking*, p. 85; *Parler*, p. 93.
27. Nietzsche, "Utility," p. 164.
28. Eve Kosofsky Sedgwick, *Touching Feeling* (Durham: Duke University Press, 2003), p. 8.
29. Nancy, "Finite History," *The Birth to Presence*, p. 164.
30. Federico García Lorca, "The Poet Speaks by Telephone to His Beloved," trans. Rafael Campo in *Diva*, p. 94.

WORKS CITED

Abelard. *The Letters of Abelard and Heloise.* Trans. Betty Radice. Harmondsworth: Penguin, 1974.
Aelred of Rievaulx. "A Rule of Life for a Recluse." Trans. Mary Paul Macpherson, OCSO. *Treatises and the Pastoral Prayer.* Kalamazoo: Cistercian, 1971. 41–102.
Agamben, Giorgio. *The Coming Community.* Trans. Michael Hardt. Minneapolis: University of Minnesota Press, 1993.
———. *Stanzas.* Trans. Ronald L. Martinez. Minneapolis: University of Minnesota Press, 1993.
———. "*Corn*: From Anatomy to Poetics." *The End of the Poem.* Trans. Daniel Heller-Roazen. Stanford: Stanford University Press, 1999. 23–42.
———. *La comunità che viene.* New edition. Turin: Bollati Boringhieri, 2001.
———. *L'aperto: L'uomo e l'animale.* Turin: Bollati Boringhieri, 2002.
Alarcón, Francisco X. *From the Other Side of Night = Del otro lado de la noche.* Tucson: University of Arizona Press, 2002.
Angela of Foligno. *Complete Works.* Trans. Paul LaChance, O.F.M. New York: Paulist, 1993.
Apter, Emily, and William Pietz, eds. *Fetishism as Cultural Discourse.* Ithaca: Cornell, University Press, 1993.
Aspland, C. W. ed. *A Medieval French Reader.* Oxford: Clarendon, 1979.
Auerbach, Erich. *Mimesis.* Trans. Willard R. Trask. Princeton: Princeton University Press, 1953.
Augustine. *On Christian Doctrine.* Trans. D. W. Robertson, Jr. Saddle River: Macmillan, 1958.
———. *Confessions.* Trans. R. S. Pine-Coffin. Harmondsworth: Penguin, 1961.
———. *Confessions.* Volume 1. Ed. James J. O'Donnell. Oxford: Oxford University Press, 1991.
Bachelard, Gaston. *The Poetics of Space.* Trans. Maria Jolas. New York: Orion Books, 1964.
———. *La poétique de l'espace.* Fifth edition. Paris: Presses Universitaires de France, 1967.
Bal, Mieke. *Louise Bourgeois' Spider: The Architecture of Art-Writing.* Chicago: University of Chicago Press, 2001.
Barthes, Roland. *The Pleasure of the Text.* Trans. Richard Miller. New York: Hill and Wang, 1975.

Barthes, Roland. *Oeuvres complètes*. Ed. Éric Marty. Volume 2. Paris: Seuil, 1994.

Bauerschmidt, Frederick Christian. *Julian of Norwich and the Mystical Body Politic of Christ*. Notre Dame: University of Notre Dame Press, 1999.

Beckwith, Sarah. *Christ's Body: Identity, Culture, and Society in Late Medieval Writings*. London: Routledge, 1993.

———. "Passionate Regulation: Enclosure, Ascesis, and the Feminist Imaginary." *South Atlantic Quarterly* 93.4 (Fall 1994): 803–24.

Bernard of Clairvaux. *On the Song of Songs*. Trans. Killian Walsh and Irene Edmonds. Kalamazoo: Cistercian, 1971.

Bersani, Leo. *Homos*. Cambridge, MA: Harvard University Press, 1995.

Bewes, Timothy. *Reification, or The Anxiety of Late Capitalism*. London: Verso, 2002.

Bonaventure. *Itinerarium Mentis in Deum*. Trans. Philotheus Boehner, O.F.M. Saint Bonaventure, NY: Franciscan Institute/Saint Bonaventure University, 1956.

———. *The Life of St. Francis. The Soul's Journey into God, The Tree of Life, The Life of St. Francis*. Trans. Ewert Cousins. New York: Paulist, 1982. 177–327.

Boswell, John. *Christianity, Social Tolerance and Homosexuality*. Chicago: University of Chicago Press, 1980.

Bourdain, Anthony. *Kitchen Confidential*. New York: The Ecco Press, 2000.

Brown, Catherine. "In the Middle." *Journal of Medieval and Early Modern Studies* 30.3 (Fall 2000): 547–74.

Brown, Michael P. *Closet Space: Geographies of Metaphor from the Body to the Globe*. London: Routledge, 2000.

Brown, Peter. *The Body and Society: Men, Women, and Sexual Renunciation in Early Christianity*. Berkeley: University of California Press, 1988.

Burrus, Virginia. *"Begotten, Not Made": Conceiving Manhood in Late Antiquity*. Stanford: Stanford University Press, 2000.

———. *The Sex Lives of Saints*. Philadelphia: University of Pennsylvania Press, 2003.

Burgwinkle, William. *Sodomy, Masculinity, and Law in Medieval Literature*. Cambridge: University of Cambridge Press, 2004.

———. "Visible and Invisible Bodies and Subjects in Peter Damian." In *Troubled Vision*. Ed. Emma Campbell and Robert Mills. New York: Palgrave, 2004. 47–62.

Butler, Judith. *Gender Trouble*. Second edition. New York: Routledge, 1999.

Bynum, Caroline Walker. "The Cistercian Conception of Community." In *Jesus as Mother: Studies in the Spirituality of the High Middle Ages*. Berkeley: University of California Press, 1982. 59–81.

———. "The Body of Christ in the Later Middle Ages: A Reply to Leo Steinberg." In *Fragmentation and Redemption: Essays on Gender and the Human Body in Medieval Religion*. New York: Zone, 1991. 79–117.

Caby, Cécile. *De l'érémitisme rural au monachisme urbain: Les camaldules en Italie à la fin du Moyen Âge*. Rome: École française de Rome, 1999.

Campbell, Emma. "Separating the Saints from the Boys: Sainthood and Masculinity in the Old French *Vie de Saint Alexis*." *French Studies* 57.4 (2003): 447–62.

Campo, Rafael. *Diva*. Durham: Duke University Press, 1999.

Camille, Michael. "Gothic Signs and the Surplus: The Kiss on the Cathedral." In *Contexts: Style and Values in Medieval Art and Literature*. Ed. Daniel Poirion and Nancy Freeman Regalado. Special edition of *Yale French Studies*. New Haven: Yale University Press, 1991. 151–70.

WORKS CITED

Camus, Albert. *La peste.* Paris: Gallimard, 2005 [1947].
Canettieri, Paolo. "*Laude* di Iacopone da Todi." In *Letteratura italiana: le opere.* Volume 1. Ed. Alberto Asor Rosa. Turin: Einaudi, 1992. 121–52.
Carson, Anne. *Eros the Bittersweet.* Normal: Dalkey Archive Press, 1998 [1986].
———. *Plainwater.* New York: Knopf, 1995.
Cazelles, Brigitte. "Modèle ou mirage: Marie l'Egyptienne." *The French Review* 53.1 (October 1979).
———. *Le corps de sainteté: d'après Jehan Bouche d'Or, Jehan Paulus, et quelques vies des XIIe et XIIIe siècles.* Geneva: Droz, 1982.
Cazelles, Brigitte and Phyllis Johnson. *Le Vain Siecle Guerpir* (Chapel Hill: University of North Carolina, 1979).
de Certeau, Michel. *L'Écriture de l'histoire.* Paris: Gallimard, 1975.
———. *The Mystic Fable.* Volume 1. Trans. Michael B. Smith. Chicago: University of Chicago Press, 1992.
Chadwick, Henry. *The Early Church.* Harmondsworth: Penguin, 1967.
Chambers, Ross. *Facing It: AIDS Diaries and the Death of the Author.* Ann Arbor: University of Michigan Press, 1998.
Chimisso, Christina. *Gaston Bachelard: Critic of Science and the Imagination.* London: Routledge, 2001.
Christine de Pizan. *The Book of the City of Ladies.* Trans. Earl Jeffrey Richards. New York: Persea, 1982.
———. *La città delle dame.* Ed. Earl Jeffrey Richards. A cura di Patrizia Caraffi. Milan: Luni, 1997.
Cioran, E. M. *Tears and Saints.* Trans. Ilinca Zarifopol-Johnston. Chicago: University of Chicago Press, 1995.
The Complete Parallel Bible. Oxford and New York: Oxford University Press, 1993.
Copeland, Rita ed. *Criticism and Dissent in the Middle Ages.* Cambridge, UK: Cambridge University Press, 1996.
Curtius, Ernst Robert. *European Literature and the Latin Middle Ages.* Trans. Willard R. Trask. New York: Pantheon/Bollingen, 1953.
Damisch, Hubert. *A Theory of /Cloud/: Toward a History of Painting.* Trans. Janet Lloyd. Stanford: Stanford University Press, 2002 [1972].
Dante. *Inferno.* Trans. Allen Mandelbaum. Berkeley: University of California Press, 1980.
———. *Purgatorio.* Trans. W. S. Merwin. New York: Knopf, 2000.
Davies, Oliver. "Later Medieval Mystics." In *The Medieval Theologians.* Ed. G. R. Evans. Oxford: Blackwell, 2001. 221–32.
Dean, Tim. "Strange Paradise: An Essay on Mark Doty." http://www.english.uiuc.edu/maps/poets/a_f/doty/strange.htm.
De Man, Paul. "The Rhetoric of Temporality." In *Blindness and Insight: Essays in the Rhetoric of Contemporary Criticism.* Minneapolis: University of Minnesota Press, 1983. 187–228.
Dembowski, Peter F. *Les vies de Marie l'Egyptienne. Versions en ancien et en moyen français.* Geneva: Droz, 1977.
D'Erasmo, Stacey. *A Seahorse Year.* New York: Houghton Mifflin, 2004.
Dinshaw, Carolyn. "A Kiss Is Just a Kiss." *Diacritics* 24.2–3 (Summer/Fall 1994): 205–26.

WORKS CITED

Dinshaw, Carolyn. *Getting Medieval: Sexualities and Communities, Pre- and Post-modern.* Durham: Duke University Press, 1999.

Doty, Mark. *Atlantis.* London: Jonathan Cape, 1996.

———. *Sweet Machine.* New York: Harper Flamingo, 1998.

———. "Rooting for the Damned." In *The Poets' Dante.* Ed. Peter S. Hawkins and Rachel Jacoff. New York: Farrar, Straus and Giroux, 2001. 370–79.

———. *Still Life with Oysters and Lemon.* Boston: Beacon, 2001.

Dronke, Peter. *The Medieval Lyric.* Third edition. Cambridge: D. S. Brewer, 1996.

Duby, Georges. *A History of Private Life.* Trans. Arthur Goldhammer. Volume 2. Cambridge, MA: Belknap, 1988.

Edelman, Lee. *Homographesis: Essays in Gay Literary and Cultural Theory.* New York: Routledge, 1994.

Elliott, Dyan. "Pollution, Illusion and Masculine Disarray." *Constructing Medieval Sexuality.* Ed. Karma Lochrie, Peggy McCracken and James A. Schultz. Minneapolis: University of Minnesota Press, 1997. 1–23.

Enders, Jody. *The Medieval Theater of Cruelty.* Ithaca: Cornell University Press, 1999.

Euripides. *Iphigeneia in Tauris.* Trans. Richmond Lattimore. New York: Oxford University Press, 1973.

———. *Iphigeneia at Aulis.* Trans. W. S. Merwin and George E. Dimock, Jr. New York: Oxford University Press, 1978.

Ferguson, Frances. *Pornography, the Theory: What Utilitarianism Did to Action.* Chicago: University of Chicago Press, 2004.

Fradenburg, Louise and Carla Freccero. "Introduction." *Premodern Sexualities.* New York: Routledge, 1996.

Frantzen, Allen J. *Before the Closet: Same-Sex Love from Beowulf to Angels in America.* Chicago: University of Chicago Press, 1998.

Freud, Sigmund. "Fetishism." *Standard Edition of the Complete Psychological Works of Sigmund Freud.* Trans. James Strachey. Volume 21. London: Hogarth, 1961.

Garber, Marjorie. *Vested Interests: Cross-Dressing and Cultural Anxiety.* New York: Routledge, 1992.

Gaunt, Simon. *Troubadours and Irony.* Cambridge: University of Cambridge Press, 1989.

———. "Saints, Sex, and Community: Hagiography." *Gender and Genre in Medieval French Literature.* Cambridge: University of Cambridge Press, 1995.

———. "Straight Minds / 'Queer Wishes' in Old French Hagiography: *La vie de Sainte Euphrosine.*" *Premodern Sexualities.* Ed. Carla Freccero and Louise Fradenburg. New York: Routledge, 1996. 155–73.

Gallagher, Nora. *Things Seen and Unseen: A Year Lived in Faith.* New York: Knopf, 1998.

Genet, Jean. *Pompes funèbres. Oeuvres complètes.* Volume 3. Paris: Gallimard, 1953.

———. *Funeral Rites.* Trans. Bernard Frechtman. New York: Grove, 1969.

Goldin, Frederick, trans. *German and Italian Lyrics of the Middle Ages.* Garden City: Anchor, 1973.

Guilhem de Montanhagol. *Les poésies de Guilhem de Montanhagol.* Ed. Peter T. Ricketts. Toronto: Pontifical Institute of Medieval Studies, 1964.

Guinizelli, Guido. *The Poetry of Guido Guinizelli.* Ed. and trans. Robert Edwards. New York: Garland, 1987.

Gumbrecht, Hans Ulrich. "Intertextuality and Autumn / Autumn and the Modern Reception of the Middle Ages." In *The New Medievalism.* Ed. Marina S. Brownlee, Kevin Brownlee, and Stephen G. Nichols. Baltimore: Johns Hopkins University Press, 1991. 301–30.

———. *In 1926: Living at the Edge of Time.* Cambridge: Harvard University Press, 1997.

———. *The Production of Presence.* Stanford: Stanford University Press, 2003.

Gunn, Thom. *Collected Poems.* New York: Farrar, Straus and Giroux, 1994.

Harpham, Geoffrey Galt. *Shadows of Ethics: Criticism and the Just Society.* Durham: Duke University Press, 1999.

———. "Ascetics, Aesthetics, and the Management of Desire." In *Religion and Cultural Studies.* Ed. Susan L. Mizruchi. Princeton: Princeton University Press, 2001. 95–109.

Haver, William. *The Body of This Death: Historicity and Sociality in the Time of AIDS.* Stanford: Stanford University Press, 1996.

Heidegger, Martin. "The Origin of the Work of Art." In *Basic Writings.* Ed. and trans. David Farrell Krell. San Francisco: Harper San Francisco, 1993.

Horner, Shari. *The Discourse of Enclosure: Representing Women in Old English Literature.* Albany: SUNY Press, 2001.

Howie, Cary. "Rude Theory: The Rough Trade of the Fabliaux." In *Comic Provocations.* Ed. Holly A. Crocker. New York: Palgrave, 2006. 163–74.

Huizinga, Johan. *The Waning of the Middle Ages.* New York: Doubleday Anchor, 1956.

Huston, Bo. *Remember Me.* New York: Amethyst, 1991.

———. "Meditations in Zurich." In *Life Sentences: Writers, Artists and AIDS.* Ed. Thomas Avena. San Francisco: Mercury House, 1994. 73–106.

Iacopone da Todi. *Laude.* Ed. Franco Mancini. Bari: Laterza, 1974.

———. *Lauds.* Trans. Serge and Elizabeth Hughes. New York: Paulist, 1982.

Jantzen, Grace. *Julian of Norwich.* New edition. Mahwah, NJ: Paulist, 2000 [1987].

Jordan, Mark. *The Invention of Sodomy in Christian Theology.* Chicago: University of Chicago Press, 1997.

———. *The Ethics of Sex.* Oxford: Blackwell, 2002.

Julian of Norwich. *A Revelation of Love.* Ed. Marion Glasscoe. Exeter: University of Exeter Press, 1993 [1986].

Kay, Sarah. "The Sublime Body of the Martyr: Violence in Early Romance Saints' Lives." In *Violence in Medieval Society.* Ed. Richard W. Kaeuper. Woodbridge: Boydell, 2000. 3–20.

Kierkegaard, Søren. *Fear and Trembling.* Trans. Howard V. Hong and Edna H. Hong. Princeton: Princeton University Press, 1983.

Kruger, Steven F. "Medieval/Postmodern: HIV/AIDS and the Temporality of Crisis." In *Queering the Middle Ages.* Ed. Steven F. Kruger and Glenn Burger. Minneapolis: University of Minnesota Press, 2001. 252–83.

Lacoue-Labarthe, Philippe. *La poésie comme expérience.* Paris: Christian Bourgois, 1986.

Lacoue-Labarthe, Philippe. *Poetry as Experience*. Trans. Andrea Tarnowski. Stanford: Stanford University Press, 1999.

Landoni, Elena. *Il "libro" e la "sentenzia." Scrittura e significato nella poesia medievale: Iacopone da Todi, Dante, Cecco Angiolieri*. Milan: Vita e Pensiero, 1990.

Leclercq, Jean. *Saint Pierre Damien: Hermite et Homme d'Église*. Rome: Edizioni di Storia e Letteratura, 1960.

Leonardi, Lino and Francesco Santi. "La letteratura religiosa." In *Storia della letteratura italiana*. Volume 1. Ed. Enrico Malato. Rome: Salerno, 1995. 339–404.

Lerer, Seth. "*Transgressio Studii*: Writing and Sexuality in Guibert of Nogent." *Stanford French Review* 14.1–2 (Spring–Fall 1990): 243–66.

———. "The Genre of the Grave and the Origins of the Middle English Lyric." *Modern Language Quarterly* 58.2 (June 1997): 127–61.

Lisicky, Paul. *Lawnboy*. New York: Turtle Point Press, 1998.

Loughlin, Gerard. *Alien Sex: The Body and Desire in Cinema and Theology*. Oxford: Blackwell, 2004.

McIntosh, Mark. *Mystical Theology*. Oxford: Blackwell, 1998.

Margoni, Ivos. *Fin'amors, mezura e cortezia: Saggio sulla lirica provenzale del XII secolo*. Milan: Cisalpino, 1965.

Margaret of Oingt. *The Writings of Margaret of Oingt: Medieval Prioress and Mystic*. Trans. Renate Blumenfeld-Kosinski. Newburyport, MA: Focus Library of Medieval Women, 1990.

Marie de France. *Lais*. Ed. Karl Warnke. Paris: Poche, 1990.

Matthews, Scott. *Reason, Community, and Religious Tradition: Anselm's Argument and the Friars*. Aldershot: Ashgate, 2001.

Menocal, María Rosa. *Writing in Dante's Cult of Truth: From Borges to Boccaccio*. Durham: Duke University Press, 1991.

Menestò, Ernesto. "La figura di Iacopone da Todi." In *Iacopone da Todi: Atti del XXXVII Convegno storico internazionale, Todi, 8–11 ottobre 2000*. Spoleto: Centro italiano di studi sull'alto medioevo, 2001. 3–19.

Merleau-Ponty, Maurice. *Phenomenology of Perception*. Trans. Colin Smith. London: Routledge, 2002 [1958].

Milbank, John, Catherine Pickstock, and Graham Ward, eds. *Radical Orthodoxy: A New Theology*. London: Routledge, 2000.

Milbank, John, and Catherine Pickstock. *Truth in Aquinas*. London: Routledge, 2001.

Milbank, John. *Being Reconciled: Ontology and Pardon*. London: Routledge, 2003.

Moore, Stephen D. *God's Gym: Divine Male Bodies of the Bible*. London: Routledge, 1996.

———. *God's Beauty Parlor, and Other Queer Spaces in and around the Bible*. Stanford: Stanford University Press, 2001.

Muske-Dukes, Carol. "A Private Matter." In *The New Yorker* (December 23–30, 2002): 126–27.

Nancy, Jean-Luc. *La communauté désoeuvrée*. Paris: Christian Bourgois, 1986.

———. *The Inoperative Community*. Ed. Peter Connor. Trans. Peter Connor, Lisa Garbus, Michael Holland, and Simona Sawhney. Foreword by Christopher Fynsk. Minneapolis: University of Minnesota Press, 1991.

———. *The Birth to Presence*. Stanford: Stanford University Press, 1993.

WORKS CITED

Nancy, Jean-Luc. *Le sens du monde*. Paris: Galilée, 1993.
———. *The Sense of the World*. Trans. Jeffrey S. Librett. Minneapolis: University of Minnesota Press, 1997.
———. *Being Singular Plural*. Trans. Robert D. Richardson. Stanford: Stanford University Press, 2000.
———. *La communauté affrontée*. Paris: Galilée, 2002.
Newman, Barbara. *From Virile Woman to WomanChrist: Studies in Medieval Religion and Literature*. Philadelphia: University of Pennsylvania Press, 1995.
Nichols, Stephen G. "Deflections of the Body in the Old French Lay." *Stanford French Review* 14.1–2 (Spring–Fall 1990): 27–50.
Nietzsche, Friedrich. *Unfashionable Observations*. Trans. Richard T. Gray. Stanford: Stanford University Press, 1995.
Parker, Patricia. "Metaphor and Catachresis." In *The Ends of Rhetoric*. Ed. John Bender and David Wellbery. Stanford: Stanford University Press, 1989.
Peck, George T. *The Fool of God: Jacopone da Todi*. University, AL: University of Alabama Press, 1980.
Pelosi, Pietro. *Guido Guinizelli: Stilnovo inquieto*. Naples: Liguori, 2000.
Peter Damian. *Life of St. Romuald of Ravenna* 49. Trans. Henrietta Leyser. *Medieval Hagiography: An Anthology*. New York: Garland, 2000.
———. *Opere di Pier Damiani: Lettere 22–40*. Ed. G. I. Gargano and N. D'Acunto. Rome: Città Nuova, 2001.
Peter of the Morrone (Celestine V). "L'Autobiografia di Pietro Celestino." In *Celestiniana*. Ed. Arsenio Frugoni. Rome: Istituto storico italiano per il medio evo, 1954/1991.
———. *Autobiography*. Trans. George Ferzoco. *Medieval Hagiography: An Anthology*. Ed. Thomas Head. New York: Garland, 2000.
Phillips, Adam. *Houdini's Box*. London: Faber and Faber, 2001.
Pickstock, Catherine. *After Writing: On the Liturgical Consummation of Philosophy*. Oxford: Blackwell, 1998.
Plato. *Republic*. Trans. Desmond Lee. Harmondsworth: Penguin, 1974.
———. Trans. Alexander Nehamas and Paul Woodruff. Indianapolis: Hackett, 1995.
Pozzi, Giovanni. "Iacopone poeta?" In *Alternatim*. Milan: Adelphi, 1996. 73–92.
Rambuss, Richard. *Closet Devotions*. Durham: Duke University Press, 1998.
Rhetorica ad Herennium. Trans. Harry Caplan. Loeb Classical Library. Cambridge, MA: Harvard University Press, 1989.
Ricco, John Paul. *The Logic of the Lure*. Chicago: University of Chicago Press, 2002.
Robertson, Duncan. "Authority and Anonymity: The Twelfth-Century French Life of St. Mary the Egyptian." In *Translatio Studii: Essays by His Students in Honor of Karl D. Uitti for His Sixty-Fifth Birthday*. Ed. Renate Blumenfeld-Kosinski, Kevin Brownlee, Mary B. Speer, and Lori J. Walters. Amsterdam and Atlanta: Rodopi, 2000.
Roden, Frederick S. "Aelred of Rievaulx, Same-Sex Desire and the Victorian Monastery." In *Masculinity and Spirituality in Victorian Culture*. Ed. Andrew Bradstock, Sean Gill, Anne Hogan, and Sue Morgan. New York: St. Martin's, 2000. 85–99.
Romanelli, Franco, ed. *Il cavaliere e l'eremita*. Milan: Luni Editrice, 1987.

Rondeau, Jennifer Fisk. "Conducting Gender: Theories and Practices in Italian Confraternity Literature." In *Medieval Conduct*. Ed. Kathleen Ashley and Robert L. A. Clark. Minneapolis: University of Minnesota Press, 2001. 183–206.

Rose, Gillian. *Mourning Becomes the Law: Philosophy and Representation*. Cambridge: University of Cambridge Press, 1995.

Rossi, Luciano and Richard Straub, ed. and trans. *Fabliaux érotiques*. Paris: Livre de Poche, 1992.

Rousseau, Jean-Jacques. "Essay on the Origin of Languages." In *On the Origin of Language*. Trans. John H. Moran. Chicago: University of Chicago Press, 1966.

Roy, Bruno. "Getting to the Bottom of Saint Caquette's Cult." In *Obscenity: Social Control and Artistic Creation in the European Middle Ages*. Ed. Jan M. Ziolkowski. Leiden: Brill, 1998.

The Rule of Saint Benedict. Trans. Abbot Parry OSB. Leominster: Gracewing, 1995.

Santi, Francesco. "La mistica di Iacopone da Todi." In *Iacopone da Todi: Atti del XXXVII Convegno storico internazionale, Todi, 8–11 ottobre 2000*. Spoleto: Centro italiano di studi sull'alto medioevo, 2001. 47–70.

Schnapp, Jeffrey T. "Touch and Transport in the Middle Ages." Unpublished manuscript.

Sedgwick, Eve Kosofsky. *Between Men: English Literature and Male Homosocial Desire*. New York: Columbia University Press, 1985.

———. *Epistemology of the Closet*. Berkeley: University of California Press, 1990.

———. *Touching Feeling*. Durham: Duke University Press, 2003.

Silverman, Kaja. *The Threshold of the Visible World*. New York: Routledge, 1996.

———. *World Spectators*. Stanford: Stanford University Press, 2000.

———. "Total Visibility: Rethinking Jeff Wall's Early Work." Lecture given at Stanford University, March 2003.

Southern, R. W. *Western Church and Society in the Middle Ages*. Harmondsworth: Penguin, 1970.

Spence, Sarah. *Rhetorics of Reason and Desire: Vergil, Augustine, and the Troubadours*. Ithaca: Cornell University Press, 1988.

Steinberg, Leo. *The Sexuality of Christ in Renaissance Art and in Modern Oblivion*. Second edition. Chicago: University of Chicago Press, 1996.

Swanberg, Ellen. "*Oraisons* and Liaisons: Romanesque Didacticism in *La Vie de Sainte Marie l'Egyptienne*." *Romance Notes* 23:1 (Fall 1982).

Tillman, Lynne. *Haunted Houses*. London: Serpent's Tail, 1995 [1987].

Turner, Denys. *The Darkness of God: Negativity in Christian Mysticism*. Cambridge: University of Cambridge Press, 1995.

———. *Eros and Allegory*. Kalamazoo: Cistercian, 1995.

Uitti, Karl D. "The Clerkly Narrator Figure in Old French Hagiography and Romance." *Medioevo romanzo* 2.3 (1975).

Underhill, Evelyn. *Jacopone da Todi: A Spiritual Biography*. London: Dent, 1911.

Vauchez, André. *Saints, prophètes, et visionnaires: Le pouvoir surnaturel au Moyen Age*. Paris: Albin Michel, 1999.

Vesely, Dalibor. "The Architectonics of Embodiment." In *Body and Building: Essays on the Changing Relation of Body and Architecture*. Ed. George Dodds and Robert Tavernor. Cambridge, MA: MIT Press, 2002. 28–43.

"Vie de Saint Marine." Ed. Léon Clugnet. *Revue de l'Orient Chrétien* 8 (1903).
Ward, Graham. *Cities of God.* London: Routledge, 2000.
Weinrich, Harald. "Le style et la mémoire." In *Qu'est-ce que le style?* Ed. Georges Molinié and Pierre Cahné. Paris: Presses Universitaires de France, 1994. 339–54.
——. "La poésie en enfer." *Cahiers d'Histoire des Littératures Romanes / Romanistische Zeitschrift für Literaturgeschichte* 19.3–4 (1995): 387–94.
Williams, Charles Allyn. *The German Legends of the Hairy Anchorite.* Champaign: University of Illinois Press, 1935.
Williams, Linda. *Hard Core: Power, Pleasure, and the Frenzy of the Visible.* Second edition. Berkeley: University of California Press, 1999.
Wojnarowicz, David. *Close to the Knives: A Memoir of Disintegration.* London: Serpent's Tail, 1991.
Wood, Jeryldene M. *Women, Art, and Spirituality: The Poor Clares of Early Modern Italy.* Cambridge: Cambridge University Press, 1996.
Wyschogrod, Edith. *Saints and Postmodernism: Revisioning Moral Philosophy.* Chicago: University of Chicago Press, 1990.
Zizek, Slavoj. *The Sublime Object of Ideology.* New York and London: Verso, 1989.
——. *The Fragile Absolute.* New York and London: Verso, 2000.
——. *Did Somebody Say Totalitarianism?: Five Interventions in the (Mis)use of a Notion.* New York and London: Verso, 2001.
Zumthor, Paul. *Parler du Moyen Age.* Paris: Minuit, 1980.
——. *Speaking of the Middle Ages.* Trans. Sarah White. Lincoln: University of Nebraska Press, 1986.

INDEX

Aelred of Rievaulx, 39, 71
Agamben, Giorgio, 23, 40, 107–8
Alarcón, Francisco X., 10
amateurism, 6, 148
anachronism, 15, 146
anaphora, 130–8
 and analogy, 131
 and asymmetrical reciprocity, 133
 and synecdoche, 134
Ancrene Wisse, 40
Angela of Foligno, 18, 94–5
animals, 23
antiphrasis, 105–6
apophasis, 90
 and abbreviation, 91
 and irony, 88–9
Aquinas, Thomas, Saint, 179 n. 14
ascesis
 and anality, 89–90
 and paranoia, 149
Auerbach, Erich, 139
Augustine, Saint, 1, 3, 4, 8, 12, 113–14, 116, 119, 120, 133, 154 n. 3, 159 n. 2, 181 n. 13

B-52's, The, 104
Bachelard, Gaston, 17–18
Bal, Mieke, 2–3
Barthes, Roland, 146–7
Bauerschmidt, Frederick, 127, 178 n. 5
Beckwith, Sarah, 9, 95, 99
belatedness, 104, 113–15, 120–1, 174 n. 24, 175 n. 28, 177 n. 67
Benedict, Saint, 38–9, 78

Bernard of Clairvaux, Saint, 94
Bersani, Leo, 170 n. 69
Bewes, Timothy, 153 n. 3
birth, 62, 66, 95–9, 101,
Bonagiunta da Lucca, 6–7, 103–5, 107–11, 122
Bonaventure, Saint, 3, 40, 83, 85, 169 n. 58
Boswell, John, 71
Brown, Catherine, 139
Burgwinkle, William, 167 n. 28, 178 n. 2
burning, 18, 108, 113, 121, 137
Burrus, Virginia, 160 n. 7, 161 n. 23
Butler, Judith, 104–5
Bynum, Caroline Walker, 165 n. 1, 171 n. 83

Camille, Michael, 167 n. 32
Campbell, Emma, 62
Campo, Rafael, 14
Camus, Albert, 139
Carson, Anne, 4, 9–10, 153–4 n. 10
Cazelles, Brigitte, 45, 50, 52, 54, 56
Celestine V, Pope, 71
Certeau, Michel de, 44, 47, 59, 66
Le chevalier au barisel, 74
Chambers, Ross, 170 n. 67, 177 n. 66
Christine de Pizan, 106
Cioran, E. M., 160 n. 10
claustrophobia, 10, 14, 155 n. 10
coming, 66, 147
community, 115–22
choral, 112–14, 136

comparison, 145–6
convenientia, 57, 81, 143

Damian, Peter, Saint, 6, 73–81
Damisch, Hubert, 162 n. 27, 169 n. 60
Dante, 71, 82, 108–9, 140, 175 n. 30
deixis, 34, 35, 101, 112, 113, 118, 122, 143
de Man, Paul, 93
Dembowski, Peter, 40–1
D'Erasmo, Stacey, 11
differential repetition, 54, 55, 131, 150
Dinshaw, Carolyn, 78, 111–12
Doty, Mark, 7, 112–16, 121–2, 175 n. 30, 177 n. 70
drag, 94, 95, 103–5, 107–8, 110, 114, 115–16, 122, 137, 150, 173 n. 8, 177 n. 67
Dronke, Peter, 173 n. 8
Duby, Georges, 58–9

Edelman, Lee, 6, 141, 167 n. 27
Elliott, Dyan, 72
emergence, 7, 12, 24–6, 33, 37–8, 62, 65, 66, 68, 119, 138
Enders, Jody, 59
experience, 36, 64–5, 70, 71, 73, 82, 108–9, 165 n. 1
eyes, 4, 9, 10, 11, 27–8, 30–1, 56, 66, 82, 98, 128, 154 n. 11, 172 n. 98

Ferguson, Frances, 181 n. 19
fetishism, 12–13, 15, 24, 29, 32, 100, 141, 142, 158 n. 73, 181 n. 19
Fradenburg, Louise, 13
Frantzen, Allen, 12–13
Freccero, Carla, 13

Gallagher, Nora, 31
Garber, Marjorie, 105
Garin, 15
Gaunt, Simon, 41, 42, 105, 156 n. 17, 164 n. 58
Genet, Jean, 24
Gerson, Jean, 72–3

Guinizzelli, Guido, 6–7, 103–11
Guilhem de Montanhagol, 83–4
Gumbrecht, Hans Ulrich, 13, 158 n. 59, 176 n. 45
Gunn, Thom, 67

hands, 34, 55–7, 107, 108, 129, 134, 140, 143, 163 n. 41–2
hair, 22–3, 49
Harpham, Geoffrey Galt, 14, 89, 144, 145
Haver, William, 118–19
Heidegger, Martin, 12, 20, 25–6, 29, 30, 122
as saint, 21
hell, 51
scholarship in hell, 141
historicism, 4, 12, 13, 146, 148–51, 176 n. 45, 180 n. 4, 181 n. 19
holding, 10, 12, 20, 30, 107, 139
as holding back, 26, 37, 110
as being held, 152
Horner, Shari, 9
Huizinga, Johan, 115
Huston, Bo, 120–1

Iacopone da Todi, 6, 70–1, 82–101, 162 n. 37
idleness, 40, 55, 61
immanence, 2, 21, 27, 70, 100, 131, 142, 175 n. 28
impurity, 5, 15, 29, 65, 108, 111, 118
intensification, 5, 7, 10, 19, 34–6, 62, 95, 113, 137
and death, 36
as intervention, 29
and tradition, 143

Jantzen, Grace, 178 n. 4
Jehan Bouche d'Or, Saint, 5, 50–63, 124
Jehan Paulus, Saint, 22–3, 52
Johnson, Phyllis, 45
Jonah, 60–2
Jordan, Mark D., 74–5, 79, 160 n. 15
Julian of Norwich, 8, 127–34

Kay, Sarah, 157 n. 46
Kierkegaard, Søren, 174 n. 16
Kruger, Steven F., 180 n. 4
kissing, 47–8, 78, 111, 120, 137, 140–1, 151

Lacan, Jacques, 100, 164 n. 68
Lacoue-Labarthe, Philippe, 20, 64, 66
Leclercq, Jean, 166 n. 15
Lerer, Seth, 57, 174 n. 24
Lifshitz, Sébastien, 151
Lisicky, Paul, 143
liturgy, 26, 28–9, 31, 34–5, 53–4, 76–7, 118, 135, 151
Lorca, Federico García, 152
Loughlin, Gerard, 2

Marguerite of Oingt, 95
Marie de France, 8, 123–7
Marie l'Egyptienne, Saint, 5, 40–50
Marina, Saint, 62–3
masturbation, 55, 57, 58, 75, 79, 129
measure, 82–5, 109
mediation, 8, 62, 127–38
  and immediacy, 9, 78, 127
middles, 15, 128, 151
Menocal, María Rosa, 4
Merleau-Ponty, Maurice, 179 n. 15
metonymy, 19, 40, 69–70, 76, 118
  as aftermath, 120
  and allegory, 91–3
  and anaphora, 137–8
  and containment, 81
  and gender, 99–100
  and irony, 105, 107, 111
  and the materiality of writing, 56, 86–7
  and metaphor, 6, 142, 168 n. 47
  and representation, 96
  and synecdoche, 3
  between time and space, 116
Milbank, John, 34, 132, 163 n. 41, 179 n. 16
miracles, 30–6, 56, 57, 61, 67, 68, 72, 99

Moore, Stephen, 96, 171 n. 80, 172 n. 89
mouths, 21, 56, 61, 77–8, 134, 138
Muske-Dukes, Carol, 122

Nancy, Jean-Luc, 31, 98–9, 110, 117, 135, 150–1, 176 n. 35, 179 n. 10
Newman, Barbara, 129
Nichols, Stephen, 126
Nietzsche, Friedrich, 149

ontological difference, 127–36
opposition, 119–20, 149
Ozon, François, 129

parataxis, 10, 126, 130
participation, 5, 7, 33–5, 78, 81–2, 91, 112, 116, 144, 168 n. 47, 170 n. 61
Phillips, Adam, 10, 29
Pickstock, Catherine, 34–5, 163 n. 41, 163–4 n. 55, 177 n. 65, 179 n. 12
Plato, 4, 30, 96
possession, 17, 148

Rambuss, Richard, 9, 36
restlessness, 39, 40, 111
Ricco, John Paul, 142
Robertson, Duncan, 50
Romuald, Saint, 74, 80
Rondeau, Jennifer Fisk, 71, 96
Rose, Gillian, 116–18, 120
Rousseau, Jean-Jacques, 105

Scarry, Elaine, 90
Schnapp, Jeffrey, 173 n. 11
Sedgwick, Eve Kosofsky, 149, 178–9 n. 9
sequence, 2–3, 38, 106, 162 n. 27
Silverman, Kaja, 30–1, 33, 100, 172 n. 94, 177 n. 67
Six Feet Under, 25–6
sodomy, 75–81, 87, 89, 166 n. 21
Spence, Sarah, 3
Steinberg, Leo, 37–8
Swanberg, Ellen, 51

Tillman, Lynne, 37, 167 n. 25
tongues, 6, 10, 88, 91
touch, 7, 57, 67, 88, 89, 92, 93, 96, 100, 111–12, 114, 118, 137, 151–2
   and the risk of detachment, 112
   and the touchable, 120
   without touching, 127
traherence, 7, 105, 108, 112, 114, 118, 120, 137
   see also drag
transcendence, 2, 35, 77, 80–2, 95, 107, 116, 117, 144, 151
   and the transcendental, 133
Turner, Denys, 86, 90, 168 n. 47, 170 n. 70

Uitti, Karl, 43–4
Underhill, Evelyn, 90–1, 95–6

version, 22, 45, 50, 55, 58, 62–3, 77, 82, 88
Vesely, Dalibor, 81

Ward, Graham, 34, 135–6
Weinrich, Harald, 140
Williams, Linda, 161 n. 21
Wojnarowicz, David, 84, 172–3 n. 98
Wyschogrod, Edith, 24

Zizek, Slavoj, 4, 32, 175 n. 30
Zumthor, Paul, 147–9